D1156978

Nongovernmental Forces and World Politics

Werner J. Feld

The Praeger Special Studies program—utilizing the most modern and efficient book production techniques and a selective worldwide distribution network—makes available to the academic, government, and business communities significant, timely research in U.S. and international economic, social, and political development.

Nongovernmental Forces and World Politics

A Study of Business, Labor, and Political Groups

PRAEGER SPECIAL STUDIES IN INTERNATIONAL POLITICS AND PUBLIC AFFAIRS

Praeger Publishers   New York   Washington   London

Library
I.U.P.
Indiana, Pa.
382   F332n
c.1

PRAEGER PUBLISHERS
111 Fourth Avenue, New York, N.Y. 10003, U.S.A.
5, Cromwell Place, London S.W.7, England

Published in the United States of America in 1972
by Praeger Publishers, Inc.

All rights reserved

© 1972 by Praeger Publishers, Inc.

Library of Congress Catalog Card Number: 70-165834

Printed in the United States of America

When in the spring of 1970 Ernst Haas asked me to prepare a paper for the American Political Science Association's (APSA) annual meeting on the changing incidence and impact of nongovernmental organizations on the international system, I did not realize that this endeavor would finally culminate in a book. But the absence of any comprehensive treatment of the subject and the paucity of available data induced me to make an initial effort at dealing systematically with this largely unexplored field. Clearly the traditional preoccupation of political scientists with the nation-state as the main actor in the international system has obscured the growing influence which nongovernmental forces have exerted in world politics, although recently a broader recognition of these important forces can be observed.

It has been the multinational enterprise (MNE) which among influential nongovernmental entities has so far received most attention and much of the literature which has developed on the relationship of MNEs to governmental authorities and indirectly to the international system has come from the pens of economists and business administration specialists. On account of its tremendous economic and financial potential, the MNE continues to retain center stage in the research and publications on nongovernmental forces. The second category of these forces on which scholarly inquiries have focused has been the great variety of traditional international nongovernmental organizations (NGOs) pursuing interests in almost any endeavor of human activity. However, in this area the research has been more sporadic and less intensive than the efforts expended on international business. Other categories of nongovernmental forces such as international labor, transnational parties, guerilla groups, student movements, and church groups with transnational objectives have received less attention by political scientists or scholars of other disciplines.

While this book attempts to examine all major categories of nongovernmental forces in a systematic manner, the varying availability of materials and space considerations made it necessary to concentrate more heavily on multinational business, international labor, and the traditional NGOs than on other types of nongovernmental entities. In view of the much broader capabilities especially of the first two groups to influence world politics on a global basis, this eclectic approach seems fully warranted. I hope, however, that this book will stimulate political scientists and international relations specialists to engage in research in the areas which were treated only superficially in this volume and collect hard data which are sorely lacking.

Much additional work needs to be done also on refining the concepts of the international political system. A full understanding of the structure of this system and its modes of transformation requires much more thought and perhaps the construction of new models which relate closer to changing realities. Some initiatives in this direction are underway and are likely to prove very useful if they succeed.

I would like to take this opportunity to express my sincere gratitude to Professors Joseph Nye and Patrick Sewell for reading the first draft of the introductory chapter and offering many valuable suggestions which were mostly adopted. I also want to thank Professor John Wildgen of my Department for his fine collaboration and his expertise in computer operation and analysis which became so evident in his contribution to Chapter 6. I have benefited greatly from the presentations of papers and comments made by the participants at the research conference on Multinational Corporations in the Global Political System held at the University of Pennsylvania in April 1971, and of the panel on Transnational Relations during the APSA annual convention in September 1971. My gratitude also goes to the students in my graduate seminar on the topic of the book; their comments, views, and insights have been most helpful. Despite the many contributions made by the individuals referred to, it goes without saying that any error or omission is exclusively my responsibility.

The index was prepared by Mrs. Valerie Steele whose dedication made it possible to accomplish this difficult task in a very short time. Above all, however, I must thank Mrs. Jan Davis, who never tired of retyping the manuscript, subjecting herself to long hours of taking dictation on parts of the manuscript, offered many invaluable editorial and substantive suggestions, and did her usual perfect job of typing the final draft. Lastly, I must thank my wife for her patience in suffering through "another book."

CONTENTS

LIST OF TABLES

LIST OF FIGURES

Nongovernmental Forces
and World Politics

The long-standing view of states being the exclusive actors in the international system has been questioned increasingly during the last 25 years. From the Peace of Westfalia in 1648 to World War I the states were indeed the predominant actors in the international arena and only the Catholic Church and, during the nineteenth century, the International Red Cross occasionally played a significant part in international politics. Since the end of World War I, however, a growing number of intergovernmental organizations (IGOs) such as the League of Nations, the International Labor Organization (ILO) and various other organizations[1] began to assume meaningful roles in international affairs and today universal and regional IGOs as exemplified by the United Nations and the European Economic Community (EEC) have been accepted as important actors in the international system. Although they lack the traditional characteristics of the nation-state, i.e. comprehensive governmental control over people living in a clearly defined territory, many IGOs have been accorded limited international legal personality, a legal status somewhat akin to that of states. This legal status entitles IGOs to conclude international agreements and sue before international tribunals, and allows some of their officials to enjoy diplomatic privileges and immunities as necessary for the exercise of organizational functions.

Proceeding beyond the states and IGOs as actors in the international system this book will focus on the growing number of non-governmental entities that especially during the last decade have made themselves felt in the world arena either through purposeful action transcending national boundaries or through unintended effects of border-crossing activities in which some of these entities are engaged. Most of these entities function in two or more countries, but they can also be exclusively national units provided that they possess the necessary power to produce significant economic and political effects beyond their national borders. Best known among these diverse entities, a few of which date back to the nineteenth century, are the multinational corporations or enterprises (MNEs). They often possess considerably greater material resources than many nation-states which enables them under certain conditions to exert more powerful influences in the international sphere than the governments of many middle-sized and small states. A striking example is General Motors (GM) which in 1970 on a world-wide basis produced goods and furnished services amounting to nearly $19 billion and which employed globally approximately 700,000 people. While it is not possible to compare the General Motors figure for goods and services produced with the gross national product (GNP) of nation-states because the former includes double counting of intermediate goods bought from other firms and the latter includes investment expenditure on new machines and construction, it is interesting to point out that Switzerland's GNP is almost $2 billion less than the goods and services furnished by General Motors.[2] If one equates GM's 700,000 employees with the total civil service, national and local, of a state, General Motors compares favorably with New Zealand. Looking beyond the giantism of GM, one finds that in 1970, 197 American and European multinational corporations each produced goods and provided services amounting to over $1 billion while more than half of the 140-odd countries of the world had a GNP below that figure. Although the power of states rests on other elements than productive capacities and financial resources inasmuch as military prowess as well as political assets and skills make up a significant part of a country's overall capabilities in the international arena, the figures given demonstrate the potential power of MNEs in world affairs. This power is enhanced by the fact that MNEs own property and operate in a dozen or more countries which enables them to escape the full control of the governments of individual countries in which they function.[3] In view of their multinational operations, they have special opportunities to influence the politics and policies of these countries either directly or through transnational transactions and thus are capable of affecting the operation of the international system.[4]

In addition to MNEs, transnational joint business ventures have also the capability of influencing the international system. Often based on the border-crossing collaboration of legally independent enterprises, these ventures have become an increasingly popular entrepreneurial arrangement. It enables the partners to exert coordinated influences on the governments of the countries where their companies are located which in turn may bring about changes in the international system. Examples of these ventures are the well-known transnational collaboration between Fiat and Citroen in the European Common Market and similar undertakings between firms in developed and developing countries.[5]

A second major category of nongovernmental entities of significance for world politics consists of national and international labor organizations. Powerful American labor unions have responded to the challenge of multinational corporations moving some of their operations into countries with lower labor costs by seeking to organize workers in the countries where new production facilities have been established and inducing indigenous labor to bargain up wages. International labor organizations such as the International Confederation of Free Trade Unions (ICFTU) or the regionally confined European Confederation of Free Trade Unions (formerly the European Secretariat of the ICFTU) have been seeking to strengthen labor unions in developing countries by providing money and consultation services. It is not unreasonable to assume that the long-range effects of these and other activities by powerful labor union organizations are likely to be gradual changes in the social, economic, and political conditions in some of the countries involved.

International trade union federations also fall under a third category of nongovernmental entities pursuing transnational objectives. These entities are the traditional international nongovernmental organizations, better known as NGOs. In general, these entities are nonprofit organizations although the objectives of some of these entities include the maximization of profits of their members. Many of these NGOs have been given the formal status of consultants to IGOs which provides for them institutionalized channels for exerting influences in the international arena. International NGOs have either an internationally universal character such as the before-mentioned ICFTU, or the activities are limited to an international region. However, they may also be intranational entities such as a group of educators or religious leaders who may play internationally significant roles by appealing privately or publicly to their counterparts in another country to press their own government to adopt a specific foreign policy position. Or, in a more complex and sophisticated example, an association of manufacturers in Country A may seek to induce a labor union in Country B to urge its government to give A's government a free hand to exploit the markets or raw materials in a third country or region. As a pay-off, the manufacturer's association promises to cut back exports of a given item to Country B, thereby enhancing the union's job and bargaining opportunities due to the increased demand for the domestically produced item.[6]

A final catch-all category of nongovernmental entities capable of affecting international politics is comprised of diverse political groups which may purposefully act across national boundaries or whose activities may have transnational effects. Perhaps the most interesting groups are national parties collaborating across national boundaries for a variety of purposes. For example, Communist parties in democratic countries such as France and Italy where they have a "nongovernmental" status have pursued joint objectives in their respective or third countries whose ultimate goal is to alter the existing international system. With the establishment of the European Coal and Steel Community in 1952, followed later by the EEC and Euratom, one has also witnessed relationships among the Christian Democratic, Liberal, and Socialist parties of the six Member States which suggest possible transnational efforts toward changes in the regional subsystem of Western Europe. These efforts have been made inside and outside the European Parliament in which deputies are seated by party affiliation and not by nationality. Finally, one should note the attempts made during the last few years to create truly "European" parties dedicated specifically to the promotion of European unification. These parties, for example the Europa Partei and the Parti Socialist Europeen, have not been very successful but they exist, nevertheless.

Other transnational political forces are guerillas and liberation fronts. The recent history in Indo-China and the Middle East has brought to the fore many dramatic examples of how these groups are capable of influencing international politics.[7]

Finally, large national foundations at times pursue certain international objectives and thereby engage in transnational activities. An example has been the interest of the Ford Foundation during the late 1950s and early 1960s to assist financially those groups in Western Europe which were aiming for and supporting the political unification of the region.

IMPLICATIONS FOR INTERNATIONAL RELATIONS THEORY

The emergence of nongovernmental entities as forces in world politics raises a number of theoretical questions. Should these new forces be recognized as actors in the international system which from 1648 to the early part of the twentieth century had been overwhelmingly dominated by the governments of sovereign states? Is the struggle for power characteristic of world politics and traditionally based on the strategic assets as well as the military, political, and economic strength of nation-states entering a new phase reducing the significance of the historical roles of soldiers and diplomats as main agents for shaping the international system? Will the new agents be the managers of MNEs, the leaders of internationally-oriented labor unions, the directors of NGOs of various kinds, and the leaders of political groups acting across national boundaries as these entities become increasingly influential participants in international politics? Has the concept of the state-centered international system become obsolete and should it be either scrapped entirely or modified to take account of the new nongovernmental forces in world politics? This book will seek to provide some answers to these questions by assessing the implications of the impact which nongovernmental entities have now and are likely to have in the future on the process of world politics. The book will begin by setting forth briefly a conceptual framework of the international system with consideration given to the position accorded to and possible roles played by nongovernmental forces in this system. It will then proceed to an analysis of various nongovernmental entities capable of affecting world politics through their activities and attempt to evaluate the actual and potential influence and impact of these entities on the international system. In the conclusions a balance sheet will be drawn as to how effective nongovernmental entities have been in bringing about changes in world politics and how much these changes justify modifications in the concept of the international system. The book will also speculate regarding the impact which the growing network of nongovernmental organizations might have on regional and global integration of polities and societies as well as the effect of this network on the prospects for international peace. In this connection, the consequences of the pursuit of different, often conflicting, interests by nongovernmental entities in the international arena will be examined critically and the implications flowing from their ability to present a variety of demands in a coordinated fashion to different governments and IGOs will be assessed. Such actions, if successful on a large scale, could serve to create a new, powerful type of international pluralism, strengthen the forces of functionalism on a regional and world-wide basis, and undermine the traditional concept of nation-state authority in the international field.

THE CONCEPTUAL FRAMEWORK

In the foregoing pages, the term "international system" has been used repeatedly and now needs to be made more explicit and to be defined. As James E. Dougherty and Robert L. Pfaltzgraff, Jr. point out[8] "system" is probably the most widely used term in political science and international relations literature today, yet means different things to different people. For this study an appropriate starting point is Anatol Rapoport's suggestion that a whole which functions as a whole by virtue of the interdependence of its parts is called a system.[9] Talcott Parsons has added a dynamic dimension to the concept of "system" by focusing on the goal orientation of actors in social systems as well as on the interaction of system actors. In fact, interaction among acting subjects is crucial to Parson's framework. If actors gain satisfaction, they develop a vested interest in the preservation and functioning of the system. Mutual acceptance of the system by the actors creates an equilibriating mechanism in the system although, according to Parsons, equilibrium does not imply static self maintenance or a stable equilibrium. An ordered process of change, perhaps transformation, and growth are possible and adaptation to changes in the system's environment is a fundamental prerequisite of social systems.[10]

Talcott Parsons conceives society to consist of an interlocking network of acting systems. Thus, smaller systems (subsystems) exist within larger systems and a change in one subsystem affects the whole system and the other subsystems. This poses the problem of boundaries between systems as well as between systems and their environments. Moreover, every system has inputs and outputs; inputs may emanate from the systems environment or from other systems (their outputs) to which the first system is connected. They may create disturbances within the system, lead to system transformation, or strengthen system maintenance.

The above considerations are relevant and applicable for the international system as used in this study. However, since our concern is with the international political system, a specific definition is required to describe this system. Seen from a world-wide perspective, this system consists of the global pattern of transnational interactions springing from two main sources. These sources may be efforts, often undertaken on several levels, to induce desired value-allocating behavior of national and intergovernmental decision-makers or value-allocating responses by such decision-makers to intended or unintended effects of border-crossing activities.[11] The initiatives producing transnational interactions may not only be specific demands for governmental or IGO behavior often backed up by various kinds of persuasion or threats, but also movements of border-crossing persons, capital, and services, the installation of different facilities in various countries, and communications across national boundaries. Changes in the pattern of transnational interactions are likely to result in changes in the relationships among the actors of the system, perhaps strengthening the positions of some, weakening those of others.

While the above definition given for the international political system centers on the pattern of interactions rather than the actors, a more detailed identification of the latter is needed. The main actors are decision-makers of national governments and to a lesser degree those of IGOs, but leadership groups of nongovernmental entities with specific resources to generate transnational interactions with national governments and IGOs must also be accorded actor status in the international system. The underlying reason for these entities to qualify as international actors may well be, as E. Raymond Platig argues, that few governments if any have total control over the people residing in their territories. To the extent that their control is less than total, individual groups within states can and do enter into independent border-crossing relations and activities, thus affording them the opportunity of becoming direct actors in the international system.[12] Arnold Wolfers traces international actor status of nongovernmental entities to the fact that men identify themselves and their interests with corporate bodies other than the nation-state.[13] While considering Platig's argument as the more potent one, it should be pointed out that national governments at times encourage and support financially and otherwise the transnational activities of national and international nongovernmental entities, especially if such activities tend to buttress governmental objectives. As Platig himself states, the practice of governments vary greatly as to when and to what degree they attempt to encourage, monitor, restrict, manage, or control the international transactions resulting from initiatives other than their own.

In the definition of the international system, the term "state," commonly used to identify the system actors, has been avoided. The reason is that this term is nothing but shorthand for a hierarchical set of processes and institutions to evolve authoritative decisions for a territorially defined segment of world society. Since our study is concerned with those decisions which give rise to transnational interaction or are made in response to such interactions it seems appropriate to identify the decision-makers as the real actors in the international system. In this connection it is recognized that the process of making the pertinent decision may involve diverse governmental and nongovernmental bureaucratic groups and individuals who, as Graham T. Allison observes,[14] see different faces of an issue in question and whose judgments may be the result of "compromise, confusion, competition, and coalition." Nevertheless, some individual or specific group in the hierarchical structure must take the final responsibility for a particular decision and thereby can be identified as the "decision-maker" committing the government or a nongovernmental entity to a specific action or nonaction.

It is also recognized that considerations of domestic politics often play a major role in shaping a governmental decision regarding external affairs. For this reason, it is frequently difficult, if not impossible, to sort out the domestic and external political motivations of a particular decision. This can lead to the argument that it does not make sense any longer to distinguish between national and international politics and that therefore the concept of the international system has become obsolete. While without doubt the linkages between national and international politics bearing on all phases of governmental decision- and policy-making are numerous and their number may be increasing, it does not follow that the concept of the international system has lost its usefulness. Rather, this concept continues to provide an important level of analysis, especially for this study of new potential forces in world politics, because it focuses on the worldwide interrelationship of actors in the international arena. It will permit one to draw conclusions from the changes in the global pattern of transnational interaction as to the improvement, disturbance, or transformation of the system as a whole or its subsystems and thereby furnishes a valuable framework for evaluation.

A few observations must now be made about the subsystems and the environment of the global international political system. In many, but not all cases, the subsystems are bounded geographically and are affected by their ties to and their membership in the global system.[15] The environment of the international political system consists of all those events and conditions, both human and nonhuman, which are nonpolitical in nature, yet may affect the behavior of national governments and other actors as well as the operation of the system.[16] Obviously the boundaries between the international political system and its subsystem on the one hand, and the environments on the other hand, cannot be drawn distinctly. It is equally obvious that the interaction between the political and economic systems is very rich.

The variety of interest represented by nongovernmental entities and the manifold objectives pursued by them in the international system suggest that inputs into the system may emanate from diverse segments of its environment. In some cases it is the physical environment which triggers transnational activities of nongovernmental entities. For example, multinational corporations faced with increasing costs of air pollution control in developed countries may decide to move production facilities to certain developing countries where the level of air pollution has remained low. Or the increasing recognition of the wealth of oceans stimulates the formation of cooperatives of fishermen, conservation societies, or certain MNEs to pursue new international goals which often may be in conflict with each other.[17]

The chains of actions set in motion by border-crossing activities of nongovernmental activities and by their effects vary greatly and may involve governmental as well as nongovernmental actors. Coalitions may be formed between nongovernmental entities in the same or different countries for purposes of bringing about direct or indirect changes in the international system. Alliances may be sought by nongovernmental entities with home and other governments as well as with intergovernmental agencies to enlist their aid in the pursuit of specific cross-national objectives, and side payments for this aid may be promised or made. In turn, governments and IGOs may seek the support of nongovernmental entities for attaining international objectives of their own or those of other nongovernmental entities in which they have a particular interest. In some cases international subsystems may become the vehicle for bringing about changes in the global political system. For example, successful attempts by nongovernmental entities within the Common Market to achieve political unification would result not only in the transformation of the EEC subsystem but also produce a material change in the global political system.

The targets to which demands by nongovernmental entities are addressed also vary from case to case as does the leverage behind these demands. The latter depends largely on the objectives and perceived resources of organizations engaged in transnational activities, the intensity of the demands, the appropriate choice of strategies and tactics, and the skill of their application. Unintended effects of these activities may engender not only responses from national governments, and IGOs, but also from other nongovernmental actors. The great variety of these international and transnational relations and interactions can best be seen by Figure 1.1 which borrows from the concepts of J. S. Nye and Robert D. Keohane,[18] but has been expanded. This figure depicts four types of relations and interactions: (1) intranational between nongovernmental actors themselves or between nongovernmental and governmental actors; (2) transnational relations and interactions between nongovernmental actors themselves; (3) transnational relations and interactions between the latter group and governmental or IGO actors; and finally (4) the classical relations and interactions between governments and IGOs.

PROBLEMS OF EVALUATION

To bring some order into the confusing array of relationships as shown in Figure 1.1, and to establish a guide for systematic

FIGURE 1.1

Network of Transnational and Intranational Relations and Interactions Involving Nongovernmental and Governmental Actors

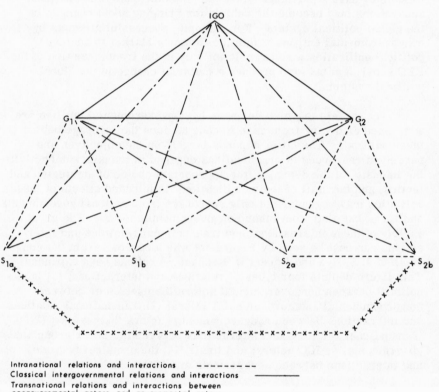

Intranational relations and interactions	‒ ‒ ‒ ‒ ‒ ‒ ‒ ‒
Classical intergovernmental relations and interactions	———————
Transnational relations and interactions between nongovernmental actors and governmental actors	— ‧ — ‧ — ‧ —
Transnational relations and interactions between nongovernmental actors	x‒x‒x‒x‒x

12

research and analysis, a distinction must be made between three significant phenomena: (1) the nongovernmental initiatives giving rise to transnational interactions, (2) the effects on national governments and IGO organs, and (3) the consequences for the global international political system and its subsystems. In most cases the sequence of action will lead through national governments and IGOs to the international system but occasionally nongovernmental initiatives for transnational interactions may have direct consequences for the international system, especially its environment. Moreover, the effects and consequences produced are likely to have a feed-back effect on current or planned activities of nongovernmental entities. Figure 1.2 demonstrates this relationship graphically.

Although nongovernmental initiatives giving rise to transnational interactions vary according to the nongovernmental entities employing them, they can be divided generally into two categories: actions with nonpolitical objectives, and specific demands and actions with political content. In the first category for example, fall foreign investments by MNEs which are basically made for economic reasons, but are potent tools for ultimate social and political change. Another example would be the transfer of technology and management skill by an MNE from one country to another. In the field of international labor an example may be strikes induced in foreign countries to raise the levels of wages or produce better working conditions. A good example for the second category, demands and actions with political contents,

FIGURE 2.1

Cause-Effect Schema of Nongovernmental Activities
Affecting the International System

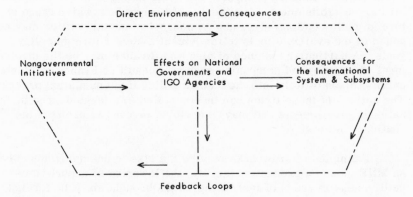

would be pressure by guerilla groups on the governments whose planes
have been hijacked successfully, and demands of transnational business collaboration ventures for changes in fiscal laws in the countries
in which the partners operate.

As varied as the initiatives for transnational interactions are
the effects on national governments and IGOs. The effects can be
classified generally into benefits, drawbacks, and indeterminate.
Benefits enhance the economic and political capabilities and assets
of national governments and IGOs and enlarge their range of foreign
policy options. Drawbacks consist of the weakening of these capabilities and assets and the narrowing of the range of foreign policy
options. Indeterminate effects are those which in a specific case
could either result in long-range benefits or eventually bring drawbacks to national governments or IGOs. The effects may have been
intended by the nongovernmental entity or they were unintended as
in the case of inflationary pressures created in Western Europe by
the large-scale outflow of American investment dollars. Finally,
it should be pointed out that what may be perceived as a benefit by
one governmental or IGO decision-maker, may be viewed as a drawback by another, a predicament which can render the evaluation of a
particular effect quite difficult.

Examples of benefits brought about by nongovernmental activities
may be increased employment, greater exports, greater independence
from imports through successful import substitution, higher wages,
and technological advances for industries. Sometimes nongovernmental entities may also provide social facilities such as new hopsitals
or schools which in turn enhance economic and political stability.
The increase in economic growth and technical know-how may also
provide greater resources for enlarged foreign economic and military
aid as well as enhance prospects for establishing a larger independent
military establishment. Another benefit might be a wider range of
foreign policy options inasmuch as nongovernmental entities may be
added to the available tools to implement a state's foreign policy
goals. A particular instance of high significance may be the involvement of state-owned companies such as Renault of France or Monte-
catini-Edison of Italy into the foreign policy implementation process.
The actions of these firms can be controlled to a large degree by the
national governments and may, therefore, be used to promote the
"national interest."

Examples of drawbacks may be the rise in unemployment when
an MNE closes a production facility, the lowering of export com-
petitiveness in cases of increasing wages brought about by foreign

labor unions, or disturbances of national plans characteristic especially of dirigistic countries and developing nations. Governments may also be weakened in their capabilities by growing constraints on policy-making inasmuch as some of the activities of nongovernmental entities cause serious dilemmas for government decision-makers which may reduce the range of policy options. Consider the example of a proposed investment of an MNE which might reduce widespread unemployment in a particular country and add to its technological potential in an economic sense, but at the same time may involve the assumption of a controlling interest over strategic industries of this particular country. In addition, nongovernmental entities may seek to impose their private foreign policies upon national and IGO decision-makers, impeding or supporting the pursuit of whatever particular state or IGO may perceive as its national or organizational interests. All of these factors are likely to introduce higher degrees of dependence and interdependence decreasing the ability of some governments and IGOs to influence other international actors. Of course, what actually constitutes a benefit or disadvantage depends to a large degree on the perceptions of national and IGO decision-makers and those perceptions are influenced by cultural, historical, and social factors which affect the level of tolerance of individual governments.

Examples of indeterminate effects may be found primarily when attitudes of governments, elites, and nonelites are changed by nongovernmental activities.[19] As Nye and Keohane point out, buying a Toyota or a Fiat may very well influence one's attitudes toward the Japanese and Italians. Face-to-face interactions between citizens of different states may alter the opinions and perceptions of reality on the part of various segments of the population. Advertising by MNEs and news items regarding these enterprises or with respect to labor organizations may create new myths, symbols, and norms that might provide greater legitimacy for their activities. As a result, shifts in loyalties may occur from traditional attachments to states or tribes to new reward-producing institutions or centers of power.

The consequences for the global international system and its subsystems will also vary from case to case. They may best be evaluated in terms of changes in collaboration and conflict among governments. In other words, some of the effects on national and IGO decision-makers caused by nongovernmental transnational activities will induce greater international collaboration while others will tend to increase world-wide or regional conflict. For example, activities by MNEs, international labor, and the traditional NGOs might lead to greater harmonization of conflicting state policies and laws, thus producing a higher degree of collaboration among the states involved. A secondary consequence may be progress toward societal and political integration. The ultimate consequence could well be the promotion of world peace and world government. A somewhat ideal- istic example would be the introduction of the United Nations into the position of regulating and supervising the activities of multinational corporations which would involve the making of world-wide rules for these entities and necessitate the establishment of enforcement agencies.

However, many of the activities of MNEs are also likely to produce tensions among governments and thereby could contribute not only to a higher level of conflict on the international scene but eventually also to the outbreak of wars. In this respect much will depend on the equitability of benefits distributed by various nongovern- mental entities among the nations of the world since national govern- ments of both advanced as well as developing countries will continue to be jealous if other countries appear to derive greater advantages from these activities than their own nations.

Listing and describing some of the effects which may be produced by the transnational initiatives of nongovernmental entities however falls short of measuring the impact on the international system. While changes may be observed in policies by governmental and nongovern- mental actors, it is very hard to translate these changes into specific consequences for the international system as a whole. One reason is that most changes in the international system are brought about by multiple causes. Second, even if one were able to isolate monocausal- effect relationships in particular cases, meaningful data may not exist. To assemble such data may require far-reaching and costly interview surveys, but even if these could be undertaken, their yield may not meet the expectations. Finally, to evaluate fully the degree of change necessitates the identification of goals and the determination of the extent of goal attainment. Especially in the field of international business, this information is likely to be difficult to come by because respondents probably would not be anxious to reveal their accomplish- ments or their failures. The problems of measurement are com- pounded by the fact that the impact on the international system is often only indirect, perhaps the result of a chain of events in which both nongovernmental and governmental actors participate. For example, multinational corporations with parent companies located in Country A make investments in Country B leading to substantial control of one of that country's strategic industries such as electronics. The government of Country B seeks to counteract this control by inducing transnational technological collaboration between its remaining individual electronics firms and similar firms in Country C, a collaboration which may lead eventually to an alliance between Countries B and C. This in turn may upset relations between Countries C and D causing a variety of reactions affecting the international system.

In the face of the above problems one may be compelled to draw more or less qualitative conclusions regarding cause and effect relationships with respect to changes in the policies and actions of the various actors in the international system. One can also look at various actions by nongovernmental entities and establish certain indicators and draw inferences for an estimate of the impact and consequences which these actions may have or are likely to have on the international system. For example, various aspects and trends of investments, profitability, and the degree of control of major industries by foreign enterprises may provide indicators from which inferences regarding actual and potential changes in the international political system might be drawn. Other indicators, especially for traditional NGOs and various political groups, may be trends in the strength of headquarter staffs, financial resources, their capabilities to interact with and influence intergovernmental organizations and national governments. Of course, as will be seen in the following pages, the use of these indicators depends on the availability of pertinent data. Such data are more plentiful for international business activities and traditional NGOs than for other categories of nongovernmental entities. However, some impressions can be gained for the latter categories from newspaper accounts and case studies produced by various authors.

Whatever the consequences for the international system flowing from transnational NGO initiatives may be, they are likely to entail novel relationships among the new nongovernmental and traditional governmental actors as well as changing relationships among the latter. New patterns of strategies may be introduced to induce desired behavior of actors who, in turn, need to sensitize themselves to meet the new challenges to their established position in the international system.

NOTES

1. A few of these organizations were founded between 1815 and World War I.

2. Fortune, May 1971, pp. 170-201; and United Nations, Yearbook of National Account Statistics, 1969, Vol. II, International Tables, pp. 15-21.

3. Cf. Raymond Vernon, "Multinational Enterprises and National Sovereignty," Harvard Business Review XLV, 2 (March-April, 1967), 156-72, and his "Economic Sovereignty at Bay," Foreign Affairs XLVII, 1 (October, 1968), 114.

4. There is a need for research into the international activities of such famous banking houses as Rothschild and the emerging industrial enterprises of the eighteenth and nineteenth century in order to determine their influence and impact on the international system existing at their time.

5. Cf. Werner J. Feld, Transnational Business Collaboration Among Common Market Countries (New York: Praeger Publishers, 1970), and Wolfgang G. Friedman and George Kalmanoff, Joint International Business Ventures (New York: Columbia University Press, 1961).

6. This and the preceding example are taken from J. David Singer, "The Global System and its Sub-systems: A Developmental View," in James N. Rosenau, Linkage Politics (New York: The Free Press, 1969), pp. 25-6. For additional examples of complex border-crossing linkages between intranational entities see also Singer article.

7. Guerillas may be regarded as falling into the same category as the time-honored levée en masse which has been given legal status under international law although there is disagreement regarding the rights and obligations of such groups. For details see Oscar Svarlien, Introduction to the Law of Nations (New York: McGraw-Hill, 1955), pp. 378-80. Pirates could also be considered as historical examples of nongovernmental entities affecting in one way or the other the international system. Examples include Uruj Barbarossa in the 1500s and his brother, Khair-ed-Din who was appointed Governor-General of Algiers by the Sultan Selim of Constantinople. In the 1600s Ali Pichinin became the greatest Barbary corsair. Some familiar pirates include Jean Lafitte, Captain Kidd, "Calico Jack," "Black Bart," and "Blackbeard," all of whom had some effect on the international system of their time.

8. James E. Dougherty and Robert L. Pfaltzgraff, Jr., Contending Theories of International Relations (Philadelphia: J. B. Lippincott Co., 1971), p. 102.

9. Anatol Rapoport, "Foreword," Walter Buckley, ed., Modern Systems Research for the Behavioral Scientists (Chicago: Aldine Publishing Company, 1968), p. xvii.

10. Talcott Parsons and Edward A. Shils, eds., Toward a General Theory of Action (New York: Harper and Row, Torchbooks, 1962).

11. For another definition of the international political system see William D. Coplin, Introduction to International Politics (Chicago: Markham Publishing Company, 1971), p. 296 Cf. also Charles A. McClelland, Theory and International System (New York: Macmillan Company, 1966), pp. 90-112. For the term "political" cf. David Easton, A Framework for Political Analysis (Englewood Cliffs, N.J.: Prentice-Hall, 1965), especially pp. 47-57.

12. E. Raymond Platig, "International Relations as a Field of Inquiry," in James N. Rosenau, ed., International Politics and Foreign Policy (New York: The Free Press, 1969) pp. 6-19, especially pp. 16-17.

13. Arnold Wolfers, Discord and Collaboration (Baltimore: Johns Hopkins Press, 1962), p. 23.

14. Graham T. Allison, "Conceptual Models and the Cuban Missile Crisis," American Political Science Review, LXIII, 3 (September 1969), p. 708. See also his Essence of Decision (Boston: Little, Brown and Co., 1971), pp. 162-81; and Werner Feld, "National Bureaucracies of the EEC Member States and Political Integration: A Preliminary Inquiry," in Robert Jordan, ed., International Administration: Its Evolution and Contemporary Applications (London: Oxford University Press, 1971), pp. 228-44.

15. National systems may also be seen as subsystems of the global international system and therefore linkages between national and international politics may also be studied on systems terms. See also McClelland, Theory and International System, pp. 104-5.

16. Rosenau, International Politics, pp. 73-75. For a more extensive analysis of the global system and its subsystems see Singer, "The Global System and its Sub-Systems."

17. Cf. Edward Miles, "Transnational Processes and International Organization: Outer Space and the Oceans," International Organization, XXV, 3 (Summer 1971), 602-25.

18. J. S. Nye and Robert D. Keohane, "Transnational Relations and World Politics: An Introduction," International Organization, XXV, 3 (Summer 1971), 351-52. Our study, however, does not follow

Nye and Keohane's restrictive definition of transnational interactions
according to which the term refers to "the movements of tangible
and intangible items across state borders when at least one actor
is not an agent of a government or intergovernmental organization"
(p. 332). We will simply use the term as synonymous to border-
crossing or transcending national boundaries and thereby avoid
terminological conflicts with such terms as Philip C. Jessup's
"Transnational Law" in his Transnational Law (New Haven: Yale
University Press, 1956), p. 2; and Karl Kaiser's Transnationale
Politik in an article of the same title in Politische Vierteljahresschrift,
Vol. X (Special Issue 1969), pp. 80-109. Both of these authors use the
term "transnational" in a broader sense and include relations and
interactions between governments. Nye and Keohane have also coined
another term: "transgovernmental." (Figures 1 and 2 of "A Conclusion," in "Transnational Relations," pp. 721-48). It refers to
interactions between sub-units of governments and IGOs. While the
author can think of many examples of such interaction, especially in
the context of the European Community, he considers them essentially
as taking place between governments and IGOs, mostly as part of the
decision-making process in both national governments and IGOs. Use
the of term "international" refers to the totality of transnational
relations or global perspective.

19. Nye and Keohane, "Transnational Relations," pp. 337-38.

2

**MULTINATIONAL
BUSINESS ENTERPRISES:
TRANSNATIONAL
INITIATIVES**

During the last few years much more has been written about the multinational enterprise than about any of the other nongovernmental entities. As a result, by now a very respectable literature has been developed on this subject, both in terms of books and even more so in scholarly and popular articles.[1] A number of very extensive research projects, such as the Ford Foundation-financed project at Harvard University under the guidance of Professor Raymond Vernon, are underway or are in the planning stages. These projects seek to investigate every facet of the multinational enterprise and attempt to assess the meaning of this rapidly expanding new phenomenon in the business world.

The rise of the MNE and its world-wide expansion have indeed been spectacular. The dynamic nature of the MNE is dramatically demonstrated by the claims of some authors, though contested by others, that goods currently produced under international investments amount to over $400 billion.[2] In 1968, half of this amount (about $200 billion) had been produced by foreign subsidiaries of American MNEs, an impressive figure when compared with United States export sales of only $34.6 billion that year and a GNP of $360 billion for the whole EEC area. American industry abroad had thus become the third largest economy in the world, outranked only by those of the domestic United States and the Soviet Union. Since over the last two decades foreign investments of MNEs and the resulting output of goods have been growing approximately twice as fast as world GNP, the world economy could well be more than half internationalized by the end of the century provided that these rates are maintained.[3] It has been estimated by some observers that by as early as 1980, 75 percent of the world's production capacity will be controlled by a small group of 300 multinational corporations. In turn, these 300 corporations might employ as much as 20 percent of the labor force on this planet.[4] Although other students of the MNE seem to consider these assertions as exaggerated,[5] Howard V. Perlmutter advances several reasons which make such a development very plausible.[6] Among these reasons are the ability of giant firms such as Unilever, IBM, Nestlé, Standard Oil of New Jersey, or Philips to obtain capital from anywhere in the world if they need it, although many of these giants not only generate sufficient revenue to be self-financing, but on occasion lend money to banks. Moreover these large MNEs have developed world-wide production and distribution systems which make it possible to launch new products anywhere in the world and reach several billion customers all over the globe. They have the financial resources to undertake research and development activities necessary to make and exploit breakthroughs in science and technology. They can diversify their risks by global investment patterns reducing their vulnerability to the economic and political cycles of a given state and to takeovers or acquisition moves by other companies.

The scenario of the future whereby 300 MNEs control a large part of world production and employment does not negate the ability of undersized or small regional or "microglobal" multinational companies of finding a positive niche in the world economy.[7] At the same time, it demonstrates forcefully the dynamic nature inherent in large-scale, profit-oriented, entrepreneurial activities supported by powerful resources. Employment of such a large percentage of the world's labor force by a relatively small number of MNEs could have interesting implications for a shifting of loyalties of these workers from national governments to new corporate bodies which might be in a better position to fulfill their economic and social needs and expectations than state authorities.

WHAT IS THE MNE?

Despite the fact that so much ink has been expended on examining the MNE, there is little agreement as to its definition, nor in fact as to its name. Some authors talk about international corporations,[8] others call it multinational firms or transnational firms and even supranational firms. Howard Perlmutter has prepared a list of these definitions:

An international firm is one in which international operations are consolidated in a line office on the division level and [which] as a matter of policy, is willing to consider all potential strategies for entering foreign markets—up to direct investment.

A multinational firm is one in which, structurally and
policy-wise, foreign operations are coequal with domestic,
(and) management is willing to allocate company resources
without regard to national frontiers to achieve corporate
objectives. Decisions remain nationally-biased for ownership and headquarters management remains uninational.

A transnational firm is a multination firm managed and
owned by persons of different national origins. Decisions
thus become free of national bias.

A supranational firm is a transnational firm legally dena-
tionalized by permitting it exclusively to register with, be
controlled by, and pay taxes to, some international body
established by multinational convention.[9]

Other authors such as Jonathan F. Galloway consider multinational
enterprises only those which have 25 subsidiaries,[10] while Jack N.
Behrman prefers a very restricted definition according to which an
MNE is characterized by central control of a parent company, a common strategy for the entire enterprise, and integration of operations
of affiliates with each other and the parent.[11] The author of this book
prefers a broader definition which does not place the emphasis on
integration of production. Therefore for this study the MNE is regarded as a number of affiliated business establishments which function simultaneously in different countries, are joined together by ties
of common ownership or control, and are responsible to a common
management strategy. From the headquarters company (and country)
flow direction and control, and from the affiliates (branches, subsidiaries, joint enterprises) products, revenues, and information.
Management may be organized in either monocentric or polycentric
fashion. In the former case, top management is centered in one headquarter company; in the latter case, management has been divided
into geographic zones and a separate headquarters company has been
established for each zone.[12]

THE PATTERN OF GROWTH

The degree of impact which MNE transnational activities have
on national governments and the consequences of their activities for
the international system obviously are closely related to the growth
enjoyed by multinational enterprises, especially during the last 25
years. The rate and geographic pattern of this growth and the type
and nature of the expanding multinational operations may suggest in
a general way the directions and intensity of present and future effects

on nation-states and IGOs caused by these activities and their eventual consequences for the international system and its subsystems. One may also hypothesize that the growing incidence of multinational business enterprises is an indirect indicator of relative success in the attainment of international goals pursued by these entities.

The growing incidence of multinational enterprises can be seen from case studies of 187 U.S. corporations with subsidiaries in at least six foreign countries undertaken by Raymond Vernon at the Harvard Graduate School of Business. Table 2.1 shows the increase in the number of these corporations that have expanded beyond the national boundaries since 1901 and the proliferation in the number of their foreign subsidiaries. While the number of parent systems engaged in activities outside the United States rose by about 800 percent, their foreign subsidiaries exhibited a phenomenal 60-fold expansion.

Analyzing Table 2.1 we find that the earlier very rapid rate of the parent system expansion has slowed down since 1955, while subsidiary proliferation has continued to move upward. In fact, a saturation point in the number of large U.S. multinational parent systems seems to have been reached, but most of these corporations continue to enlarge their foreign operations, perhaps to preempt international production and marketing opportunities and to stifle the aspirations of ambitious newcomers whether they be Americans or of another nationality. The proliferation has been greatest in Europe (about 43 percent), followed by Latin America (23 percent) and Canada (13 percent).

The remarkable expansion of the number of foreign subsidiaries has spread not only toward the markets for the products of multinational corporations, but also to the sources of raw materials. A more detailed breakdown of the international growth and scope of certain U.S. multinational corporations in the petroleum and nonpetroleum extractive industries is found in Tables 2.2 and 2.3. These tables show multinational operations by function (extraction, manufacturing, and marketing) as well as by geographic area. These data, perhaps more than any descriptive effort, show the at times explosive growth of U.S. multinational corporations in the petroleum and nonpetroleum extractive industries attesting to the potential power of these entities to exert influences on the international system. Of course, the nine American oil companies do not control by themselves the petroleum of the world. Especially since World War II, British, French, and Italian oil companies have also gone "multinational" and have taken advantage of the enormous rise in the world demand for oil as well as of the discovery of rich new finds all over the world.

Library
I.U.P.
Indiana, Pa.

382 F332n
c.1

TABLE 2.1

Increase of Multinational Corporations
and Their Subsidiaries of Selected U.S. Corporations, 1901-67

Country or Region	Expansion in Number of Parent System										
	1901	1913	1919	1924	1929	1939	1950	1955	1960	1965	1967
Outside U.S.	23	47	74	93	123	153	168	182	186	187	186
Canada	6	27	54	65	92	123	137	158	176	179	174
Latin America	3	9	16	23	36	72	113	143	179	185	182
Europe	22	37	45	64	95	116	129	154	180	187	185
EFTA	18	29	38	50	86	102	113	130	166	183	181
European Community	15	25	29	47	63	80	84	116	166	185	179
Southern Dominions	2	8	14	21	34	63	77	95	129	154	154
Asia + Other Africa	0	4	8	12	23	33	51	71	103	153	158
Japan	0	1	3	3	7	10	9	26	50	111	117
Other Asia + Africa	0	3	7	11	23	30	49	63	87	123	133
Arab World	0	2	2	2	4	7	11	17	26	32	37
Black Africa	0	0	0	1	4	4	3	8	24	53	62

The Proliferation of Foreign Subsidiaries

Country or Region	1901	1913	1919	1924	1929	1939	1950	1955	1960	1965	1967
Outside U.S.	107	255	390	591	987	1,763	2,289	3,114	4,796	7,379	7,927
Canada	9	36	86	123	215	353	473	600	792	1,017	1,048
Latin America	12	27	49	86	139	315	606	856	1,341	1,813	1,924
Europe	83	173	218	327	530	883	904	1,165	1,872	3,140	3,401
EFTA	36	80	104	136	242	419	449	562	881	1,335	1,405
European Community	43	83	101	156	238	370	397	513	869	1,540	1,675
Southern Dominions	3	13	22	33	53	120	172	250	399	639	648
Asia + Other Africa	0	6	15	22	50	92	134	243	392	770	906
Japan	0	1	3	4	8	11	11	57	68	197	233
Black Africa	0	0	0	1	6	4	9	42	65	142	166
Arab World	0	3	3	3	7	16	29	43	56	77	88

Source: James W. Vaupel and John P. Curran, The Making of Multinational Enterprise (Boston: Division of Research Graduate School of Business Administration, Harvard University, 1969), pp. 11, 123.

TABLE 2.2

Geographical Distribution of U.S.- Controlled Multinational
Enterprises in Petroleum,
1910-67[a]

Crude Oil Operations[b]	1910	1920	1930	1938	1957	1967
Number of enterprises engaged in such operations	1	5	6	7	9	9
Number of countries in which engaged	1	5	12	20	22	31
Number of country-operations in :[c]						
Canada	1	2	1	2	7	13
Europe	1	2	3	8	9	11
Southern dominions	0	0	0	0	1	5
Latin America & Caribbean	0	6	15	18	18	28
Other	0	1	5	13	29	46
Total country-operations	2	11	24	41	64	103

Subsidiaries of All Types	1913	1919	1929	1939	1957	1967
Number of subsidiaries by area:						
Canada	1	16	22	40	135	220
Europe	59	70	137	202	333	626
Southern Dominions	2	2	4	10	32	68
Latin America & Caribbean	8	10	41	68	202	329
Other	3	4	8	31	84	199
Number of subsidiaries by function:						
Extraction	3	7	20	27	33	60
Manufacturing	16	19	43	52	92	279
Sales	36	43	78	110	156	289
Other[d]	7	13	39	65	208	325
Unknown	11	20	32	97	297	489
Total subsidiaries	73	102	212	351	786	1,442

[a]The U.S. enterprises covered in the table are: Cities Service, Continental, Gulf, Mobil, Philips, Standard Oil of California, Standard Oil of Indiana, Standard Oil of New Jersey, and Texaco.

[b]Crude oil operations are commonly carried on through foreign branches of U.S. companies rather than subsidiaries. In this portion of the table, therefore, the frequency shown is a hybrid; it represents the sum of (a) the number of subsidiaries in crude oil operations and (b) the number of parent companies represented through branches in a country in the areas indicated. The figures are subject to larger error than those in the lower half of the table.

[c]Europe includes the United Kingdom, Ireland, and Turkey. The Southern Dominions are: Australia, New Zealand, Rhodesia, and South Africa.

[d]Includes "Holding," "Research and Development," "Serving and Entertaining," "Banking," "Transportation," and "Name Protection."

Source: Raymond Vernon, "Foreign Enterprises and Developing Nations in the Raw Materials Industries," (mimeo 1969), p. 6.

26

TABLE 2.3

Geographical Distribution of Eight U.S.- Controlled Multinational
Enterprises in Non-Petroleum Extractive Industries
1910-67[a]

Non-Petroleum Extractive Operations	1910	1920	1930	1938	1946	1957	1967
Number of enterprises engaged in such operations	3	4	4	4	4	8	8
Number of countries in which engaged	1	4	9	12	13	18	20
Number of country-operations in:[b]							
Canada	0	2	1	1	1	9	6
Europe	1	1	2	3	3	4	3
Southern Dominions	0	0	1	4	4	6	11
Latin America & Caribbean	3	7	8	23	21	27	21
Other	0	0	2	2	2	11	9
Total country-operations	4	10	14	33	31	57	50

Subsidiaries of All Types	1913	1919	1929	1939	1945	1957	1967
Number of subsidiaries by area:							
Canada	1	3	6	8	8	23	46
Europe	1	1	2	6	6	15	111
Southern Dominions	0	0	1	6	6	14	47
Latin America & Caribbean	3	9	10	38	36	66	92
Other	0	0	3	2	2	26	62
Number of subsidiaries by function:							
Extraction	3	9	12	33	31	57	39
Manufacturing	2	2	2	6	6	33	152
Sales	0	0	0	2	2	8	55
Other[c]	0	1	3	11	11	28	71
Unknown	0	1	5	8	8	18	41
Total subsidiaries	5	13	22	60	58	144	358

[a]The U.S. enterprises covered in the table are: Aluminum Company of America, American Metal Climax, American Smelting and Refining Co., Carborundum Co., Engelhard Industries, Kaiser Industries Corporation (including Kaiser Aluminum and Chemical), Phelps Dodge Corporation, Reynolds Metal Co., Scovill Manufacturing Co. Some major raw material producers are omitted from the table such as Anaconda and Kennecott. This is due to the inadequacies of our mechanistic selection process, which required that the companies selected have manufacturing operations in six countries or more in 1963.

[b]See Table 2.2, note c for definitions of terms.

[c]For definitions, see Table 2.2, note d.

Source: Adopted from Raymond Vernon, "Foreign Enterprises and Developing Nations in the Raw Materials Industries" (mimeo., 1969), p. 10.

While nonpetroleum extractive industries have also recorded a rapid expansion of interests since 1910, Table 2.3 reveals that the spread in extraction activities is very much slower than that in manufacturing and marketing; in fact, extraction subsidiaries showed an absolute decline between 1957 and 1967. Moreover, West European firms such as Pechiney of France and others have also moved into the multinational game and are now engaged in extraction activities in foreign countries.[13]

Although American multinational corporations have shown the most spectacular growth during the last 50 years, multinational parent companies are now found in many countries. Table 2.4 shows the number of parent companies in the U.S. and the major countries of Western Europe, as well as the number of countries where affiliates are located. Table 2.5 provides a geographic distribution of the countries in which parent companies in the countries listed in the preceding Table have subsidiaries and affiliates. Finally, Table 2.6 lists the corporations which have subsidiaries and affiliates in 29 countries or more. The reader should note that the figures given in all three tables are for the number of countries, not the number of subsidiaries and affiliates in an individual country which may be considerable.

From Table 2.4 we can gather that there are 3,357 parent companies in 15 European countries and in the U.S. with affiliates in one foreign country only, and 7,276 with affiliates in one or more. Of these parent companies, U.S. corporations constitute 36 and 33 percent respectively. There are 678 parent companies which have affiliates in at least ten or more countries and 177 in twenty or more countries. Of these, U.S. parent companies constitute 21 and 42 percent respectively. These percentages suggest that the multinational operations of individual U.S. corporations cover a larger number of countries than those of European companies, but it says nothing about the size of individual corporations. Considering that the 7,276 parent companies have a total of 27,310 links with foreign countries in which they have affiliates, the average company has links in 3.75 countries. In the case of European parent companies alone, the average drops only slightly to 3.66 countries, suggesting that European MNEs are catching up with their American counterparts.

The geographic distribution of the links of the parent companies with foreign countries as shown in Table 2.5 reveals that 57 percent of these links are with Europe, 19 percent with the Americas (excluding the United States, which is listed under Europe because it relates more to the developed European countries than to the developing

TABLE 2.4

Number and Location of Parent Companies and the Number of Countries[a] in Which Parent Companies Have Had Affiliates, as of 1970

Number of Countries / Country of Parent	1	2	3	4	5	6	7	8	9	10-14	15-19	20+	Total Parents	Total Countries
Austria	21	5	6	1	1	1	2	0	—	2	—	—	39	105
Belgium	137	41	12	14	7	8	2	4	—	7	1	2	235	594
Denmark	54	26	19	13	4	3	—	1	3	4	—	1	128	2,354
France	211	107	55	45	24	14	14	7	9	32	10	10	538	2,023
Germany (West)	448	196	89	53	38	23	22	18	13	31	12	11	954	2,926
Italy	57	17	12	9	9	4	2	1	—	1	2	6	120	459
Luxembourg	10	1	1	1	1	2	—	1	—	1	—	—	18	55
Netherlands	92	50	34	15	24	9	6	6	5	17	3	7	268	1,118
Norway	54	16	6	6	4	4	—	—	—	3	1	—	94	220
Portugal	3	1	1	—	—	—	—	—	—	—	—	—	5	8
Spain	11	1	2	—	—	—	1	—	—	—	—	—	15	26
Sweden	93	42	38	9	16	6	8	3	7	17	7	9	255	1,159
Switzerland	213	74	34	41	21	8	10	5	9	19	7	6	447	1,456
United Kingdom	725	289	163	100	85	57	55	34	26	85	23	50	1,692	7,116
United States	1,228	335	175	115	82	76	58	72	36	146	70	75	2,468	9,691
Total	3,357	1,201	647	422	316	215	180	152	108	365	136	177	7,276	27,310

[a]Country of the parent company is excluded.

[b]Total number of parent companies established in a given country.

[c]Total number of links from parent companies in the country to foreign countries. Two or more affiliates of a particular company in a given foreign country is counted as one link.

Source: <u>Yearbook of International Organizations</u> (13th edition, 1970–71).

TABLE 2.5

Number of Parent Companies for Each Major Industrialized Country Having Subsidiaries
and Associates in a Given Foreign Country
(Data as of 1970)

Country of Subsidiary or Associate	Austria	Belgium	Denmark	France	Germany (West)	Italy	Luxembourg	Netherlands	Norway	Portugal	Spain	Sweden	Switzerland	United Kingdom	United States	Totals
Europe and U.S.																
Austria	—	4	4	43	297	10	3	19	1	—	—	27	83	54	100	645
Belgium	2	—	9	136	138	25	3	141	4	1	2	39	87	233	460	1,280
Denmark	2	3	—	10	39	3	2	16	24	—	—	104	18	80	100	401
France	3	101	24	—	387	58	7	90	9	1	4	55	158	340	575	1,812
Germany (West)	27	31	58	153	—	39	17	136	21	2	3	111	260	337	702	1,897
Italy	11	28	13	136	183	—	5	44	3	—	—	38	137	158	455	1,211
Luxembourg	1	31	6	20	39	18	—	6	1	—	—	2	14	39	52	229
Netherlands	2	42	19	58	191	10	6	—	10	—	2	60	73	247	464	1,184
Norway	1	3	24	14	16	2	1	7	—	—	—	104	14	46	63	295
Portugal	—	14	2	24	24	6	—	18	1	—	4	19	19	60	54	245
Spain	2	28	4	138	148	24	2	33	2	—	—	26	47	134	249	837
Sweden	2	5	46	15	63	5	2	20	44	—	—	—	32	107	175	516
Switzerland	11	24	11	116	291	36	5	43	13	—	1	57	—	183	421	1,212
United Kingdom	5	29	39	118	179	14	3	83	22	—	3	91	99	—	1,362	2,047
United States	4	18	13	84	145	20	1	46	12	—	—	66	67	482	—	958
Subtotal	73	361	272	1,065	2,140	270	47	702	167	4	19	799	1,108	2,500	5,233	14,769
Other Europe																
Cyprus	—	1	—	—	—	1	—	—	—	—	—	1	—	21	4	28
Finland	—	2	8	2	11	—	—	—	3	—	—	74	10	21	41	176
Greece	1	5	1	13	25	7	—	13	2	—	—	3	9	21	33	133
Ireland	—	6	1	9	22	1	—	14	1	—	—	5	9	368	80	516
Turkey	4	2	2	10	18	5	—	6	—	—	—	5	7	10	18	87
Other Western Europe	1	—	1	5	4	2	—	1	—	—	—	1	6	64	23	108
East Europe	7	—	—	—	1	1	—	1	—	—	—	3	1	1	—	15
Subtotal	13	16	13	39	81	17	—	39	6	—	—	92	42	506	199	1,063
Africa	2	132	20	564	171	52	3	118	18	3	1	33	52	1,417	378	2,964
Americas (excl. U.S.)	10	59	23	251	325	92	5	158	16	1	6	164	160	1,117	2,744	5,131
Asia	6	13	22	76	155	18	—	80	10	—	—	47	61	712	707	1,907
Australasia and Oceana	1	13	4	28	44	10	—	21	3	—	—	24	33	864	431	1,476
TOTAL	105	594	354	2,023	2,916	459	65	1,118	220	8	26	1,159	1,456	7,116	9,691	27,310
			582		2,683		97									

Source: Yearbook of International Organizations (13th Edition, 1970-71).

countries of Latin America), 11 percent with Africa, 7 percent with
Asia, and 5 percent with Australia. These percentages indicate that
the majority of multinational operations remain concentrated in the
developed countries but that the Third World is beginning to attract
a growing number of MNE affiliates. While the United States has the
largest number of multinational corporations with affiliates in most
countries, followed by the United Kingdom and West Germany, it is not
surprising that in Africa, because of former colonial ties, affiliates
of MNEs based in the United Kingdom and France exceed those of
the American MNEs by 300 percent and 150 percent respectively. In
Australia the U.K. firms also have twice as many affiliates as those
of the United States.

     Table 2.6 lists 47 MNEs with affiliates in 29 countries or more.
It should be noted that this listing does not imply that the top company
is the largest firm in terms of sales, assets, and employees. In fact,
the company operating in the largest number of countries as far as
affiliates or subsidiaries are concerned is the Shell Transport and
Trading Company headquartered in the United Kingdom which operates
in 85 countries. This company is not listed in the Fortune rankings,
either because it is not considered an "industrial" company (it is
mainly concerned with transportation) or it may be included in the
figure of Royal Dutch Shell. The two runners-up are Mobile Oil and
Gulf Oil. They are listed numbers 8 and 11 in the Fortune listing of
the 500 largest American corporations. It is interesting to note
that while in terms of links in foreign countries U.S. based companies
exceed the MNEs headquartered elsewhere, in this table U.K. headquartered companies appear 17 times whereas U.S. MNEs only 14
times.

     It should be pointed out that reliable and pertinent figures for
Japan and Canada were not available and had to be omitted from
Tables 2.4, 2.5 and 2.6. While this omission obviously causes a certain distortion in the overall picture presented, the three tables
provide useful data regarding the extensive network of multinational
corporations in the contemporary international arena. Japan's corporations have been increasing rapidly in size; 51 of these corporations,
some of them perhaps not falling in the MNE classification, are among
the 200 largest industrial companies outside the United States as listed
by Fortune in August 1971. This is four more than listed in 1970
and eight more than shown in the 1969 directory.

     While Table 2.6 offers a rank ordering of MNEs based on the
number of countries in which they have subsidiaries, it does not
provide information about the size of these corporations in terms of

TABLE 2.6

Multinational Business Enterprises with 29 Affiliates or More

Name of Enterprise	Headquarters	Country of Headquarters	No. of Countries
The Shell Transport & Trading Co. Ltd.	London	U.K.	85
Mobil Oil Corp.	New York	U.S.	62
Gulf Oil Corp.	Pittsburgh, Pa.	U.S.	61
Royal Dutch Shell	The Hague	Netherlands	61
Colgate-Palmolive	New York	U.S.	55
The British Petroleum Co. Ltd.	London	U.K.	52
Imperial Chemical Industries Ltd.	London	U.K.	46
Farbwerke Hoechst AG, Vormals Meister Lucius & Mruning	Frankfurt/M	Germany	43
The National Cash Register Co.	Dayton, Ohio	U.S.	42
International Telephone & Telegraph	New York	U.S.	40
Ente Nazionale Idrocarburi (ENI)	Rome	Italy	39
Farbenfabrieken Bayer AG	Leverkusen	Germany	39
The Wellcome Foundation Ltd.	London	U.K.	39
Glaxo Group Ltd.	London	U.K.	38
Reckitt Colman Ltd.	Hull, York	U.K.	38
Ciba AG	Basel	Switzerland	37
Phillips Petroleum Company	Oklahoma	U.S.	37
Det Østasiatiske Kompagni A/S	Copenhagen	Denmark	36
The General Electric And English Electric Co.	London	U.K.	36
Svenska Kullager Fabrieken AB	Goteborg	Sweden	36
The Rank Organisation Ltd.	London	U.K.	34
Union Carbide Corp.	New York	U.S.	34
Air Liquide, L': SA Pour L'Etude et L'Exploration des Procedes Georges Claude	Paris	France	33
British Leyland Motor Corp. Ltd.	London	U.K.	33
Firestone Tire & Rubber Company	Akron, Ohio	U.S.	33
Sandvikens Jernverk AB	Sandviken	Sweden	33
Schering AG	Berlin	Germany	33
General Electric Co.	New York	U.S.	32
Telefonaktiebolaget LM Ericsson	Stockholm	Sweden	32
Courtaulds Ltd.	London	U.K.	31
Electrical & Musical Industries Ltd.	Middlesex	U.K.	31
Gilette Co.	Boston	U.S.	31
Unilever NV	Rotterdam	Netherlands	31
Blackwood Hodge Ltd.	London	U.K.	30
Financiere Chimo, CIE	Paris	France	30
Ford Motor Company	Michigan	U.S.	30
Joseph Lucas (Industries) Ltd.	Birmingham	U.K.	30
The Singer Company	New York	U.S.	30
Standard & Chartered Banking Group	London	U.K.	30
Texaco Inc.	New York	U.S.	30
AGA AB	Lidingo	Sweden	29
Diners Club, Inc.	New York	U.S.	29
The Dunlop Co., Ltd.	London	U.K.	29
Minnesota Mining & Manufacturing	Minnesota	U.S.	29
Pechney-Progil	Paris	France	29
The Plessey Co. Ltd.	Essex	U.K.	29

sales, assets, or employees. Table 2.7 offers these data for the 20
largest corporations headquartered inside and outside the United
States for 1968 and 1970. Comparison of this table with Table 2.6
reveals that the correlation of rank orderings is quite low.

What is significant in Table 2.7 is the fact that the supremacy
of the American MNEs in terms of overall size is being challenged.
Among the 20 largest MNEs in the world in 1968, only 2 were non-
American. In 1970 that number had increased to 5. Moreover, if one
looks at the total number of corporations—not all perhaps are MNEs—
which produced sales in excess of $3, $2, or $1 billion during 1970
(the second section of Table 2.7), one finds that one-third of the corporations in the first category are non-American and that their percentage rises in the $2 and $1 billion categories. This trend can also
be seen in Table 2.8 which compares the size of U.S. and non-U.S.
firms from 1957 to 1967 and determines the relative size ratio in
1967 in terms of sales, assets, and employees. This ratio varies for
the sales figures from a high of 2.5 for the sales of the 10 top American
corporations in relation to those of the 10 top non-American firms to
1.6 for the smallest category of companies. When size is measured
by assets, the relative size ratio varies from about 2 to 1.5. In terms
of number of employees, American firms have only a slight size
advantage.

Tables 2.7 and 2.8 may offer some evidence that perhaps the
American challenge as so forcefully described by J. J. Servan-
Schreiber,[14] is being met by increasingly larger MNEs in Europe and
other parts of the world through mergers and additional financing.
This can also be seen from Figure 2.1 which provides a breakdown
of the comparative sizes of the largest MNEs by selected industries.
At the same time, non-American firms seem to become more aggressive in the sales field and are better producers of profits than their
American counterparts. This can be gleaned from the statistics
presented annually by Fortune on the 500 largest corporations inside
and the 200 outside the United States. In the 1970 report the combined
sales of the 50 largest U.S. industrial firms exceeded the sales of the
entire 200 non-American companies. In 1971 this was no longer the
case. In fact, the sales of the 200 rose by 16.7 percent, whereas those
of all the 500 American firms increased by only 4.3 percent. And
while in 1971 the profits of the 500 fell by 12 percent, those of the 200
non-American corporations decreased only 2.7 percent.[15]

Recapitulating the statistical information regarding the growth
and geographical distribution of MNEs presented in the preceding
pages one finds multinational parent system headquarters concentrated

TABLE 2.7

World's 20 Biggest Industrial Corporations, 1968 and 1970
(ranked by sales; in millions of dollars)

Rank*	Corporation	Country of Principal Affiliation	1968			1970		
			Sales	Assets	Employees	Sales	Assets	Employees
1 (1)	General Motors	U.S.	$22,755	$14,010	757,231	$18,752	$14,174	695,796
2 (2)	Standard Oil (N.J.)	U.S.	14,091	16,786	151,000	16,554	19,242	143,000
3 (3)	Ford	U.S.	14,075	8,953	415,000	14,979	9,904	431,727
4 (4)	Royal Dutch/Shell	U.K./Netherlands	9,216	14,303	171,000	10,797	16,977	184,000
5 (5)	General Electric	U.S.	8,382	5,744	400,000	8,727	6,310	396,583
6 (8)	Chrysler	U.S.	7,445	4,398	231,089	7,000	4,816	228,332
7 (6)	IBM	U.S.	6,889	6,743	241,974	7,504	8,539	269,291
8 (7)	Mobil Oil	U.S.	6,221	6,872	78,300	7,261	7,921	75,600
9 (9)	Unilever	U.K.	5,534	3,432	312,000	6,883	3,952	333,000
10(11)	Texaco	U.S.	5,460	8,687	78,475	6,350	9,924	73,734
11(13)	Gulf Oil	U.S.	4,559	7,498	60,300	5,396	8,672	61,300
12(14)	U.S. Steel	U.S.	4,537	6,391	201,017	4,814	6,311	200,734
13(10)	ITT	U.S.	4,067	4,022	293,000	6,365	6,697	392,000
14(12)	Western Electric	U.S.	4,031	2,722	176,970	5,856	3,744	215,380
15(17)	Standard Oil (Calif.)	U.S.	3,635	5,770	47,885	4,187	6,594	44,610
16(NL)	McDonnell Douglas	U.S.	3,609	1,335	124,740			
17(NL)	DuPont	U.S.	3,481	3,289	114,100			
18(NL)	Shell Oil	U.S.	3,317	4,230	39,080			
19(16)	Westinghouse	U.S.	3,296	2,271	138,000	4,313	3,358	145,000
20(NL)	Boeing	U.S.	3,274	2,186	142,400			
NL(15)	Volkswagen	Germany				4,315	2,445	190,306
NL(18)	Philips	Netherlands				4,163	5,273	359,000
NL(19)	British Petroleum	U.K.				4,062	6,320	70,600
NL(20)	Nippon Steel	Japan				3,992	5,772	101,561

Comparison of American and European Industrial Corporations
in Terms of Selected Sales 1970

	American	European
$3 billion +	24	12
$2 billion +	22	16
$1 billion +	74	49
	119	77

*Rank in ( ) indicates 1970.
NL = not listed.

Source: Fortune, May 1969 and 1971 and August 1968 and 1971.

TABLE 2.8

Size Distribution and Relative Size Comparisons of
U.S. and Non-U.S. Corporations

Size Class of Sales	Cumulative Number of Firms						U.S. as % of Total*
	1957		1962		1967		
(Millions of $)	U.S.	Non-U.S.	U.S.	Non-U.S.	U.S.	Non-U.S.	
19,999 to 26,005	—	—	—	—	1	—	100
15,345 to 19,999	—	—	—	—	1	—	100
11,724 to 15,345	—	—	1	—	2	—	100
9,033 to 11,724	1	—	2	—	3	—	100
6,931 to 9,033	2	1	3	—	4	1	80
5,318 to 6,931	3	1	3	1	7	2	78
4,080 to 5,318	5	1	4	2	9	2	82
3,131 to 4,080	6	2	7	2	12	2	86
2,402 to 3,131	11	2	11	3	28	5	85
1,843 to 2,402	16	4	20	4	37	10	79
1,414 to 1,843	22	5	29	8	50	18	74
1,085 to 1,414	33	7	41	11	73	34	68
0,823.5 to 1,085	45	8	56	23	101	61	62
0,639.8 to 0,823.5	57	18	77	36	137	87	61
0,490.1 to 0,639.8	81	27	108	61	175	112	61
0,376.0 to 0,490.1	105	51	138	88	225	142	61
0,289.5 to 0,376.0	143	67	180	118	278	185	60
0,221.4 to 0,289.5	196	88	235	155			
0,169.9 to 0,221.4			284	183			

*1967

Firms Ranked[b]	1967 Sales (billions of dollars)		Relative Size Ratio in 1967[a]		
	U.S.	Non-U.S.	Sales	Assets	Employees
1–10	82.2	32.8	2.5	1.9	1.2
11–20	30.7	15.7	2.0	2.0	1.2
21–30	25.3	12.7	2.0	1.4	1.5
31–40	20.1	10.7	1.9	1.7	0.7
41–50	15.2	9.5	1.6	1.4	1.0
51–60	13.5	8.7	1.5	1.7	0.5
61–70	12.0	8.0	1.5	1.7	0.9
71–80	10.6	7.1	1.5	1.7	0.9
81–90	9.9	6.5	1.5	1.2	1.2
91–100	9.1	5.6	1.6	1.2	0.9
101–110	8.1	5.2	1.6	1.3	0.7
111–120	7.7	4.7	1.6	0.9	0.9
121–130	7.1	4.4	1.6	1.5	1.0
131–140	6.5	4.0	1.6	1.1	0.8
141–150	6.0	3.7	1.6	1.4	0.9
151–160	5.5	3.5	1.6	0.9	1.3
161–170	5.2	3.3	1.6	1.1	1.0
171–180	4.9	3.1	1.6	1.4	0.9
181–190	4.6	2.9	1.6	1.1	1.2
191–200	4.4	2.8	1.6	0.7	0.5
1–50	173.5	81.3	2.1	1.7	1.1
1–100	228.6	117.2	1.9	1.6	1.0
1–200	288.8	154.8	1.8	1.5	1.0

[a]The relative size ratio is the ratio of total sales, assets, or employees of U.S. corporations to non-U.S. corporations within a given ranking.
[b]1-10 means the 10 largest firms (by sales size), etc.

Source: Adapted from Stephen Hymer and Robert Rowthorn, "Multinational Corporations and International Oligopoly: The Non-American Challenge", in Charles P. Kindleberger, ed., The International Corporation: A Symposium (Cambridge, Mass.: M.I.T. Press, 1970), pp. 60-61.

35

FIGURE 2.1

Comparative Size of Largest MNEs, Selected Industries*

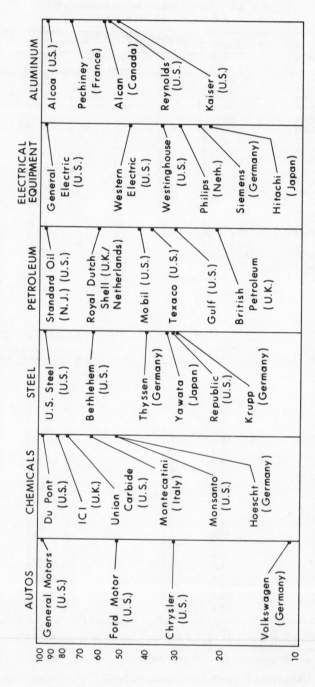

*Figure shows comparative firm sizes, by 1967 sales, of the largest firms in each industry. The leading firm is set at 100; figures, on a log scale, show relative size of others in terms of sales.

Source: Richard J. Barber, The American Corporation (New York: E. P. Dutton & Co., 1970), Chart 7.

in the advanced countries of the world although it should be noted that
a few large firms, mostly Western-controlled, have established corporate headquarters in Latin America and Africa. While the increase
in the creation of MNEs in the United States seems to have stopped, it
continues in other developed countries presenting a challenge to the
dominance of American MNEs. At the same time, the proliferation
of new subsidiaries goes on unabated, with multinational operations
in the developing nations slowly catching up with those carried out in
the advanced countries.

Attention must now be turned to the examination of specific
initiatives for transnational interaction which when employed by MNEs
may produce various effects on nation-states and IGOs, with ultimate
consequences for the global international system or its subsystems.
It should be stressed from the outset that in most cases these initiatives
will not be "politically" motivated per se, but are actions to enhance
the economic potential of the individual MNE in terms of profits, markets, research and development (R&D), or finances. In fact, interviews
with top executives of large multinational corporations by this author
and others[16] have revealed again and again that most of these executives consider themselves apolitical and only engaged in activities
to promote the growth and profits of their firms. They are anxious
to project the image of the good cooperative citizen in parent and host
countries, which, however, does not exclude close relations with the
agencies of the host government as "friend of the regime."

To systematize this examination of transnational initiatives by
MNEs several categories have been set up: (1) private foreign instruments, (2) transfer of technology, (3) changes in management structures
and practices, and (4) lobbying activities in support of specific MNE
demands. The last category clearly has the strongest direct political
thrust, but it is the first category, foreign investments, which is likely
to have the most far-reaching and diverse effects and consequences.

TRANSNATIONAL ASPECTS OF FOREIGN INVESTMENTS

International investments are potentially powerful agents of
economic, social, and political change regardless of whether they
are made in developed or developing, Free World or Communist,
countries. Their manifold effects on states, IGOs, and indirectly on
the international system can offer advantages or create conflicts as
the following examples illustrate. The investments influence the
balance of payments of the countries involved, may lead to the control
of strategic industries often considered undesirable by national

governments of the host countries, may add to the export totals of the countries in which new factories are built, and provide investing corporations with bargaining leverage regarding prospective host country laws and regulations, particularly if the infusion of capital can be shifted to a neighboring country without impunity as is possible in a customs union or free trade area. Moreover, they may affect domestic politics because wage scales and working conditions are likely to be improved in the countries where investments are made and perhaps job opportunities impaired in the countries where the parent company is located. Also, bidding up labor costs may cause inflation and borrowing of multinational companies in countries with weak currencies may tend to weaken these currencies further. Finally, investments abroad may reduce the control over the corporation that can be exercised by the parent government and thus give management greater operational latitude such as circumventing export embargoes through shipment from foreign subsidiaries. At the same time, a multinational corporation may appeal to its parent government to intervene through diplomatic channels or even stronger means in order to obtain protection against unfriendly action by host governments. But international investments may also supplement the foreign policy goals of the parent government through helping developing countries to achieve a higher economic level and thereby attain greater political stability, or promoting national security by ensuring the flow of needed raw materials.

Investments are useful indicators to measure the thrust and intensity of economic and perhaps social changes effected or expected in various parts of the world. Although world-wide investment figures are not available, Table 2.9 provides statistics on direct U.S. investments abroad and foreign investments in the United States from 1950 to 1969. It reveals that the latter have been expanding but that their rate of increase is below that of the U.S. investments abroad. Hence, the American net investment position has been growing regularly, amounting in dollar terms to more than $70 billion, with an inferred positive impact on earnings of nearly $6 billion a year.[17] However, direct investments are not the only criterion for the spread and effectiveness of foreign subsidiaries. At present, capital for investments in foreign subsidiaries often flows from Eurodollar issues floated in Europe.[18]

A geographical and functional breakdown of U.S. investments abroad can also be found in Table 2.9. The increase of these investments is most impressive in Europe, induced undoubtedly by the rapid industrial growth resulting from the lowering of trade barriers among Common Market and among EFTA countries and a consequent rising level of demand. With respect to the Third World, U.S.

TABLE 2.9

Value of Direct U.S. Investments Abroad and Foreign Investments
in the U.S., 1950-69
(billions of dollars)

	1950	1967	1968	1969	Annual Growth Rate
Direct U.S. investments (Book value mainly subsidiaries of U.S. companies)	11.8	59.3	64.8	70.8	10%
Direct foreign investments	3.4	9.9	10.8	11.8	6.5%

Growth and Distribution of U.S. Direct Investments
(billions of dollars)

Country or Region	1946	1969
Canada	2.5	21.1
Europe	1.0	21.6
Latin America	3.1	13.8
Other Areas (mainly developing countries in Asia and Africa) plus Japan, New Zealand and Australia.	0.6	14.3

U.S. Private Investments in the Third World
(millions of dollars)

Country or Region	1955	1960	1965
Latin America	$6,233	$8,387	$9,391
Africa	572	925	1,918
Middle East	1,027	1,139	1,536
Far East (includes all countries from Pakistan to Japan; it excludes Mainland China and Australia)	668	1,152	2,033

Distribution Pattern 1969

Country or Region	Total	Manufacturing	Petroleum	Mining & Smelting	Other
Europe	21.6	12.2	4.8	.07	4.5
Canada	21.1	9.4	4.4	2.8	4.5
Latin America	13.8	4.3	3.7	1.9	3.9
Other Areas (mainly developing countries in Asia and Africa)	14.3	3.6	7.1	.9	2.6
TOTAL	70.8	29.5	20.0	5.7	15.5

Sources: (Adopted from U.S. Department of Commerce, Survey of Current Business, L, 10 (October 1970), pp. 21-38; and U.S. Council of the International Chamber of Commerce.

TABLE 2.10

Value of Foreign Direct Investments in the United States, 1950-69
(in billions of dollars at ends of years listed)

Country/Region	1950	1965	1967	1969
Canada	1.0	2.4	2.6	2.8
United Kingdom	1.2	2.9	3.2	3.5
Belgium and Luxembourg	nss	.2	.2	.3
France	nss	.2	.3	.3
Germany	nss	.2	.3	.6
Italy	nss	.1	.1	.1
Netherlands	.3	1.3	1.5	2.0
Sweden	nss	.2	.2	.2
Switzerland	.3	.9	1.1	1.4
Japan	nss	.1	.1	.2
Latin America	nss	.2	.2	.2
Other	nss	.2	.2	.1
Total	3.4	8.8	9.9	11.8

nss = not shown separately

Value of Direct Investment in the United States by Major Industry
and Selected Countries, End of 1969
(billions of dollars)

Area	Total	Manu-facturing	Finance and Insurance	Petroleum	Trade and Other
All areas	11.8	2.5	2.2	2.5	1.8
Canada	2.8	1.6	.3	.1	.7
United Kingdom	3.5	1.2	1.1	.8	.4
Netherlands	2.0	.5	.1	1.3	.1
Switzerland	1.4	1.0	.3	--	a
Other Europe	1.7	.8	.3	.2	.4
Other areas	.5	.2	.1	a	.2

a = Less than $50 million

Details may not add to totals due to rounding

Source: U.S. Department of Commerce, Survey of Current Business L, 10 (October 1970), 35-36.

investments have increased in net dollar terms in all developing
countries of Africa, Asia, and Latin America, but a large part of the
funds expended have gone into oil installations. However, in terms
of percentage, the Latin American region has suffered a dramatic
decline as investments have fallen from 32.27 percent in 1955 to 17.5
percent in 1969. The Middle East also shows a reduction in this period
from 5.32 percent to 2.58 percent. However, the percentage of U.S.
investments in Africa has grown from 2.96 percent to 4.2 percent in
the same period and that in Asia from 3.46 percent to 4.75 percent.

Table 2.10 provides data on the value of foreign investments in
the United States from 1950 to 1969 and the major economic sectors
in which these investments have been made. The main investors in
the United States have been companies in the United Kingdom and
Canada but since 1965 the Netherlands and Switzerland have also taken
on important investment positions. As of the end of 1969, Canadian
and Swiss investments are concentrated in manufacturing industries,
substantial investments of the United Kingdom are in finance and
insurance, and the Dutch have their major stake in the petroleum
industry.

An overall, though rather rudimentary, view over time of direct
foreign investments by major countries and certain broad industrial
sectors can be gained from Tables 2.11 and 2.12. Table 2.11 shows
the growth for selected years of international investments by the
United States, United Kingdom, and the Federal Republic of Germany
broken down by various regions. It also provides percentages of these
investments by region. While net investment positions have grown
across the board, the percentages by region present a different picture.
They manifest substantial percentage increases of investments in the
EEC and Australia but significant percentage decreases of United
States and British investments in the developing countries. West
Germany had invested 23.5 percent of its total foreign investments
in developing countries in 1967; no figures are available for earlier
years. The regional investment percentages are mixed with respect
to EFTA and Japan while U.S. investments in Canada as well as West
German and British investments in North America have remained
relatively stable.

Table 2.12 identifies the part of the total world-wide investments
made in the developing countries which amounted to 33.45 percent.
Of the countries listed in this table—and again the fragmentary nature
of the data should be stressed—firms in Japan have the largest share
of their investments in the developing countries,[19] followed by the
French whose interest in their former colonies remains an important

TABLE 2.11

Regional Distribution of Direct Foreign Investments of the U.S., the U.K., and the Federal Republic of Germany
(billions of dollars)

		EEC	EFTA	North America	South America	Africa[a]	South Africa	Asia[b]	Japan	Australia	Developing Countries	Total
U.S.	1959	2.194	3.106	10.171[c]	8.218	.520	.343	2.026	.210	.739	10.764	29.735
	1967	8.405	9.477	18.069	10.213	1.610	.667	3.414	.868	2.345	15.237	59.267
U.K.	1960	.503	1.330	1.725	.346	.749	.620	1.171	.007	1.036	2.609	7.080
	1966	1.063	2.012	2.352	.586	1.003	1.023	1.832	.015	1.829	3.372	10.778
Germany	1965	.527	.475	.337	.337							2.079
	1967	.891	.636	.505	.391	.148	.030	.080	.017	.046	.634	3.014

Percentage Distribution

		EEC	EFTA	North America	South America	Africa[a]	South Africa	Asia[b]	Japan	Australia	Developing Countries
U.S.	1959	7.4	10.5	34.2	27.6	1.7	1.2	6.8	0.07	0.2	36.2
	1967	14.2	16.0	34.5	17.5	2.7	1.1	5.7	1.5	4.0	25.0
U.K.	1960	7.4	1.9	24.4	4.9	12.0	8.7	16.5	0.1	14.6	36.8
	1966	9.9	2.8	21.8	5.0	9.3	9.5	17.0	0.1	17.0	31.6
Germany	1965	25.3	23.0	16.2	16.2						
	1967	29.6	21.1	16.7	13.0	4.9	1.0	2.6	0.6	1.5	23.5

[a]Does not include South Africa
[b]Does not include Japan
[c]U.S. Investments in Canada

Source: Adapted from Handelskammer Hamburg, Deutsche Direktinvestitionen in Ausland (May 1969), pp. 27, 28.

42

TABLE 2.12

Direct Foreign Investment, Accumulated Assets, by Major Countries, End of 1966
(book value, in millions of dollars)

	LDC %	World	U.S.	U.K.	France	Germany	Sweden	Canada	Japan
Petroleum	45.84	25,942	16,264	4,200	d	200	a	a	a
(LDC)		(11,892)	(6,975)	(2,167)	(670)	(65)	a	a	(222)
Mining and smelting	47.45	5,923	4,135	759	a	100	a	250b	a
(LDC)		(2,801)	(1,827)	(298)	(200)b	(38)	(65)	(202)	(71)
Manufacturing	52.2	32,246	22,050	6,028	a	1,800	a	2,988b	a
(LDC)		(8,047)	(4,124)	(1,471)	(1,230)b	(645)	(96)	(332)	(270)
Other	33.67	21,472	12,113	5,015c	a	400	a	a	a
(LDC)		(7,230)	(3,915)	(2,255)	a	(97)	a	a	(33)
Total		89,583	54,462	16,002	4,000	2,500	793	3,238	1,000
(LDC)		(29,970)	(16,841)	(6,184)	(2,100)	(845)	(161)	(534)	(605)
LDC percent of total by country		33.45	30.92	38.64	52.5	33.8	20.3	16.49	60.5

Note: Italy, Holland, Switzerland, and Belgium data not available; Australia total investment is $300 million.
aNot available
bEstimate
cIncluding agriculture of 1,022 (864 in the less-developed countries, or LDC's)
dTotal French oil production estimated at 57.2 million tons in 1966

Source: Compiled from OECD, DAC (68) 14, Annex C (April 23, 1968).

factor for investments. The smallest percentages of investments made in the Third World are shown by firms in Canada and Sweden.

As in the case of the U.S. investments, a higher percentage of total investments in the Third World (nearly 50 percent) is devoted to oil and other extractive industries, and only about 22 percent to manufacturing industries for whose establishment a particularly urgent need exists in the developing nations. An analysis of the effects of international investments on developing and developed countries will be presented in the next chapters.

Another dimension of direct foreign investments by multinational corporations can be seen when these investments are related to exports and the GNP of the country where the parent system is located. Both foreign investments and exports are to a large degree manifestations of nongovernmental initiatives capable of influencing the international system. Table 2.13 reveals that in 1968 foreign investments by U.S. companies were nearly twice as large as exports, but represented only about 7.5 percent of the GNP generated during that year. The United Kingdom, ranking second in terms of number of multinational corporations and foreign investments (Tables 2.11 and 2.12), shows about equal amounts for investments and exports, but the investments constitute 15.5 percent of her GNP. On the other hand, the foreign investments of French firms are lower than France's exports (68.8 percent) and in Germany these investments constitute only about 17 percent of exports. The respective investment percentages of GNP are 7 and 3 percent respectively. It should be noted, however, that Germany's exports make up nearly 19 percent of GNP, while U.S. exports amount only to a little more than 4 percent. Thus, Germany's capability of influencing the international system through foreign investments has been relatively small, but its potential as measured by her GNP is substantial and the foreign investment trend of German firms in fact points upward.[20] In view of the frequently heard complaints about American industrial imperialism it should be pointed out that direct foreign investments of U.S. corporations are not out of line with the mean ratio of investments to GNP for the four countries analyzed in Table 2.13 (8.3 percent), and exceeds substantially only the ratio of Germany. In fact, if the figures for both foreign investments and exports are summed and then related to GNP, the U.S. shows the lowest percentage of all four countries. Thus, the overall potential of U.S. private enterprises to influence the international system and its subsystems may not be as great as the foreign investment figures alone seem to suggest and the potential of the Germans may be greater than it appears at first glance.

TABLE 2.13

Comparison of Direct Foreign Investments, Exports,
and GNP of Selected Countries, 1968
(in billions of dollars)

	U.S.	U.K.	France	Germany
Foreign investment	64.8	16[a]	8.8[a]	4.3[a]
Percent of exports	190.6	104.5	68.8	17.3
Percent of GNP	7.5	15.5	7.0	3.2
Exports	34.6	15.3	12.8	24.9
Percent of GNP	4.4	14.9	10.1	18.8
GNP	865	103	126.6	132.7
Sum of foreign investment and export as percent of GNP	11.5	30.4	17.1	22.0

[a]Estimate

Sources: Adopted from Statistical Abstract of the U.S., 1970;
Office Statistique des Communautés Européenes, Foreign Trade,
No. 6 1970; and Vereinigter Wirtschaftsdienst Bulletin, October 6,
1969.

The above figures dramatize an ongoing revolution in world
economics. From a trade standpoint, American participation in
the world economy looks very limited while that of Germany looms
very large. But, as Richard J. Barber points out, [21] trade statistics actually mask the realities of the new globalism in economics
flowing from increasing foreign investments. Instead of shipping
goods to purchasers from production facilities in one country, for
instance automobiles from Detroit, plants are established in low-cost
locations around the world from which potential customers are served.
From a business standpoint this makes perfectly good economic sense,
but it could also mean that exports from the United States may suffer.[22]

On the other hand, investment in a foreign country may often
face greater resistance than the importation of goods since it presents

a more direct challenge to established prices. Companies that were previously prepared to tolerate some competition in the form of exports by foreign firms may not be willing to tolerate competition by direct investment and will seek to drive the intruder out of the market before he gets too strong. Nevertheless, the firm making the foreign investment can win this struggle if it has the necessary financial resources. This has been proven many times by the experiences of American MNEs. With the increasing financial strength of European firms the tempting benefits of foreign investment will serve as a strong inducement for the latter to aggressively expand their transnational production and marketing facilities.[23] Of course, the availability of financial resources may not be the only limitation to foreign investments. Balance-of-payments problems may also impede the flow of international investments as the American experience has shown. This points up another relationship between investment and exports inasmuch as a vigorous export trade is at least in part the foundation for the continued outpouring of foreign investments.

FOREIGN INVESTMENT PROFITABILITY

Although marketing strategies, tariff barriers, the ease of technological research, and production and transportation costs are important motivations for business enterprises to multinationalize their operations, the maximization of profits remains always a pervasive catalyst for investments in different parts of the world. As a consequence, a major motivation for the initiation, continuation, and enlargement of foreign investments is the degree of their profitability.

Despite a number of dips, Table 2.14 and Figure 2.2, broken down for developing and developed areas over the period from 1960-1969, show the relatively high profitability of U.S. direct investments abroad. During the 1960s the average annual yield of U.S. foreign direct investments was 12.6 percent. It is important to note that yields in the developing countries were consistently higher than those in the developed countries. However, most of this difference reflects earnings in the petroleum producing countries. When rates of return on manufacturing are compared, yields in the developed countries and the Third World are about the same, amounting to about 11.8 percent for the decade. In 1969 the rate of return on all U.S. foreign direct investments rose to 13 percent, exceeding that of domestic yields.[24]

The significance of foreign earnings for American corporations can be gleaned from the second part of Table 2.14. Eight of the twenty firms listed derive 50 or more percent of their earnings from abroad, although only three have larger sales abroad than at home. In addition more than half of these companies have forty or more of their assets abroad, attesting to both their power and vulnerability in foreign countries.

In addition to the $5. 6 billion earned in 1969 by U. S. direct investments abroad, royalties and fees received by U. S. corporations from foreign affiliates, having grown sharply in recent years, reached almost $1. 4 billion in 1969. European operations contributed the largest share which is evidence that advanced technology exported from the home country produces considerable income for the American parent company.

It is noteworthy that while the profitability of U. S. investments in Europe declined during the early 1960s, the investments of European countries in the United States have shown an increase in profitability. Taken together with the better performance of non-American, especially European, industrial corporations during 1970, [25] an expansion of European operations in the American market is likely, an expansion whose beginning is already clearly visible.[26]

THE TRANSFER OF KNOWLEDGE

Transfer of knowledge as an MNE initiative for transnational interaction consists of the transmission of either technological knowledge or management skills across national boundaries. This discussion of the transfer of technology will be concerned only with proprietary technology owned by particular entities, not the kind that can be obtained through perusal of technical literature or direct purchases of hardware and service.

As Peter Drucker has pointed out, in our age of rapid change understanding the dynamics of technology and applying the proper technological strategy is essential for the success, and indeed the survival, of a business and perhaps even of an industrial nation. [27] Businessmen and perhaps also governments must be able to anticipate the direction and speed of technological change and take advantage of the opportunities that technological developments offer. With innovation often being the crucial variable for economic success in production and marketing as well as for the military-strategic position of nation-states, it is obvious that transfers of technology can play a vital role for the fortunes of MNEs and states.

TABLE 2.14

Profitability of U.S. Direct Investments Abroad, 1960-69
(in millions of dollars)

Income

Year	Europe	Canada	South Africa, Australia, New Zealand	Latin America and Other West Hemisphere	Asia-Africa*	Japan
1960	397	361	71	719	790	15
1961	486	464	103	824	876	15
1962	526	476	107	891	1,025	19
1963	507	455	97	956	1,093	21
1964	659	634	106	1,011	1,234	30
1965	768	703	140	995	1,310	47
1966	729	756	138	1,113	1,266	43
1967	849	790	138	1,190	1,505	46
1968	905	851	161	1,218	1,777	60
1969	1,026	762	209	1,277	2,294	70

*Includes a few "international unallocated countries."

Fees and Royalties
1964, 1968, 1969

	Europe	Canada	Latin America and Other West Hemisphere	Other Areas
1964	306	162	148	140
1968	511	261	226	248
1969	588	268	239	275

Source:- U.S. Department of Commerce, Survey of Current Business, L, 10 (October 1970), pp. 31 and 34.

Table 2.14 (Continued)

Some Big Players in the Global Game

	Total Sales 1967 ($000)	Number of Countries with Production Facilities	Percent Net Income Abroad	Percent Total Assets Abroad	Percent Sales Abroad
General Motors	20,026,252	24	7a	15a	14a
Standard Oil (N.J.)	13,266,015	45b	52	56	68
Ford	10,515,700	27b	92c	40	36
Chrysler	6,213,383	18	NA	31a	21ad
Mobil Oil	5,771,776	38b	45	46	NA
IBM	5,345,291	14	32	34	30d
Gulf Oil	4,202,121	48b	29	38	NA
DuPont (E.I.) de Nemours	3,102,033	16b	NA	12	4
ITT	2,760,572	60	50	47	47
Goodyear Tire & Rubber	2,637,710	35	30	22	30d
International Harvester	2,541,897	18b	10	21e	17
Caterpillar Tractor	1,472,500	14	NA	25	14
Minnesota Mining & Mfg.	1,231,066	24	29	29	30
Singer	1,137,653	28b	NA	58	50d
Corn Products	1,072,940	33	49	47	46
Anaconda	1,047,815	9	57	44	32
Colgate-Palmolive	1,025,351	43b	NA	50	55d
National Cash Register	955,455	10	51	41	44
Massey-Ferguson	844,764	22b	NA	84	90
H. J. Heinz	690,863	15	57	55e	47
Warner-Lambert Pharmaceutical	656,822	47	33	32	33
Pfizer	637,776	32	52	50	48
American Standard	599,807	21b	39	30	28
Abbott Laboratories	303,341	24	26	27	26
U.S.M. Corp.	283,528	25	57	50	54

[a]Excludes Canada.
[b]Includes unconsolidated affiliates and manufacturing franchises.
[c]Ford's profits in the U.S. were substantially reduced by the auto strike.
[d]Includes export sales from the U.S.
[e]Percent of net assets abroad.

Source: Sanford Rose, "The Rewarding Strategies of Multinationalism", Fortune, September 15, 1968, pp. 100 ff.

FIGURE 2.2

Rates of Return on U. S. Direct Investments Abroad
and Domestic Manufacturing Excluding Petroleum

All Industries Abroad

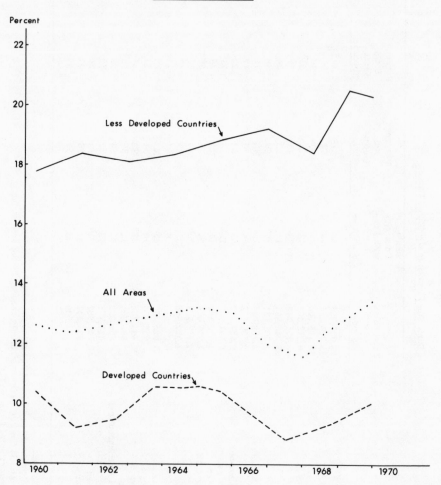

Source: U. S. Department of Commerce, Survey of Current
Business, L, 10 (October 1970), p. 33.

50

Technology can be transferred by licensing agreements and through the medium of the MNE either by the use of existing multinational facilities or investment in a new facility in a foreign country. Licensing agreements, which do not require any border-crossing capital or foreign ownership of industrial installations, have been successful vehicles for large numbers of patent and technological know-how transfers. In many cases independent national private firms are involved and in some instances these agreements have led to transnational business collaboration arrangements between two companies of different nationalities encompassing joint production and marketing activities.[28]

About two-thirds of the licensing arrangements are found in the industrial countries of Europe, Canada, and Australia. In Latin America and Asia these agreements are relatively new, but constitute a growing method of transnational business. In Africa, they are concentrated in the Republic of South Africa. Generally, in the Third World the agreements require more assistance with plant facilities, machinery, and marketing than potential licensors are prepared to offer. At the same time, fewer potential licensees limit the opportunities.[29]

Since some technical knowledge is not offered under licenses without substantial equity ownership—especially U.S. companies are becoming increasingly reluctant to part with technology without such a safeguard—[30] facilities of MNEs in host countries have become the means for the inflow of new technologies. In some instances, formal licensing arrangements have also been made within multinational corporate structures, but whether such agreements are legally acceptable, is a matter of dispute.[31] In any case, such agreements could restrict the flow of know-how which otherwise should become available from the parent company's pool of knowledge and expertise comprising research skills, production techniques, and management capability. And it is precisely this combination which can make transfer of technology through the structures of the MNE so important. A possible additional advantage of such knowledge transmission is that the parent company may charge its subsidiary less than the market price for the knowledge it transmits resulting either in lower prices for the host country consumer or higher profits for the subsidiary.

A midway house for the transfer of technology between the fully-owned affiliate of an MNE and licensing agreements is the joint equity venture formed by a multinational corporation and a host country company. While under this arrangement the involvement of MNE management is reduced, there is likely to be a better appreciation of local economic conditions and needs, thereby enhancing the relations with the host government. [32]

For the transfer of managerial skills across national boundaries the MNE is also a potent agent. These skills are in short supply in many industrially advanced countries, but are most urgently needed in the Third World. Few business executives even in Europe are trained to meet the problem of rapid technological change and the demands of competitive markets. American management methods and training have proven to be most successful in facing up to the many problems challenging modern business.

Skills within an MNE can be transferred in several ways. Management personnel and instructors can be sent from the parent company to affilitates in the host countries and potential managers in the affiliates can be sent for training to the parent company headquarters. Management conferences in which personnel from affiliates in different countries participate may be scheduled and handbooks and guides distributed by the parent company. This leads to the adoption of new management techniques on a company-wide basis benefiting the operations in all affiliates. [33]

CHANGES IN MNE MANAGEMENT STRUCTURES
AND PRACTICES

In the description of the MNE it has been stated that its top management may be organized either in a monocentric or polycentric fashion. It is the author's contention that changes in management structures can serve to trigger a variety of transnational interactions with definite objective and perceptual effects on the relationships between MNE affiliates and host countries and with eventual consequences for the international system. Such changes may be instrumental in projecting new corporate images, can affect the attitudes of MNE employees in geographic regions, and tend to modify the perceptions of host country governmental leaders and other elities.

What kind of structural changes in the management of MNEs are likely to produce the above effects? One thinks of movements of location of the international headquarters company from the country of the parent firm to another country. The advantage of such a shift may be greater autonomy and less likelihood of inteference by the parent organization, better integration of international operations, greater financial feasibility for border-crossing transfers of

earnings and assets, and spreading the political and financial risks
of the MNE as a whole. Negative aspects include loss of parent
company country diplomatic protection which may be questionable in
any case, and perhaps closer scrutiny by home country tax and trade
authorities. [34]

Another pertinent change may be the shift from monocentric to
the polycentric organization of headquarters management which would
create several international headquarters in different parts of the
world. A further change with implications for transnational interactions would be the establishment of what Kolde[35] calls the "world
company. " In such a structure domestic parent and international
operations would be integrated by subordinating domestic to multinational affairs. The top echelons of the parent company would be
oriented toward a global point of view and the dualistic structure
distinguishing between the domestic operations of the parent corporation
and its international activities would be eliminated. Under such a
system, the single and several headquarters could be anywhere in
the world with the result that the headquarters staff will become
multinational in managerial responsibility and outlook. The operating
units would then be organized under the territorial principle and
adapted to the economic, cultural, and political pecularities of individual regions. Under such conditions area expertise may take pre-
cedence over functional and product knowledge for general management
positions on the operational level which could lead to greater accept-
ability of MNE affiliates in certain countries than under other organizational schemes.

Finally, modifications in the structures of affiliates may influence
MNE-host government elections. Fully-owned subsidiaries or branches
which do not possess their own legal personality but are physical off-
shoots of the parent companies may be changed into jointly-owned
subsidiaries or other kinds of joint ventures. The new partners may
be citizens of the host country, the host government itself, or a state-
owned or state-controlled development corporation, a device frequently
used in developing countries. At times these changes may not be
made voluntarily, but by order of the host government. It is not
inconceivable that in some instances the process may be reversed
whereby the MNE will buy out partners in joint subsidiaries or ventures to obtain full management control.

As has already been intimated, the changes in management
structure will entail certain changes in management practices which,
in turn, influence and are influenced by the orientation of upper-rank
MNE executives. The orientations of these executives can become

crucial factors influencing the nature of interactions between MNE affiliates, host country governments, and in some cases IGO institutions, through attitudinal changes produced in governmental leaders and politically powerful elites. However, it should be noted that a polycentric structure does not automatically engender polycentric orientations but may set the stage for a propensity toward such orientations. Howard V. Perlmutter distinguishes three basic orientations of headquarters executives which correlate to some degree with the management structures described above[36] and therefore are useful for our discussion. These orientations are ethnocentric, polycentric, and geocentric.[37]

> The ethnocentric attitude can be found in companies of any nationality—even those firms with extensive overseas holdings and years abroad. The attitude revealed in executive actions and experienced by foreign subsidiary managers, is: "We, the home nationals of X company, are superior to, more trustworthy and more reliable than any foreigners in headquarters or subsidiaries. We will be willing to build facilities in your country if you acknowledge our inherent superiority and accept our methods and conditions for doing the job."
>
> Ethnocentric attitudes are revealed—in the communication process where "advice," "counsel," and directives flow from headquarters to the subsidiary in a steady stream, bearing this message: "This works at home; therefore, it must work in your country."
>
> Executives in both headquarters and affiliates express the national identity of the firm by associating the company with the nationality of the headquarters: this is a "Swedish company," "a Swiss company," "an American company, ..."
>
> Crucial to the ethnocentric concept is the current policy that men of the home nationality are recruited and trained for key positions everywhere in the world. Foreigners feel like "second class" citizens.
>
> The ethnocentric orientation of home company executives toward the host and home nation-state's objectives is to identify with the home country interests while ignoring or considering the host country interests as secondary. More resources and better resources are allocated to the home

market (where risk is generally considered lower). Headquarters executives insist that pay-offs to home country
should be the primary consideration. HQ believes that
the host country executives should not be permitted to
have information that might help the host country to compete with the home country.

Polycentric attitudes are those which, by experience or by
the inclination of a senior executive begin with the assumption that host-country cultures are different and that foreigners are difficult to understand. Local people are
considered to know what is best for them, and the part of
the firm which is located in the host country should be as
"local in identity" as possible. The senior executives at
headquarters believe that their multinational enterprise
can be held together by good financial controls. A polycentric attitude, literally, advocates a loosely connected
group with quasi-independent subsidiaries as centers—
more akin to a confederation.

Executives in the headquarters of such a company are apt
to say: "Let the Romans do it their way. We really don't
understand what is going on there, but we have to have
some confidence in them. As long as they earn a profit,
we want to remain in the background." They assume that
since people are different in each country, standards for
performance, incentives, and training methods must be
different. Local environmental factors are given greater
weight.

The polycentric attitudinal orientation is to identify with
the host country, and be very permissive about the rein-
vestment of funds in each country. Resources generated
in the host country are considered to "belong" to the host
country. The primary concern of the home country executives is with local acceptance. Building small inefficient
plants, which are labor intensive, is justified. In general
these HQ executives appear to need to avoid conflict, or
to seek compromises with the host country political
leaders.

The third attitude which is beginning to emerge at an accelerating rate is geocentrism. Senior executives with this
orientation do not equate superiority with nationality.
Within legal and political limits, they seek the best men,

regardless of nationality, to solve the company's problems anywhere in the world. The senior executives attempt to build an organization in which the subsidiary is not only a good citizen of the host nation but is a leading exporter from this nation in the international community and contributes such benefits as (1) an increasing supply of hard currency, (2) new skills and (3) a knowledge of advanced technology. Geocentrism is summed up in a Unilever board chairman's statement of objectives: "We want to Unileverize our Indians and Indianize our Unileverans."

The ultimate goal of geocentrism is a world-wide approach in both headquarters and subsidiaries. The firm's subsidiaries are thus neither satellites nor independent city states, but parts of a whole whose focus is on worldwide objectives as well as local objectives, each part making its unique contribution with its unique competence. Geocentrism is expressed by function, product, and geography. The question asked in headquarters and the subsidiaries is: "Where in the world shall we raise money, build our plant, conduct R&D, get and launch new ideas to serve our present and future customers?"

This conception of geocentrism involves a collaborative effort between subsidiaries and headquarters to establish universal standards and permissible local variations, to make key allocational decisions on new products, new plants, new laboratories. The international management team includes the affiliate heads.

The Geocentric orientation among home country executives is evidenced in the desire to promote national capability objectives of the host country in the context of world-wide standards. The parent company executives promote a world-wide consultative process (probably beginning on a regional basis) to promote interdependence of nation-states marketing, production, and R&D. HQ provides information about world-wide markets, thus acting as a mediator between the nation-state and customers, and about global technological changes. The geocentric orientation necessarily involves some de-identification with home country objectives.

Table 2.15 relates the orientation of headquarters executives to organizational functions and activities of MNEs which perhaps

TABLE 2.15

Three Types of Headquarters Orientations Toward Subsidiaries in an
International Enterprise

Organization Design	Ethnocentric	Polycentric	Geocentric
Complexity of organization	Complex in home country, simple in subsidiaries	Varied and independent	Increasingly complex and interdependent
Authority; decision making	High in headquarters	Relatively low in headquarters	Aim for a collaborative approach between headquarters and subsidiaries
Evaluation and control	Home standards applied for persons and performance	Determined locally	Find standards which are universal and local
Rewards and punishments; incentives	High in headquarters, low in subsidiaries	Wide variation; can be high or low rewards for subsidiary performance	International and local executives rewarded for reaching local and world-wide objectives
Communication; information flow	High volume to subsidiaries orders, commands, advice	Little to and from headquarters. Little between subsidiaries	Both ways and between subsidiaries. Heads of subsidiaries part of management team
Identification	Nationality of owner	Nationality of host country	Truly international company but identifying with national interests
Perpetuation (recruiting, staffing, development)	Recruit and develop people of home country for key positions everywhere in the world	Develop people of local nationality for key positions in their own country	Develop best men everywhere in the world for key positions everywhere in the world

Source: Howard V. Perlmutter, "Attitudinal Patterns in Joint Decision Making in Multinational Firms - Nation State Relationships," in M. F. Tuite, M. Radnor, and R. Chisholm, eds. International Decision Making, (Chicago: Aldine Publishing Company, 1972).

better than anything else demonstrates the potential impact of these orientations on the interactions between multinational affiliates and their governments.

LOBBYING AND EXERTION OF INFLUENCE

The final initiative available to MNEs for setting into motion transnational interactions is lobbying to press national governments and IGOs for the acceptance of their demands and objectives. As has already been observed, many business executives claim to be "apolitical," only interested in the pursuit of greater profits and wider markets. However, they are known not to shun various channels to bring their needs and demands to the attention of the authorities for favorable consideration. In fact, it is precisely the multinational opportunities offered MNE executives which permit close coordination of lobbying activities in several countries that ultimately may lead to the harmonization of national policies and laws and, in turn, to greater political integration in areas where regional economic unions have been instituted. [38]

While undoubtedly many MNEs want to project or retain the image of the "corporate good citizen" and therefore avoid any adverse publicity associated with "lobbying," some corporations and their affiliates may not be disturbed by aggressively seeking their political ends. Characterized by Charles T. Goodsell as "Back Room Heavies" they may engage in large-scale bribery such as paying large commissions or giving gifts to governmental leaders or their families, induce concessions by promising to make new investments if certain conditions are met, or threaten the intervention of the parent company government if the host government takes specific actions or refuses the demands of the MNE. [39] Some of Goodsell's examples serve to illustrate the above activities. In the 1920s, the Electric Boat Company paid huge commissions to the son of the Peruvian President to sell submarines to the Peruvian Navy. In 1965 an Italian construction consortium probably bribed the Minister of Development and Public Works along with several Peruvian congressmen to obtain the Mantaro hydroelectric contract, previously assigned to Anglo-German interests. In 1967 the presidents of three U.S. mining companies—Cerro de Pasco, American Smelting and Refining, and Anaconda—arranged a private, joint meeting with President Fernando Belaunde Terry, at which they showed him several projects they had in mind for Peru, but only if Article 56 of the Mining Code were liberalized (it was shortly thereafter). ITT, for years majority stockholder in the Peruvian Telephone Company, launched telephone expansion projects in the 1960s and then deliberately halted them, making resumption of the work contingent on a rate increase. In 1967, the President of ITT cabled Secretary of State Dean Rusk regarding a pending telephone bill in the Peruvian Congress which threatened ITT's control, requesting the intervention of the State Department at the highest level. In 1969 California tuna interests did their best to generate pressure in the U.S. Congress to provide naval escorts to their tuna clippers when they invaded Peru's 200-mile coastal fishing jurisdiction and in 1971 W. R. Grace proposed to a U.S. congressional committee that part of Peru's sugar quota payments he held back as a fund to compensate victims of nationalization.

To achieve these objectives MNE headquarters and especially affiliate executives may determine important target groups in the host country with which they maintain continuing relationships. The targets are not only government officials, but also general public and special interest groups, trade unions, news media, shareholders, supplier and customer organizations, universities, and last but not least, other companies. Functional departments within the MNE and its affiliates are assigned the task of dealing with various target groups. This means that for example the marketing department would deal with customer organizations, the personnel department with trade unions, the financial department with shareholders, and the public relations department with the news media and the general public. Some large corporations such as Royal Dutch-Shell or Standard Oil of New Jersey have set up large-scale organizations resembling the foreign ministries of national governments. These organizations engage in carefully coordinated information and intelligence gathering operations through a network of representatives in the major capitals of the world. At the same time, these representatives are used to present their companies' viewpoints on pertinent issues to the national governments in whose countries they are stationed and seek to influence national decision-makers in the direction desired by the corporation management. Periodically, these representatives are called back to headquarters to discuss "foreign policy" problems and to receive new instructions.

The formulation of "foreign policy" objectives by MNEs is not always easy. Different regional headquarters, especially in polycentrically organized corporations, may have conflicting policy priorities stemming from varying economic and political activities in the countries in which they operate. For example, one regional headquarter or subsidiary may advocate flexibility or concessions with respect to a particular national government demand, while other headquarters may insist on a hard-nosed attitude world-wide, arguing that flexibility in one country may induce other governments to request equal concessions. In fact, such differences of opinion can emerge within the MNE management of one country subsidiary as Goodsell relates with respect to the problems of the International Petroleum Company (IPC) in Peru. The IPC management was split into behavioral camps, unofficially known as "Hawks" and "Doves." The first group opposed innovative concessions to the Peruvians on the grounds that some of the more than 100 governments with which IPC's parent, the Standard Oil Company of New Jersey, must deal, would demand the same. The Doves believed that appropriate flexibility was the only way to save the company in Peru. The Hawk leadership was in part comprised of former managers of IPC's field operations at Talara (rather than of the Lima office). As it happened, several former Talara managers had been promoted in recent years to the top echelons of Standard Oil, which may help to explain why the Hawk approach prevailed, at least until the last minute.[40]

To make the lobbying process effective and successful a variety of frequently overlapping coalitions need to be formed. These coalitions are not limited to intranational groups, but may reach regional and world-wide dimensions. They may be formed vertically embracing the MNE's customers as well as suppliers and their trade associations, and they may reach out horizontally to companies with related or common interests and again their trade associations. The closest allies for the MNE are the specialized interest groups in their own industries. For example, in the oil industry the American Petroleum Institute is the permanent basis of useful intercorporate alliances. The API serves as a meeting ground for some 8,000 individual members from most segments of the industry. While much of its efforts are devoted to technical research, there is also continuing concern with fundamentals of national oil policy and the behavior of governmental agencies in Washington and in state capitals. The policies, financial contributions, and leadership of the API are clearly dominated by the large international oil companies and API statements of position generally echo their interests. However, the international oil companies do not rely solely on the API; rather they form coalitions with such groups as the National Foreign Trade Council, the Committee for Economic Development, the Chamber of Commerce of the United States, and the Venezuelan Chamber of Commerce whose objectives the international oil MNEs frequently back up. Depending on the particular goals the oil corporations pursue, they may also seek support from such diverse groups as teachers associations, the Congress of Parents and Teachers, state bar Associations, the American Legion, the Veterans of Foreign Wars, water conservation associations, soil conservation district supervisors, and the Federation of Women's Clubs.[41]

MNEs also engage in formal and informal government alliances in order to press the pursuit of their objectives. This does not mean that the oil companies or other MNEs should be viewed simply as Machiavellian manipulators and the governments as innocent by- standers or agents. Rather, in many cases, alliances stem from an assumption of mutual needs. Nevertheless, returning to the example of the international oil companies, it appears that on many occasions the State Department has taken its policies right out of the executive suites of these companies. This process has been helped by the fact that a close, informal relationship has existed between a number of public officials with backgrounds in the oil business and their continuing connection with the oil industry. These relationships can best be described by quoting several paragraphs from Engler's book.

> Several oilmen, including Edwin W. Pauley, J. Howard Marshall, and J. R. Parten, served on the Reparations Commission after World War II. James Forrestal, Secre- tary of the Navy and then first Secretary of Defense, had been head of the investment backing house of Dillon, Reed and Company which helped arrange corporate loans for Middle Eastern oil operations. John L. Sullivan, his successor as Secretary of the Navy, who as Assistant Secretary had handled oil matters for the Navy, has rep- resented Gulf and was active in persuading President Truman against releasing the Federal Trade Commis- sion's oil cartel report. In 1956 E. V. Murphree, presi- dent of Esso Research and Engineering and an advisor to the Atomic Energy Commission, was appointed to head the guided missile program in the Defense Department. He was succeeded by a former research director for Socony Mobil. In 1957 Mr. Eisenhower nominated to the Defense Department, as Assistant Secretary for Research and Engineering, a retired executive on pension from Gulf. A retired vice president of Standard of California who had handled his company's negotiations with the Navy and the Congress over the Elk Hills naval reserve contracts became a special assistant to the Secretary. Military pro- curement officers frequently are civilians from the oil industry or Army and Navy personnel sent to petroleum indoctrination courses sponsored by serveral of the giant companies. . . .

> [F]ormer Secretary of State John Foster Dulles, until 1949, was the senior member of Sullivan and Cromwell,

the major law firm for the Jersey Standard empire, and
involved in many international transactions and in German
property cases in the United States. (It should be noted
that Covington and Burling, the law firm of his predecessor,
Dean Acheson, has also represented Jersey.) Herbert
Hoover, Jr., a petroleum engineer and director of Union
Oil whose major associations have been with oil, was the
State Department's representative in the secret Iranian
negotiations. He later became Undersecretary of State
and was involved in questions of Middle Eastern policy
and represented his Department in many of the top-level
Suez arrangements. Winthrop W. Aldrich, head of the
Chase Bank, which has long been tied to the Rockefeller
and related oil interests, was sent to London in 1953 as
United States ambassador. . . . 42

Another potent ally of MNEs may be national and international
professional business associations which bring together executives
engaged in international business firms and in which executives of
MNEs may be able to play an important role in the determination of
association objectives. Other professional associations in the fields
of technology, science, economics, finance, and law may also be
used as coalition partners in support of MNE demands. This subject
will again be treated in a discussion of the traditional NGOs (see
Chapter 6).

Another possible ally for MNEs may be national or international
labor organizations. However, in view of the very complex, often
hostile, attitudes of organized labor toward MNEs, which has emerged
during the last few years, alliances with labor organizations may be
effective only in very specific cases. This subject will be dealt with
in greater detail in Chapter 5.

The successes of lobbying efforts are always difficult to determine and frequently do not become visible until considerable time
has elapsed. In many cases lobbying agents do not want to trumpet
their successes to the world as such publicity may be counterproductive. Of course, they are also anxious to conceal failures whenever
possible. However, whatever determination can be made of the effective influence exerted by the MNEs through lobbying must be seen
in the context of the overall effects on governmental and intergovernmental actors produced by the transnational MNE initiatives. An
analysis of these effects will be presented in Chapter 3.

NOTES

1. See for example Richard J. Barber, The American Corporation (New York: Dutton, 1970); Richard N. Cooper, The Economics of Interdependence: Economic Policy in the Atlantic Community (New York: McGraw-Hill, 1968); Frederic G. Donner, The World-Wide Industrial Enterprise: Its Challenge and Promise (New York: McGraw-Hill, 1967); John H. Dunning, The Role of American Investment in the British Economy (London: PEP, 1969); Stephen H. Hymer, "The Efficiency (Contradictions) of Multinational Corporations," Economic Growth Center, Yale University, mimeo., 1970; A. J. N. Judge, "Multinational Business Enterprises," in Yearbook of International Organizations, 1968; Charles P. Kindleberger, American Business Abroad (New Haven: Yale University Press, 1969); Howard V. Perlmutter, "The Tortuous Evolution of the Multinational Corporation," Columbia Journal of World Business, No. 4, 1969; Sidney E. Rolfe and Walter Damm, eds., The Multinational Corporation in the World Economy (New York: Praeger Publishers, 1970); Jack N. Behrman, National Interests and the Multinational Enterprise: Tensions Among the North Atlantic Countries (Englewood Cliffs, N. J.: Prentice-Hall, 1970); Rainer Hellmann, The Challenge to U.S. Dominance of the International Corporation, translated by Peter Rouf (New York: University Press of Cambridge, Mass., Dunellen, 1970); Allan W. Johnstone, United States Direct Investment in France: An Investigation of the French Charges (Cambridge, Mass.: M.I.T. Press, 1965); Charles P. Kindleberger, ed. The International Corporation: A Symposium (Cambridge, Mass.: M.I.T. Press, 1970); Harry, Magdoff, The Age of Imperialism: The Economics of U.S. Foreign Policy (New York: Monthly Review Press, 1969); Edith T. Penrose, The Large International Firm in Developing Countries: The International Petroleum Industry, (London: George Allen & Unwin, 1968); A. E. Safarian, Foreign Ownership of Canadian Industry, (Toronto: McGraw-Hill Co., of Canada, 1966); Michael Tanzer, The Political Economy of International Oil and the Underdeveloped Countries (Boston: Beacon Press, 1969); Raymond Vernon, Sovereignty at Bay: The Multinational Spread of U.S. Enterprises, (Harvard Multinational Enterprise Series, (New York: Basic Books Publishers, 1971); and Isaiah A. Litvak and Christopher J. Maule, Foreign Investment and the Experience of Host Countries (New York: Praeger Publishers, 1970.

2. Cf. Judd Polk, "The Rise of World Corporations," Saturday Review (November 22, 1969), pp. 32 ff. On the other hand see the comments made by Erland H. Heginbotham at the conference on multinational corporations held at the University of Pennsylvania

in the spring of 1971, entitled "The Multinational Corporation and
International Production: Some Common Misconceptions. "

3. The maintenance of these rates is doubted by some students
of the MNE. See for example Raymond Vernon, "Future of the
Multinational Enterprise" in Kindleberger, The International Corporation, pp. 373-400.

4. Cf. G. P. Speeckaert, "Multinational Business Enterprises, "
Yearbook of International Organizations, 13th ed., 1970-71, pp. 1028-
89, and Philippe Heymann, "Une question de vie ou de mort: une
politique industrielle européene, Communauté Européene, No. 140,
Mars 1970, pp. 25-30. Speeckaert also reports that some observers
such as Robert Lattes believe that by 1985 only 60 MNEs will dominate
the world.

5. See Vernon, "Economic Sovereignty at Bay, " Foreign Affairs,
XLVII, I (October 1968), 114. but also Sidney E. Rolfe, "The Inter-
national Corporation in Perspective" in Rolfe and Damm, eds., The
Multinational Corporation, pp. 6 and 7.

6. Howard V. Perlmutter, "Towards Research on and Develop-
ment of Nations", address before the symposium on "International
Collective Bargaining" sponsored by the International Institute of
Labour Studies of the ILO, April 29, 1969, Geneva, Switzerland.

7. Ibid.

8. For example see Kindleberger, The International Corporation.

9. Howard V. Perlmutter, "Attitudinal Patterns in Joint
Decision Making in Multinational Firm-Nation State Relationships"
M. F. Tuite, M. Radnor, and R. Chisholm, eds., International
Decision Making (Chicago: Aldine Publishing Company, 1972), pp.
4-5.

10. Jonathan F. Galloway, "Multinational Enterprises as World-
wide Interest Groups, " Paper delivered at the Annual Meeting of the
American Political Science Association, (mimeo., September 1970).

11. J. N. Behrman, "The Multinational Enterprise: Its Initiatives and Governmental Reactions" (mimeo., March 1971). See
also his, National Interests and the Multinational Enterprise pp. 2-11.

12. Cf. E. J. Kolde, International Business Enterprise (Englewood Cliffs, N.J.: Prentice-Hall, 1968), pp. 218-20 and 251-52. See also Raymond Vernon, "Economic Sovereignty at Bay."

13. For additional details see Raymond Vernon, "Foreign Enterprises and Developing Nations in the Raw Materials Industries" (mimeo., 1969), especially the tables on pp. 6 and 10.

14. J. J. Servan-Schreiber, Le Defi Americain (Paris: Editions de Noel, 1967).

15. Fortune (August 1971), p. 150.

16. For example, Charles T. Goodsell, "The Multinational Corporation as Transnational Actor: Observations Based on Peru," Remarks at Annual Meeting of American Political Science Association, September 9, 1971; and Werner Feld, Transnational Business Collaboration Among Common Market Countries (New York: Praeger, 1970).

17. U.S. Department of Commerce, Survey of Current Business, L, 10 (October 1970), p. 27.

18. For details see U.S. Congress, Joint Economic Committee, The Euro-Dollar Market and Its Possible Policy Implications, Paper No. 12, 91st Congress, 2nd Sess., 1970.

19. For additional data on Japan see Ashok Kapoor, "The Multinational Enterprise and the Nation State in Asia", Paper presented at the Research Conference on the Multinational Corporation in the Global Political System, University of Pennsylvania (mimeo., April 1971).

20. Cf. Vereinigter Wirtachaftsdienst Bulletin, April 20, 1970.

21. Barber, The American Corporation p. 252.

22. This issue will be discussed in greater detail in the next chapter. For reactions of labor to this development, see Chapter 5.

23. Cf. also Stephen Hymer and Robert Rawthorn, "Multinational Corporations and International Oligopoly: The Non-American Challenge," in Kindleberger, ed., The International Corporation, pp. 74 and 75.

24. Domestic yields were lower than yields abroad in the early 1960s, but exceeded the latter in 1966. The gap was gradually closed during the next few years when expansion abroad was particularly strong.

25. See p. 50.

26. See James Leontiades, "The European Challenge: A Response", Columbia Journal of World Business, IV, 4 (July-August, 1970), 9-16.

27. Peter F. Drucker, The Age of Discontinuity (New York: Harper and Row, 1969), p. 48.

28. This kind of transnational arrangement will be discussed in detail in Chapter 4.

29. Cf. Kolde, International Business Enterprise, p. 278.

30. See Jack N. Behrman, National Interests and the Multinational Enterprise, p. 16.

31. Kolde, International Business Enterprise, p. 280.

32. See John H. Dunning, "Technology, United States Investment, and European Economic Growth" in Kindleberger, The International Corporation, pp. 141-76, p. 172.

33. For special experiences see Behrman, National Interests and the Multinational Enterprise, pp. 18, 19.

34. Kolde, International Business Enterprise, p. 249.

35. Ibid., p. 250.

36. See p. 35.

37. Howard V. Perlmutter, "Attitudinal Patterns in Joint Decision-Making in Multinational Firms—National State Relations," pp. 37-41.

38. See Feld, Transnational Business Collaboration, pp. 66-80.

39. Goodsell, "The Multinational Corporation as Transnational Actor."

40. Barber, The American Corporation, p. 268 refers to the
same kind of intracompany divergence of opinion when he discusses
the decision-making in a hypothetical major international corporation
regarding the location of new plants in Europe. One group may favor
a location in Belgium while another group perfers a site in France,
partly out of a desire to avoid coming into the disfavor of the French
government.

41. For greater details see Robert Engler, The Politics of
Oil (Chicago: University of Chicago Press, 1961), pp. 59-60 and
390-91.

42. Ibid., pp. 311 and 310. See also Tanzer, The Political
Economy of International Oil, pp. 41-58.

3

**MULTINATIONAL
BUSINESS ENTERPRISES:
TRANSNATIONAL EFFECTS
AND CONSEQUENCES**

While it would have been possible to relate categories of MNE
initiatives to their particular transnational effects on national governments and IGOs, the author prefers to examine these effects together
since otherwise judgments as to their benefits or drawbacks are often
difficult to make. Indeed, an effect one government may perceive as
a benefit, another may view as a drawback because each government
operates under different economic, cultural, and political conditions.
In fact, even individual political and administrative leaders within a
particular government may disagree on this score. Frequently, benefits and drawbacks need to be balanced carefully before conclusions
as to their positive or negative impact can be drawn.

Discussed first will be the primarily economic benefits, drawbacks, and indeterminate effects of MNE transnational initiatives and
their political implications. Then the counteractions available to
national governments to blunt these effects or to control the substance
and execution of MNE initiatives will be examined. Finally, there will
be an appraisal of the consequences of these initiatives and their effects
on the international system and its operation.

BENEFITS FOR GOVERNMENTAL
ACTORS

Investments and the Transmission of
Technological and Managerial Skills

Inflows of capital into a country from abroad obviously bring
certain primary benefits if the funds are not used simply to acquire

existing companies but to establish new facilities. In that case the construction industry in the host country will profit, employment will rise directly and indirectly, exports may be expanded, imports reduced if new products manufactured may become substitutes for formerly imported items, the balance of payments may be improved by a more favorable trade balance as well as the inflow of capital, and tax receipts increased although MNEs might be able to manipulate the size of the receipts.[1] In some host countries wage levels may also rise but such a development might not be an unmixed blessing everywhere since it could lead to or reinforce inflationary pressures.

Some examples will serve to illustrate the impact of the above effects on the host country. Table 3.1, shows that U.S. affiliates manufacturing in the United Kingdom, Canada, and the EEC exported between 14 and 35 percent of their total sales in 1965. In fact, they accounted for 17 percent of total exports by the United Kingdom and 48 percent of those exported by Canada. Both of these percentages were higher than the share of ownership by U.S. affiliates in the manufacturing industries of those countries[2] which suggests that the affiliates of U.S. MNEs not only made a considerable impact on the trade balance of the host countries but showed to be more export oriented than domestic companies. The new small compact cars of Ford and Chrysler, put on the market in 1970 and 1971, depend heavily for their parts on affiliates in Western Europe indicating that the benefits for Western European exports received from U.S. affiliates continue. In fact, as Figure 3.1 and Table 3.2 show, on a global basis the increase of exports from all foreign affiliates of U.S. MNEs has not only kept up with their local sales, but has considerably outstripped the latter as far as shipments to the United States are concerned. This increase was especially notable in Canada; however, even in other areas (including mostly developing countries in Africa and Asia) considerable growth of the exports to the United States can be observed.

Of course not only the affiliates of America MNEs contribute to the export sales of host countries, but other foreign affiliates may have equally beneficial effects. John H. Dunning reports that in 1969 foreign manufacturing firms as a whole accounted for 24 percent of all U.K. exports. Although U.S. firms were responsible for 17.5 percent of that figure, in some industries such as food, drink, and tobacco as well as metal manufacturing non-U.S. affiliates showed a considerably higher percentage of total exports than affiliates of American MNEs.[3] The export performance of foreign firms in the United Kingdom is especially impressive when one bears in mind that these firms account only for 12 percent of all U.K. sales and 10 percent of all assets.

TABLE 3.1

Total Sales and Export Sales of Manufacturing Affiliates
of U.S. Companies and Total Exports of
Manufactures, Selected Countries, 1965
(in millions)

Country	Total Sales	Exports	Percent	Total Manufacturing Exports	Exports as Percentage
Canada	13,445	2,537	19	5,280	48
United Kingdom	7,510	1,187	25	11,180	17
Benelux	1,589	557	35	8,860	6
France	2,665	440	17	7,330	6
Germany	4,356	1,160	27	15,920	7
Italy	1,272	184	14	5,610	3

Source: U.S. Dept. of Commerce, Survey of Current Business, (November 1966), p. 9, Table 5.

FIGURE 3.1

Sales of Foreign Manufacturing Affiliates

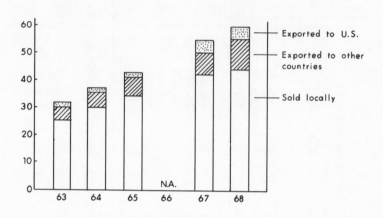

The inflow of capital also benefits the balance of payments directly, as shown by examples of Germany, Italy, and the Benelux countries. Germany received over $200 million annually during the early 1960s in the form of direct investment which bolstered its already strong payments position through an increase of reserves. Italy received an average of $400 million annually during 1961 to 1965 and the Benelux countries also received about $200 million annually.[4]

Finally, it should be noted that the formation of capital in host countries has expanded as the result of investments in MNE affiliates as can be seen from Table 3.3. This table also shows the increase in the share of profits enjoyed by countries in which MNEs operated extractive industries (oil in Venezuela and copper in Chile). The recent successful pressures of the oil producing countries to expand their share of the profits is only the latest evidence of this trend.

The contribution of technology and management skills to the operations of MNE affiliates abroad made by the parent organization often spreads beyond the confines of the affiliates. As Jack N. Behrman points out, commercial activities tend to spread managerial and technical contributions to customers and suppliers of the affiliates. Customers are provided with products of higher quality, perhaps at lower cost and better adapted to local conditions. Technical services

TABLE 3.2

Sales of Foreign Manufacturing Affiliates by Area,
Industry, and Destination, 1965, 1967, 1968
(in millions)

	All Areas	Canada	Latin America and Other Western Hemisphere	Europe	Other Areas
Local sales					
1965	34,686	10,890	5,111	14,264	4,421
1967	41,994	12,361	6,458	17,408	5,767
1968	46,465	13,369	7,213	19,195	6,688
Export to U.S.					
1965	1,789	1,380	101	231	77
1967	3,688	2,956	161	394	177
1968	4,741	3,787	212	549	193
Percent Increase of exports to U.S.					
1965–68	165	174	109	137	150
Export to other countries					
1965	5,842	1,079	314	4,190	259
1967	7,469	1,268	509	5,278	414
1968	8,470	1,392	541	6,091	446
Percent Increase of exports to other countries					
1965–68	45	29	72	45	72

Source: Adapted from U.S. Department of Commerce, Survey of Current Business, L, 10, (October 1970), 18 and 20.

include counseling the customer on his product needs and ways of
increasing his productivity. At the same time, affiliates of MNEs
can assist suppliers in the construction of their plants and equipment
layouts thereby helping in the production of a higher quality of goods
for use by the affiliate and other users in a particular foreign country.[5]

The benefits for host countries from the transplantation of
superior technological knowledge and managerial skills make themselves
felt regardless of whether this is the result of direct investment or
occurs through existing MNE facilities in the host country. According
to John H. Dunning, U.S. and Canadian agricultural machinery companies
in Britain were credited with accelerating the mechanization of farming,
resulting in an eight-fold increase in the number of tractors between
1938 and 1955.[6] Prior to investment by U.S. companies, France did
not have a local production of carbon black, and the exploitation of
French petroleum reserves was made possible by resource exploration
techniques developed by an Esso affiliate.[7]

Transfer of technology may also help to raise the productivity
in host country industries. For example, mostly as a consequence of
American technological contributions, the output of British precision
instruments increased tremendously and the availability of advanced
instrumentation also raised the productivity of other British industries.[8]

Another significant benefit for the economy of host countries
can be the reduction of prices for goods produced by superior technology. However, in many cases, the prices remain unchanged, resulting in larger returns for the MNE. Then the only benefit for the
host government would be enlarged tax receipts which of course by
itself can be important, especially for small countries. Perhaps for
this reason as well as to ensure the continuity of the benefits from
technology for their country, host governments are anxious to have
research and development institutes established in their own countries.
As a consequence, they seek to induce MNEs by a variety of means,
including threats, to locate at least some of their research facilities
within their boundaries.

Finally, benefits from MNE investments and transfers of technology and managerial skills may bolster efforts to promote regional
development in host countries. Responding to special inducements
and incentives by national governments and their subdivisions, MNEs
have located new affiliates in depressed regions more often than have
national companies because such action is likely to make them more
welcome in a new host country. During the period from 1959 to 1966,

TABLE 3.3

Host Country Benefits
Plant and Equipment Expenditures of U.S. Subsidiaries
as Percentage of Local Area's Gross Domestic
Fixed Capital Formation on Machinery and
Equipment, 1965

	Percent
Belgium	4.5
France	4.0
West Germany	4.1
Italy	5.0
Netherlands	4.8
EEC	4.5
United Kingdom	10.0

Source: John H. Dunning, "Technology, United States Investment, and European Economic Growth," in Charles P. Kindleberger, ed., The International Corporation: A Symposium (Cambridge, Mass.: M.I.T. Press, 1970).

Host Country Share of Pre-Tax Profits of
Foreign Investors in Raw Material
Enterprises
(Percent)

	Venezuela (oil)	Chile (copper)
1933	n.a.	16
1940	58[a]	28
1950	51	28
1955	52	69
1960	68	65
1965	66	69[b]

[a]1943.
[b]1964.

Source: Adopted from Raymond Vernon, "Foreign Enterprises and Developing Nations in the Raw Materials Industries" (mimeo, 1969), p. 14.

foreign-owned companies acceded to Belgian incentive projects for
locating plants in the provinces by a ratio of three-to-one compared
with Belgian companies.[9]

Benefits for Parent Company Governments

Benefits not only accrue to host countries of MNE affiliates, but
also to the countries where the parent company is located. Foreign
investments and transfers of technological and managerial know-how
may supplement foreign aid objectives of parent country governments
in developing countries. In the United States a special agency, The
Overseas Private Investment Corporation, was established in 1970 to
stimulate investments in the Third World and to provide insurance
and guarantee programs. In countries such as France and Italy where
the state either owns large industrial enterprises or. controls them on
the basis of being a major shareholder, foreign investments by these
enterprises can become potent instruments of foreign policy implementation everywhere. Selective legal or administrative restrictions
on the transfer of technology by any kind of MNE to their foreign
affiliates also may serve parent company governments as persuasive
foreign policy tools.

MNEs involved in extraction industries can offer benefits inasmuch
as they provide for their home governments relatively secure sources
of raw materials without which advanced industrial economies cannot
function successfully. It should be noted that these materials are not
only necessary for strategic purposes, especially for countries such
as the United States which engages in stockpiling programs of strategic
materials, but also for other industrial uses. Table 3.4 illustrates
the need for raw materials for one particular product, jet engines.[10]

On the other side of the ledger, sales of MNEs to their affiliates
may expand the export totals of the parent company and thereby provide
gains for parent country governments. A survey published in 1969[11]
asserted that in 1965 one-third of U.S. total exports was accounted
for by only 300 U.S. multinational corporations which had 3,600 affiliates abroad. The U.S. parent companies exported $8.5 billion in
that year of which $4.4 billion was through these affiliates. Approxi-
mately one-third of U.S. nonagricultural exports was intracompany
trade of enterprises with direct foreign investments. The largest
exports were in industries characterized by MNEs: soap, cosmetics,
and automobiles; the smallest in ones not so characterized: steel and
aircraft. Moreover, foreign affiliates of U.S. enterprises bought
substantial quantities from U.S. sources other than parent companies

TABLE 3.4

Critical Materials Used for Jet Engines

	Pounds Used in Jet Engine	Imports as Percent of Consumption	Where This Material Is Produced (in percent)
Tungsten	80-100	24	U.S. (30) South Korea (19) Canada (12) Australia (8) Bolivia (8) Portugal (7)
Columbium	10-12	100	Brazil (54) Canada (21) Mozambique (18)
Nickel	1,300-1,600	75	Canada (71) New Caledonia (20)
Chromium	2,500-2,800	100	South Africa (31) Turkey (19) S. Rhodesia (19) Philippines (18) Iran (5)
Molybdenum	90-100	0	U.S. (79) Canada (10) Chile (9)
Cobalt	30-40	100	Zaire (Congo-Kinshasa) (60) Morocco (13) Canada (12) Zambia (11)

Source: Harry Magdoff, The Age of Imperialism (New York: Monthly Review Press, 1969), p. 52, Table XI.

(about $600 million in 1965) and perhaps 50 percent of U.S. non-agricultural trade stemmed from MNEs and their affiliates. However, while these figures seem to support the claim that parent companies of MNEs are contributors to a country's export totals, the survey also pointed out that a large number of MNEs did report no exports from the United States to their foreign affiliates which suggests that there is not necessarily a favorable link between the existence of MNEs and their contribution to exports of the country where the parent company is located. In fact, there is some evidence for the argument that the establishment of production facilities set up by MNEs abroad might be harmful to the balance of trade of the parent company country inasmuch as "jobs are exported" rather than goods.[12]

Changes in MNE Structures and Management Methods

The effect of changes in corporate structures and management practices of MNEs on host countries is difficult to determine. Nevertheless, one can speculate that a change from a monocentric to a polycentric structure will be viewed as beneficial by those countries in which the new headquarters companies are located. The higher level of MNE decision-making in the host country flowing from such changes is likely to draw indigenous talent into the executive suite of the new headquarters and may entail the establishment of new management and research facilities. Host governments may perceive that the MNE's executives will be guided more by the interests of the host country than previously and thus a more favorable climate is created for MNE-host government relations, especially if the executives adopt polycentric orientations as described earlier.[13] Additional attitudinal changes of host governments may occur where executives of MNEs and their affiliates become strongly geocentric-oriented provided that such an attitude is accepted as supporting the objectives of governmental elites in the host countries. Host government leaders may then encourage MNEs to develop their affiliates as world-wide bases with global capabilities, admit specialists and managers from around the world for employment in MNE affiliates, promote equitable pay-offs to other countries on rational rather than emotional criteria, and seek to solve internal problems in collaboration with MNE affiliates.[14]

If the leadership in the parent company country follows a neutralistic nonalignment type philosophy and foreign policy or perhaps harbors ambitions for a world-wide community, it is not inconceivable that government-MNE relations might be improved by changes of the parent company structure from the monocentric to the polycentric

model. In such an event, the considerations outlined for host governments in the preceding paragraph would also apply mutatis mutandis
to possible actions by home governments. However, in the face of the
domestic political realities in which most national governments operate,
it is much more likely to encounter ethnocentric attitudes of governmental and political elites. Governmental leaders would probably
insist that home country firms expand and capture larger sectors of
the world market, repatriate as much of the profits as possible to the
home country as quickly as this can be done, and expect the executives
of the foreign affiliates of the MNE to identify with national interests
of the home country as opposed to the host country.[15]

Changes in MNE management practices leading to the initiation
of transnational integration of production facilities among existing or
new affiliates also cause various effects in the countries in which the
affiliates are located. The introduction of integrated production may
require the opening of a new plant or the enlargement of an old one
which cannot but have favorable implications for employment and
technological know-how in a particular country. However, it may also
necessitate the closing of plants or simply lay-offs of workers, and
politically this can be a very sensitive matter.

If the transnational integration of production facilities among
MNE affiliates were to assume the form of an evermore tightly knit
web, it would entail a growing integration of the national economies of
the countries drawn into the web. The result would be much greater
interdependence among these countries, which could be regarded as
an asset, as well as an increasing degree of "dependence" of each
country on foreign governmental and nongovernmental forces and
decisions, which many governmental decision-makers might be
reluctant to accept. In case these countries are engaged in an economic
integration scheme such as a Common Market or a free trade area,
the rational presumption should be that such dependence would not be
harmful since in fact it is an objective of the scheme. But we know
from the experiences of the Latin American Free Trade Association
(LAFTA), the Central American Common Market, and even the European
Common Market that national decision-makers tend to resist any
forces they cannot fully control since they are fearful of losing their
national prerogatives and positions of power. Nevertheless, an increasing degree of economic interdependence among several countries
will generate potent, well-coordinated pressures by MNE affiliates
and their "allies" in the ranks of governmental elites to do everything
possible for the smooth functioning of the integrated production processes. However, the national decision-makers are likely to be reluctant to take the necessary steps such as the harmonization of laws,

administrative procedures, and policies to satisfy the petitioners, but gradual and slow progress may well be forthcoming ultimately. Sometimes it is argued that the maximization of international welfare resulting from the integrated production methods of MNE affiliates should convince the national governments of the value of this approach. But national governments are mainly concerned about national welfare maximization which is likely to bolster their own power position and rarely have a genuine inclination to promote the common interests of mankind. Thus, the integrating force of MNEs may not be welcomed by national governments, or only so far as national interests can be satisfied. This has been demonstrated clearly by the European Community Commission's industrial policy proposal of 1970 which was oriented subtly against American MNEs despite the fact that U.S. corporations had taken better advantage of the EEC unitary market provisions than their European counterparts and thereby had given a greater lift to the integration process of Europe.

Benefits for the Third World

The economic and social effects of MNE investments and transfer of technological and managerial knowledge can be most striking when the receiving countries are part of the developing world. However, as noted above,[16] a high percentage of total investment by American and other MNEs is devoted to oil and other extractive industries, and only about 22 percent to manufacturing industries for whose establishment a particularly urgent need exists in the developing nations.[17] Nevertheless, even extractive industries often create new social infrastructures of schools, housing, health facilities, and transportation necessary to conduct their business. In addition, local engineers and technicians can learn from exposure to the advanced training and experience of their counterparts brought in by management from the advanced countries.[18] However, investments in manufacturing industries are likely to produce more lasting benefits in developing areas because the technological and managerial skills introduced into developing countries are likely to spread as educational levels for the population rise. In some developing countries in Asia, such as India, Pakistan, Ceylon, and the Philippines, and in some Latin American countries such as Argentina and Brazil, there is actually no dearth of persons who already have the general education and a good natural ability to fit the cast of the contemporary effective manager.[19] Therefore, new industries can eventually be established and run by citizens of these and other developing countries, causing an overall improvement in social and economic standards which, in turn, may contribute to greater political stability of the new nations.

A few examples illustrate the favorable impact of MNE's on Third World host countries where affiliates are located. Sears pioneered the modern supermarkets of Mexico and established a large number of native manufacturing industries to furnish goods for its retail stores. United Fruit Company, despite its reputation as an "exploiter," expanded the real incomes and welfare of the peoples in Central America where it operated and contributed immeasurably to the control of disease in the area. International Basic Economic Corporation, an organization controlled by the Rockefeller family with affiliates in 33 developing countries and concentrating upon agribusiness, promoted innovations in food production and was active in the construction of low-cost housing.20

Developing countries with large-scale unemployment and relatively well-educated populations have benefited from the establishment of MNE affiliates which used low-cost labor for the manufacture of parts for electronics and other high-technology products to be sold in established markets, mainly in the advanced countries of the world. Taiwan, South Korea, and Singapore are some of the countries that have benefited from such investments and as a consequence the economic levels of their people as a whole have risen. Other developing countries, such as Mauritius,21 have geared their current development plans to attracting appropriate MNEs for similar purposes.

Indirect benefits for developing countries may stem from multinational bank affiliates and partnership arrangements with local banks. For example, the Mellon National Bank and Trust Company has a 25 percent stake in the Bank of London and South America (BOLSA) which in turn has branches in various South American countries. New York's First National City Bank has a 40 percent stake in National and Grindley's Bank, Ltd. in London, whose main operations are in India, Pakistan, the Middle East, and East Africa. The pooled financial resources of U.S. and British banks are made available for investments and other purposes in the Third World.22

While potential contribution of MNEs to the development of the Third World is large, much depends on the political stability and the attitude of their governments toward private investment. If the stability is high and the attitudes favorable, private investment is encouraged and MNEs can fulfill their roles as expanders of economic development. As Neil Jacoby points out, the remarkable evolution of such countries as Mexico, Malaysia, and Taiwan have testified to this truth.23 However, governmental instability and unfavorable attitudes are not the only source of political risks with which MNEs may be faced in developing countries. Others are social unrest and disorder, recent or impending independence, armed conflict, and private vested interests. The extent of these risks depends to a large degree on how beneficial or damaging governmental and political elites view the effects of MNE initiatives and activities with respect to their countries and especially their own goals, ambitions, and expectations. This then requires an examination and analysis of actual and perceived draw-backs of MNE initiatives for national governments.

DRAWBACKS AND PROBLEMS FOR
GOVERNMENTAL ACTORS

Certain drawbacks caused by MNE activities can affect both developed and developing countries, but some of them may be more difficult to cope with by the latter. Moreover, perception of dis-advantages and costs may be more extensive among Third World governmental leaders as problems arising from newly gained in-dependence and "nation-building," as well as from former relations with colonial masters, tend to color their views.

Obviously, the closing of plants either in the country where the parent company is located or in the host countries of affiliates if more favorable production facilities are found elsewhere will be regarded as a drawback because it reduces employment opportunities and may affect unfavorably the potential for exports. But the establishment of new plants can also have disadvantages by creating pressures on wages and inducing or reinforcing inflationary trends. Moreover, the location of new plants desired by MNEs can cause problems. For example, during the last few years many foreign MNEs considered the Rhine River area as the most suitable region to set up production facilities in the European Common Market. For France this location posed problems since she has only a relatively small piece of her territory in this area and therefore felt less favored than some of the other EEC countries.[24]

Inflationary pressures in host countries may also be fueled by large-scale inflows of capital, but other aspects of investment flows between parent companies and their foreign affiliates may be even more vexing. Once affiliates are established by direct investments, they may seek to obtain additional finances locally. Such tapping of the local capital markets may either be by voluntary decision of the MNE or prompted by the parent company's government imposing mandatory controls on the outflow of funds as was done in 1968 by the United States.[25] In any case, the entry of large multinational corpora-tions into a host country's capital market may well dry up the normal sources for financing upon which smaller national companies usually depend. Despite attempts by host countries to prohibit bank loans to "foreign" firms, the question arises as to whether or when long-established affiliates of MNEs can be characterized as "foreign." But even if affiliates of American MNEs were prevented from using the local capital market, they could, in Europe at least, resort to the Eurodollar market. Borrowings in Eurodollars exceeded $3 billion in 1967 and the total amount of Eurodollars in 1970 was estimated to exceed $50 billion.26 However, it should pointed out that the Eurodollar borrowings had at least an indirect negative impact on the national financial market and therefore were somewhat of a drawback for certain host countries.

The mandatory controls devised by the U.S. government also required extensive repatriation of earnings on foreign investments and other short-term financial assets held in foreign countries by parent companies. This provision could not but arouse the displeasure of host governments which complained that the imposition of capital controls by the American government challenges the sovereignty of the host country by dampening its economic growth and altering the investment projections in the host country. It should noted that the U.S. provisions were much less stringent for investments and reinvested earnings in developing countries. Nevertheless, these controls were convincing evidence for many observers that the U.S. MNE had indeed become an instrument of American foreign policy providing through its affiliates a potent channel into the economies of the host countries.27

The suspicion that the MNE is a tool of the foreign policy of the parent country government is not new and can find much justification in the history of the colonial empires and of American actions in Latin America. Of course, powerful governments may also become instruments for achieving objectives pursued by MNEs when an influential corporation calls for help in a particular host country. Moreover, apprehension regarding the MNE can be aroused simply by its ability to shift important resources such as the infusion of capital or the transfer of knowledge from one country to another with relative impunity. This places the MNE in a strong bargaining position when it comes to determining the present or future conditions of its operations in a particular country. The combination of powerful resources with world-wide operations affects not only host governments, but also control by the parent company country inasmuch as it furnishes the MNE with sufficient operational latitude to circumvent such rules as export embargoes by shipment from foreign affiliates.

Host governments may also be apprehensive about the ability of

multinational companies to affect tax receipts unfavorably. This can
be done through allocation of production to facilities in low-tax countries or through the manipulation of profits on items that can be moved
across national boundaries from one subsidiary to another for assembly
or sales so that the most profit per item accrues in the countries with
the lowest tax rates. [28]

All the above factors are apt to produce fears in the minds of
governmental and political leaders that MNE operations can be a
liability to their country inasmuch as they may impose serious constraints on the scope of the national decision-making process by reducing the availability of options and forcing solutions not perceived
as in accordance with the national interest. In industrially advanced
countries these fears may stem from three major concerns: foreign
domination of industries, technological dependence, and disturbance
of national plans. [29]

Foreign Domination of Industries

The concern that the industries of host countries will be dominated
by affiliates of foreign MNEs stems, as Jack N. Behrman observes,
from three sources: the giant size of MNEs and their affiliates, their
concentration on key industrial sectors, and their aggressive behavior.
Data provided in Chapter 2[30] testifed to the size of U.S. MNEs. This
may be emphasized by observing that the sales of the five largest U.S.
corporations equal Italy's GNP, that GM's sales are larger than those
of the 17 largest German companies, and GE's turnover is five times
that of the entire French electronics industry. [31] European indus-
trialists claim that competition is possible from plant to plant, but
not from company to company because the U.S. MNEs could, by concentrating their power in one place, drive out all competition. Moreover, foreign control of industries in host countries seems to concentrate often in the largest firms. In 1963, 40 percent of foreign-
controlled Canadian firms were companies with assets over $100
million each.   Foreign ownership in the French chemical industry
is also concentrated in a few large companies which accounted for
25 percent of total industry-wide sales. Similar situations exist in
Australian and British industries. Among the nearly 1,500 subsidiaries
owned by foreign companies in Britain in 1964, the top seven companies,
ranked by investment, accounted for 25 percent of total investment
and 14 percent of their total earnings. Since the large affiliates of
U.S. and other parent companies frequently have a higher rate of
profit and reinvest a larger share of these profits than smaller companies—basically a benefit to host countries—they pose a threat to

smaller domestically owned firms. This is viewed as a danger by
many Europeans who do not want to be condemned to Canada's fate
which is regarded as being nearly 50 percent "owned" by U.S. enterprises.[32]

Equally distasteful to the governments and people of many advanced
host countries is the thought that certain industrial sectors should fall
under the domination of foreign MNEs. This is especially the case
when it involves technology-oriented and growth sectors which have
strategic significance for a country's national security. Such control
provides these firms with potential means to influence the international
behavior of host governments, or at a minimum to restrict their freedom of external action.

Few precise data are available on the domination of individual
industries by foreign firms in particular countries. Some illustrative
examples are found on Tables 3.5 through 3.8 which show the degree
of foreign control over industrial sectors and selected industries in
Canada and Western Europe. Table 3.5 and the first part of Table 3.8
indicate that in Canada (1963) and Germany (1968) foreign control was
heaviest in the field of petroleum products where it reached 74 percent
and 84 percent respectively in the two countries. In Canada foreign
control is also strong in manufacturing as well as mining and smelting
industries amounting to about 60 percent. As expected, a large number
of the controlling multinational companies in Canada and Germany are
American. Table 3.6 evidences the high percentages of U.S. ownership
in the Canadian automobile and rubber industries which in 1963 were
97 and 90 percent respectively.[33] Table 3.7 confirms that a high percentage of the largest Canadian firms are foreign controlled, i.e. more
than 50 percent equity-controlled. Twenty six of these firms are controlled by 25 U.S. based MNEs. These companies, both Canadian and
U.S. are listed in this table. The second section of Table 3.8 shows
the increasing shares of oil refining capacities in the EEC which have
fallen under the control of U.S. firms. By 1970 the refining capacities
of the Benelux countries were more than 50 percent controlled by U.S.
companies, whereas in France this percentage reached 20 percent. The
third section of this table presents the foreign ownership share in selected industries in France and the U.S. share in U.K. industries estimated on the basis of their percentage of sales of various products.
In both countries the carbon black industries hold top honors.

As far as West European industry as a whole is concerned, the
largest U.S. investment has been in the oil, chemical, transportation
equipment, metals, machinery, electrical, and food sectors. From
1963 to 1967 takeover bids by U.S. companies in the automobile industry

TABLE 3.5

Foreign Control of Selected Industries in Canada
(Percentages)

	End of 1959			End of 1963		
	Canada	U.S.	Other	Canada	U.S.	Other
Manufacturing	43	44	13	40	46	14
Petroleum and natural gas	27	67	6	26	62	12
Other mining and smelting	39	53	8	41	52	7
Railways	98	2	0	98	2	0
Other utilities	95	4	1	96	4	0
Merchandising and construction	91	6	3	88	7	5
All industries	68	26	6	66	27	7

Source: The Canadian Balance of International Payments 1963, 1964, and 1965 and International Investment Position, Dominion Bureau of Statistics, Canada.

TABLE 3.6

Percentage Ownership of Canadian Industries and Sales by U.S. Affiliates

	Percentage Ownership of Total Capital 1963	Percent of Total Sales 1961
Automobiles	97	—
Rubber	90	77
Electrical apparatus	66	45
Chemicals	54	43
Agricultural machinery	50	42
Pulp and paper	35	30
Transport equipment	33	67
Beverages	17	20
Textiles	13	18
Iron and steel mills	2	40

Sources: Adapted from The Canadian Balance of International Payments 1965, Dominion Bureau of Statistics, Canada; and Jack N. Behrman, National Interests and the Multinational Enterprise: Tensions Among the North Atlantic Countries (Englewood Cliffs, N.J.: Prentice-Hall, 1970), p. 40.

TABLE 3.7

Fortune's 500 U.S. Firms, Control of Leading
100 Canadian Firms, 1966

Canadian Company			U.S. Parent Company	
Rank by Sales	Name		Rank by Sales	Name
1	Imperial Oil		3	Standard Oil, N. J.
3	Ford Motor		2	Ford
10	British American Oil		10	Gulf Oil
16	Canadian General Electric		4	General Electric
24	Texaco Canada		7	Texaco Inc.
26	International Harvester		18	International Harvester
32	Canadian Westinghouse		19	Westinghouse Electric
33	Dupont of Canada		12	DuPont de Nemours
34	Crown Zellerbach		108	Crown Zellerbach
35	International Business Machines		9	IBM
36	Union Carbide		27	Union Carbide
45	Goodyear Tire & Rubber		21	Goodyear Tire & Rubber
48	Dow Chemical		50	Dow Chemical
50	British Columbia Telephone		22	General Telephone & Electronics
51	Chemcell		77	Celanese
53	Weldwood		76	U.S. Plywood
63	General Food		38	General Foods
64	Proctor & Gamble		26	Proctor & Gamble
81	Columbia Cellulose		77	Celanese
86	H. J. Heinz		129	H. J. Heinz
94	Hudson Bay Oil & Gas		33	Continental Oil
95	Canadian Canners		162	California Packers
99	Dominion Dairies		25	National Dairies
100	Ontario Steel Products		123	Rockwell-Standard

Source: Isaiah A. Litvak and Christopher J. Maule, "Foreign Investment in Canada," in Isaiah A. Litvak and Christopher J. Maule, eds., Foreign Investment: The Experience of Host Countries (New York: Praeger Publishers, 1970), p. 89.

TABLE 3.8

Foreign Control of Selected Industries in Europe

Germany, 1968

Average Foreign Control 18.7 percent of which
U.S. Share is 44 percent

Petroleum products	84
Food processing	48
Fibers, rubber and asbestos	35
Electric equipment	31.4
Steel, machinery, autos	25

Source: Vareingter Wirtschaftdienst Bulletin, October 6, 1969.

Refinery Production Capacities—U.S. Share
(percent)

	Jan. 1964	Jan. 1969	Jan. 1970
Germany (West)	31.2	37.9	38.2
France	19.6	16.8	20.1
Italy	23.0	27.9	27.8
Netherlands	39.0	47.5	54.8
Belgium/Luxembourg	17.0	43.9	46.8

Source: Rainer Hellmann, The Challenge to U.S. Dominance of the International Corporation (New York: Dunellen, 1970), p. 53.

Foreign Ownership in Selected French and U.K. Industries

France 1964 Industry	Percent of Foreign Ownership	United Kingdom 1964 Industry	U.S. Firms (% of Sales)
Black carbon	95	Refined Petroleum products	over 40
Synthetic rubber	90		
Margarine	90	Computers	over 40
Ball bearings	80	Carbon black	over 75
Agricultural equipment	70	Cars	over 50
Telecommunication equipment	65	Refrigerators	33 1/3-50
Oil distribution	60	Pharmaceuticals	over 20
Elevators	60	Tractors and agricultural machinery	over 40
Electrical lamps	50		
Office equipment & materials	50	Instruments	over 15
Tires	50	Razor blades and safety razors	approx. 55
Plumbing	50		
Automobile accessories	40		
Radio and television	35		
Electrical appliances	20		
Toys	20		
Machine tools	30		

Sources: Census of Foreign Investments (Ministry of France, 1967); and Hary Magdoff, The Age of Imperialism: The Economics of U.S. Foreign Policy (New York: Monthly Review Press, 1969), p. 61.

brought their share of the market to more than 30 percent. The share
of U.S. companies in the computer industry of the EEC countries has
been estimated in 1969 at 80 percent.[34] In Australia, foreign firms
owned about one-quarter of all business corporation assets in 1965.
They controlled about one-fourth of Brazil's rail and electrical industries and about 18 percent of its manufacturing.[35]

In addition to the possible constraints on a country's foreign
policy that might flow from foreign domination of industrial sectors
or individual industries, other drawbacks may be perceived by national
governments and elite groups. Some of these are alleged "trans-
atlantic decisions" for large-scale dismissals of workers in host country affiliates to which Europeans, accustomed to a high degree of
employment stability, are especially sensitive; forced alignment of
traditional farm work schedules to factory production programs as
was done by an American canning factory in France; and the creation
of labor shortages, especially in Germany, through new investments
in plants. Aggressive behavior of MNE affiliates in host countries
also has deepened the concern of national government leaders and the
public-at-large about foreign industrial dominance and has contributed
to the perception that MNE penetration of a particular country could
on balance be a liability. Aggressive behavior may range from a very
rapid rate of acquisition of national companies, especially when accompanied by extensive publicity, to the displacement of nationals in
top executive positions or their rejection from such a post in favor of
a citizen of the MNE parent company country. Other examples of
aggressive behavior looked upon as damaging to the host country and
its economy are offensive labor recruitment practices such as the use
of loudspeaker trucks placed in front of competitor's factories blaring
out attractive offers to the latter's workers,[36] or flamboyant, hard-sell
type marketing techniques including severe price-cutting. The techniques may well be the result of production over-capacities created
by new investments; on the other hand the nature of the MNE makes
it possible to sustain losses from unprofitable sales in one country
by increasing margins in affiliates elsewhere.

Technological Dependence

The benefits that may accrue to host countries from the transfer
of technological know-how were stressed above. However, while host
country governments may appreciate the benefits they derive from the
transfer of technologies, they may also be apprehensive that in the
case of serious needs such transfers may be withheld either by decision
of the headquarter company or by the government of the country in

which that company or the parent company is located. The United
States, the major "exporter" of technology in the world, has two
principal laws on its books, The Trading with the Enemy Act of 1917
and the Export Control Act of 1949, under which the U.S. government
can deny another country access to goods or technology generated by
affiliates more than 50 percent U.S. owned in that country or a third
country. Moreover, multinational corporations pursuing their own
self-interests may use the transfer of technology to bargain for more
favorable and flexible treatment. Thus, the ability of MNEs to transfer
technology to the host countries of its affiliate creates serious dilemmas
for the governmental decision-makers and conjures up vistas of intolerable dependence. Governments fear that without national sources
of technological advance their economic development will be impeded
and their military and political influences reduced. But to advance
independently requires facilities for fundamental research within the
national boundaries which is frequently beyond the financial capabilities
of domestic firms and even governments.

In attempting to solve the dilemma, governments can choose
from the following options:

1. To forego the acquisition of certain advanced technologies
such as space exploration which in fact may not contribute to their
particular needs.

2. To generate the necessary funds for setting up domestically
owned facilities for the development of needed technologies.

3. To import technology by purchase of the desired products.

4. To import technology by permitting the establishment of
foreign-owned production facilities for the desired item.[37]

For most governments the cost of purchasing technological
independence is excessive and therefore they lean toward options 1
and 4. The latter option provides some control over the MNE affiliate
which is the vehicle for importing the technology because it is located
within the borders of the host country. At the same time, as mentioned
earlier, host governments seek to reduce dependence by urging MNEs
to establish local research and development facilities. The extent to
which this request is followed varies greatly. Some have established
separate R&D institutes while others have authorized affiliates to
create appropriate R&D sections. In other cases institutes have been
set up whose main purpose is to monitor published research carried
out within the host country and surrounding areas. In most instances,

however, the bulk of research efforts is concentrated in the parent organization or is directly under its control, although affiliates are frequently encouraged to perform development work for the local market or for improving locally used processes.[38] Thus, dependence of host governments may not be eliminated, but somewhat alleviated by the above practices of MNEs.

However, even if relatively independent R&D institutes or affiliate sections are established in host countries, additional drawbacks may have to be considered. These institutes may stifle the creation of domestically owned research bases and they may adversely affect the local supply of scientific and engineering talent to locally owned R&D organizations. In fact, MNE affiliates are known to have purchased fully manned and equipped research institutes from domestic owners.[39]

The above considerations lead to the conclusion that despite the substantial benefits which host countries derive from technological transfers, they are also sources of tensions, stimulate perceptions of threat by the MNE in the minds of host governments and other elites, and carry with them some objective drawbacks as well.

Disturbance to Economic Plans

The economically advanced countries of the world have increasingly assumed responsibilities for assuring the social and economic welfare of their citizens despite continued and varying lip service given to the principle of free enterprise. Economic growth and stability as well as full employment are the major goals of the countries which they seek to reach through varying degrees of planning and the commitment of public means. France has been in the forefront of economic planning but most of the other advanced countries have also become involved in some form of governmental planning for their national economies.

Jack N. Behrman argues that the more responsibility for economic growth the government accepts, the greater its control over the economy, and the greater the possibility that the MNE will be viewed as a potential disturber of economic plans.[40] Accordingly, since France has been the most active country in planning the growth and the direction of the economy, it has been least receptive to foreign direct investments, while Germany, Britain, and Italy, less active in economic planning, have been most receptive to these investments.

Although MNEs and their affiliates can make substantial

contribution to the economic growth of the host countries, they can also inject uncertainties into the economies of these countries by altering economic factors and reducing the government's ability to predict reactions to its plans since MNEs may be able to ignore governmental persuasions and pursue policies not supportive of the national goals. In particular they may cause uncertainties and risks by creating economic disequilibria through concentration of foreign ownership in industries of the highest returns, over-investment in equipment industries resulting in overcapacities, producing deficits in the balance of payments, and causing disturbances in the labor market.

The underlying reasons why the MNE and its affiliates in a particular host country can create the above disequilibria are the options available to the management regarding the sources of funds and the direction of investments which remove it from the normal control techniques and inducements of the host government. Having alternative investment opportunities elsewhere in the world, MNE managements may not respond to the incentives which would be sufficient for a decision desired by the government of a domestically owned firm. Moreover, the ability to shift funds among the components of an MNE through intercompany sales, technical assistance fees, royalties, and allocation of headquarter expenses may have impacts on the host country's balance of payments which may be inexpedient in terms of host government goals. In addition, these shifts in funds reinforce already existing currency exchange pressures; in fact, threatening disturbances in the exchange market may have caused the fund movements because corporation treasurers wanted to safeguard or even improve their overall assets when devaluations or revaluations of national currencies appeared to be likely.[41]

Finally, MNEs can allocate export territories among its affiliates to suit their own objectives which may go as far as removing an export market entirely from a particular affiliate. Such action may reduce undesirable competition among affiliates but at the same time damage the prospects of the host country for the expansion of exports from its territory. Of course parent company governments may face essentially the same situation when, for example, the American automobile manufacturers import parts for their compacts from their European affiliates rather than produce them in the United States.

All the above actions may impinge on the ability of national governments to carry out their economic plans and programs and therefore constitute serious drawbacks for a government which has affiliates of MNEs within their national boundaries.[42]

The Developing Countries

Many of the adverse effects of MNE transnational operations suffered by the economically advanced countries also burden the governments of the Third World. However, since manufacturing facilities of MNE's are mainly located in the advanced countries, some of the problems of control over MNE affiliates examined in the preceding pages and the security concerns flowing from the availability of advanced technologies are much less significant. On the other hand, a different set of issues and problems, many psychological in origin and stemming from the needs of nation building, the natural desires of political leaders to retain their power, and from the general Third World conditions of poverty, illiteracy, and traditional political cultures, aggravates some of the drawbacks and generates additional ones.

Without doubt the governments of all developing countries wish to enhance the standard of living of their people through various means such as diversification of agricultural commodity exports, industrialization, and perhaps exports of manufactured goods. However, they lack the necessary resources—technology, skills, organization, access to international markets, and foreign exchange. The MNE possesses these resources, but suspicion and distrust on the part of governmental leaders and political elites in the developing countries color their perceptions of possible benefits and drawbacks.

What are the major reasons for this coloration of perceptions? All of the present-day Third World leaders have experienced the trauma of colonialism instilling in them a fear of foreign capital as something inherently evil because it was used for the exploitation of resources that in their view belonged to the people of their countries. In addition, many of the present-day leaders have been attracted to the socialist model of the economy either through their educational experiences or by being captivated by the apparent successes of the Soviet and Communist Chinese systems. Other leaders had backgrounds in the civil service or the military and therefore had very little comprehension of economic and business issues. In fact, in several developing countries business activity has not been viewed as an "honorable" profession compared to some forms of public service, a medical doctor, a lawyer, or joining the armed forces. In many of these countries, businessmen were considered to be too closely associated with the former colonial powers and some were accused of wanting to maintain the colonial form of government to protect their own economic interests. At the same time, political leaders in the forefront of the independent movements and the post-independence political consolidation period viewed indigenous business groups, especially the large business

enterprises, as being too narrow in their outlook and exclusively
concerned with the immediate question of profits which, in turn, made
them suspicious of the motives and methods of businessmen.

The attitudes of Third World leadership groups toward MNEs,
shaped by their backgrounds and positions held, have been reinforced
by the tasks which need to be performed to retain the position of power
assumed after independence had been gained. These tasks include the
continuous mobilization of citizens to rally around the nation, highly
visible achievements in the enhancement of their economic welfare,
and a continuous exaltation of the new nationhood which must not suffer
from any apparent infringement upon the independence and decision-
making autonomy of the government. The priority of these tasks implies
that the MNE with its transnational capabilities and large resources is
likely to be regarded as a potential threat to the leadership groups and
to the independence of their country since its control may be difficult.
Therefore the obvious benefits of an affiliate for a developing country
may be outweighed by the problem of control to assure full acceptance
by the MNE of the broad objectives of the host government. In practical
terms this often means the insistence of the government that ownership
of the MNE affiliate be at least 51 percent in its hands although minority ownership has been accepted at times. Such an arrangement is
carried out usually through the country's development corporation, a
governmental agency which is the participant in a number of these
ventures and supervises compliance with governmental regulations.
Of course, these terms are frequently not acceptable to MNEs and the
range of beneficial investments in a given developing country is greatly
reduced.

In concluding this discussion of the attitudes of Third World
leadership groups toward the MNE two observations should be made.
While attitudes described above are typical, there are exceptions from
time to time and in certain countries, often depending on precedents
of MNE investments. In addition attitude changes appear to be in the
wind. For example, in the summer of 1971 General Idi Amin, President
of Uganda, announced that the Uganda Development Corporation would
seek to reduce its financial participation in various enterprises to 25-
40 percent. Moreover, a new, younger generation of governmental
leaders and administrators may also adopt a more flexible and favorable view of the benefits of MNE activities. Offsetting these favorable
developments for MNE investments in some parts of the Third World
are tendencies of private business firms in a given country, despite
their commitment to free enterprise, to promote or support government
decisions against permitting the establishment of an MNE affiliate if
they view this as a threat to their vested interests. In fact, in such a

case they may use opposition parties, if they exist, to lobby against
admission in the event that the government is seriously considering
issuing an appropriate invitation to an MNE. Their pervasive fear is
that new competitive forces brought into the country may compel them
to abandon their traditional and often antiquated business policies.
Since a widespread regimen of control and regulations operating in
many developing countries assured competition to be restricted and
profits to flow in easily, it is not surprising that many local businessmen in their areas are anxious not to rock the boat.[43]

INDETERMINATE EFFECTS

Chapter 1 touched on attitude changes which might be caused
directly or indirectly by MNE activities when affiliates in certain
countries use advertising to project a certain image or when news
items regarding these companies appear in local newspapers, on TV,
or radio. Also mentioned was the attitude changes resulting from
host country citizens driving foreign cars such as Fiats or Toyotas
inasmuch as they create an impression about a certain MNE. It was
also stated that the effects of such attitude changes on host country
governmental decision-makers cannot be determined immediately and
can only be judged as a benefit or drawback after a considerable lapse
of time.

Here attention will be focused briefly on one aspect of each of
these examples which has interesting implications for the future effects
of the attitude changes. MNEs are relatively new institutions in the
societies of host countries and are involved in a legitimizing process
for whose success advertising of and news items regarding MNE
affiliates may play crucial and sometimes conflicting roles. The aim
of the legitimizing process is to create perceptions in host governmental leaders and elites that MNE affiliates and activities contribute
to the society, are necessary organizations, and should be granted
autonomous existence. According to Howard V. Perlmutter[44] situations
and activities for which legitimacy is sought are: (1) the multinational
firm is a model citizen and necessary to the host country's economic
growth; (2) multinational firms are so interwined in the economic life
of the host country that rescue attempts should be made in the event
of crises by host institutions such as banks, unions, or government;
(3) workers have access to greater prosperity through the multinational
firm; (4) the presence of MNE affiliates in host countries gives access
to global markets and technology and therefore benefits local business
interests; (5) the presence of multinational firms is justified on the
basis of its presence in other countries (particularly the parent country

of the firm); (6) the multinational firm must be relatively autonomous and is necessary for the home country's economic viability.

If such beliefs can be created eventually in parent and host countries, the effects of MNE activities will be viewed by the governments involved as highly beneficial. If MNEs fail to establish these beliefs, perceptions of host governments and elites are likely to be negative and the effects perceived as drawbacks and liabilities.

The effects from attitude changes stemming from citizens of host countries driving foreign cars such as a Toyota or Fiat may be especially salient if these experiences take place in Communist countries. Although Fiat's automobile manufacturing plant in the Soviet Union has just begun to ship its products throughout Russia, other Fiat factories in Eastern Europe (Yugoslavia and Poland) have produced cars for a longer period.[45] In these countries the cars sold may not only be a pertinent tool to create a favorable impression about an important Western consumer good, but may also stimulate new tastes and expectations of the public which, in turn, can bring about changes in the perceptions of governmental leaders and other elites. As a consequence Communist governments may consider it beneficial to permit some of their state-operated enterprises to engage in transnational collaboration with Western MNEs. These ventures are difficult to devise and slow in emerging, but some have borne fruit in addition to the Fiat undertaking. Examples are the joint development of digitally controlled lathes by Knap of Germany and Csepel of Hungary and the jointly owned (50-50) trading company set up in Switzerland by Zocca of Italy and a Bulgarian machine tool company.[46] In Yugoslavia changes in the law have gone so far as to permit foreign investment in domestic enterprises and the investment opportunities thus created have begun to attract Western firms.[47] As a result of all these developments West European and Japanese MNEs are seeking now to move further in the direction of an international division of labor across ideological borders. One may therefore see the emergence of what Perlmutter calls the "transideological" enterprise, a multinational operation for which not only the importance of political frontiers has diminished but which can overcome also the barriers of opposing political ideologies. And it should be kept in mind that the perception of governmental leaders to regard such transnational interactions as beneficial may be aided by the attitude changes described in the example related earlier.

Reactions and Counteractions of National Governments

The various benefits that are likely to accrue to parent and host

countries from transnational initiatives of MNEs and the drawbacks
that might also flow from these initiatives often pose serious dilemmas
for political and administrative decision-makers in the states affected.
While on the one hand these decision-makers may feel compelled to
compete for these benefits by offering different inducements such as
tax advantages to MNEs planning new foreign investments or facilities,
they are also anxious to control as much as possible the influx of
these investments or closely supervise their implementations. A
major concern has been the prevention of foreign control of strategically
important companies and industries and for this purpose host governments in the industrially advanced countries as well as the Third
World have employed weapons ranging from the stimulation of adverse
public opinion to a variety of legal measures. The most extreme of
these measures is expropriation which has been carried out in several
developing countries. In addition, host governments have attempted to
curb and supervise foreign affiliates through various regulations
which often have placed constraints on the strategies of maximizing
profits through the use of multinational operations.

Governments of countries in which parent companies are located
have also interfered with MNEs by regulating the outflow of capital
and the transfer of technology. The reactions and counteractions of
host and parent governments to MNE initiatives highlight the interaction process engendered which frequently leads to considerable tension
between nongovernmental and governmental actors as well as among
the governments of states involved. The counteractions can be divided
into three categories: foreign investment controls, countermeasures
to transfer of technology controls of parent country governments,
and operational and ownership restrictions.

Investment Controls

Investment controls can be applied by the governments of parent
companies or by host governments. Already discussed are the mandatory controls in the outflow of capital and the repatriation of profits
which the United States imposed in 1968.[48] These controls followed
a voluntary capital restraint program initiated in 1965 which was
aimed primarily toward increasing the net return of dollars through
greater return of earnings and other means to ease the pressure of
the U.S. balance-of-payments deficit. As stated above, these programs
aroused the ire and dissatisfaction of host countries of MNE affiliates
and led to attempts to frustrate and counter these regulations which
were regarded as unwarranted intrusions into the sovereign sphere
of the host governments.

Foreign investments and parent company-affiliate relations were

also affected by exchange control programs that were instituted by
such countries as Britain and France when balance-of-payments
problems caused difficulties for the national economies. The scope
of these programs varies from country to country and from period
to period. Obviously, countries with chronic balance-of-payments
problems are undesirable parent countries for MNEs since they
seriously hamper investments to be made abroad unless such funds
happen to be already in the foreign countries concerned. Some
countries such as Italy and others require authorization for the outflow
of capital destined for foreign investment because they fear that this
may deprive the country of scarce funds urgently needed for domestic
development.[49]

Investment controls also exist in the recipient countries where
MNE affiliates are to be established. Although aware of the benefits
of foreign investments, the main reason is the apprehension that key
industries might fall under foreign control, a problem which, as
discussed earlier, bothers the governments of both developed and
developing nations. Therefore, most governments have adopted special
authorization procedures, some of which are mainly administrative
and statistical checks, while others involve substantive screening.
The latter seek to discourage openly or indirectly undesirable investments, limit the presence of foreigners on management boards or the
share of foreign ownership permitted, or simply exclude nonresidents
or noncitizens from certain types of business such as banking,
communications, utilities, or extractive industries not only in the
Third World, but also in industrially advanced countries. Among the
latter, France and Japan have been most active in curtailing the
inflow of foreign investments or have given approval only after insisting
on significant modification of the investment plans for which the well-
known case of Machines Bull of France and General Electric provides
an excellent illustration.[50] A very recent example of French screening
is the denial of the request of the Heinz Company to assume control
of Grey-Poupon Mustard.[51] Although the United States set up a
special office in 1966 to encourage European investment, there are a
number of regulations both on the federal and state levels which
restrict foreign direct investment. Several federal laws prohibit
alien ownership or limit the percentage of capital in foreign hands
with respect to coastal or inland shipping, domestic radio communications, domestic air transport, the development of hydroelectric power
or atomic energy, the leasing or exploitation of mineral lands, or the
exercise of banking activities. State laws also impose a variety of
restrictions on aliens and some states require that a specific number
or percentage of incorporators or officers must be of U.S. nationality.[52]

Countermeasures to Technology
Transfer Controls

Referred to earlier was the legal power of the United States to deny technology generated by foreign affiliates of a U.S. MNE to the country in which it is located or to prohibit the export of goods produced by that affiliate to third countries when it involves so-called strategic items. Although the list of these items has been steadily reduced, this power of the United States over its MNEs clearly constitutes an infringement of the host government's own authority over activities in its territory.

What can host governments do to counter the possibility that foreign and especially U.S. owned affiliates of MNEs become tools for the foreign policy implementation of a third country through restrictions of technology transfers? One preventive step is refusal to authorize the establishment of an MNE affiliate or to insist that majority ownership is in the hands of its own citizens or of a public corporation. Another method is passage of a law which compels MNE affiliates to carry out directives and policies within carefully spelled-out areas regardless of ownership considerations. A final, very drastic measure would be the threat of expropriation, which may however be blunted by the fear of retaliation when industrially advanced countries are involved among which extensive MNE ties exist.

Clearly, it is the MNE which bears the brunt of a friction-laden situation not of its own making, a situation that it needs to avoid if at all possible. Meanwhile, the progressive reduction of tension between the United States and the Soviet Union, the resultant changes in the perception of threats to their respective survivals, and the increasing economic power of the Common Market countries and Japan relative to that of the United States, may induce the American government to resort less and less to its authority over the use of technology by affiliates of U.S. MNEs.

Operational and Ownership Restrictions by
Host Governments

To counter the effects produced by activities of MNE affiliates that host governments regard as drawbacks requires measures which are potent enough to induce behavior conforming to what is perceived as the national interests of the host country. To be fully effective

the measures would have to be very comprehensive and would have
to include the regulation of marketing arrangements within the MNE
(if greater exports were desired), intercompany pricing, intercompany
changes and profit allocation (to ensure minimum tax receipts),
remittance of dividends, transfer of capital among affiliates, and
local borrowing (to watch over the country's balance of payments).[53]
To increase the national base for technological growth, host governments would have to rule on the selection of research projects and
determine in detail how the results of the research should be pro-
tected and used.

Most host governments have shied away from day-to-day regulations of MNE affiliates in their countries because they may reduce
the attractiveness of doing business to zero and obviate the advantages
of multinational operations for the MNE concerned. Thus overzealous
regulations whose full implementation might also be very costly, may
defy their purpose by killing the golden goose. In fact, some European
governments continue to seek new investments by U.S. MNEs despite
the acknowledged drawbacks and despite the currency problem of the
dollar.[54] Nevertheless, these governments also use the existence of
these investments as a target for thinly concealed threats voiced in
support of their foreign economic policy goals. For example, during
the monetary crisis in the second half of 1971 produced by the U.S.
floating of the dollar and imposition of the 10 percent surcharge on
imports, an "information memorandum" issued by the EEC Commission pointedly referred to the profits repatriated by the U.S.
MNEs which from 1960 to 1970 had risen from $2.9 billion to $7.9
billion.[55]

Going beyond operational controls and in many respects much
more serious for MNE affiliates are restrictions on ownership imposed
by host governments. Laws to this effect may require that companies
agree to shifts in ownership by acceding to either minority or majority
interests of nationals of the host country. In some advanced countries
such as Italy and France, state-owned or state-controlled enterprises
such as IRI or Renault may be assigned the minority or majority interests.
Most developing countries also use similar arrangements whereby
either the state itself or a government-owned development agency
assumes financial partnership functions in MNE affiliates. State-
controlled financial participation has the advantage that the host
government can be informed of all actions of the MNE affiliate including
its contributions to research and development facilities and its
response to the economic planning of the government.[56] It also
sharply limits government interventions sought by parent companies
for affiliates since counterpressure of host governments on affiliates
would raise such intervention to the diplomatic level.

A good, very recent example of ownership and operational restrictions is the promulgation of the Andean Investment Code which requires foreign firms in Bolivia, Chile, Colombia, Ecuador, and Peru to turn over majority control to domestic interests within 15 to 20 years or face certain sanctions. The code also puts limits on profit remittance and authorizes local governments to have a strong voice in technology transfer decisions of the foreign firms.[57]

The ultimate action of host governments in restricting the ownership of foreign affiliates is of course expropriation. While domestic political reasons may be a very persuasive motivation for such a step, the result in terms of economic benefits for the host country may be less than satisfactory. National pride in the new ownership may not be a substitute for proper and profitable management and the government may be obliged to sign at least a temporary costly management contract with the former owners, besides paying some kind of compensation.

How far operational and ownership restrictions, with the exception of complete expropriation, will be able to alter the behavior of MNE affiliates in host countries, is difficult to determine and depends on the particular situation which MNEs and their affiliates face in different countries. These situations may be classified into five sets of constraints: (1) both governments have the same—or similar—regulations for parent companies and affiliates and enforce compliance; (2) governments are in disagreement regarding regulations and all are attempting to compel a particular behavior; (3) governments are in disagreement and some are attempting to compel particular behavior while others are not; (4) government have the same—or similar—regulations but there is no enforcement; (5) governments are in disagreement as to what is desired from the enterprise, but there is no compulsion from any government. In some of these situations, the power of the multinational company to circumvent governmental policy is increased, in others it is nearly obviated.[58] Figure 3.2 presents the five situations graphically.

In situation 1 the multinational companies retain little choice because the same response or action is required by all governments concerned. In situation 2a the multinational corproation has the choice of limiting its exposure to the governments which impose the least burdensome regulations. This has been the response of many companies to the regulations imposed in the developing countries and consequently the companies have often stayed out of the economies of some countries completely. Similarly, in Europe multinational enterprises have concentrated their activities in carefully selected countries, avoiding those which have a propensity to insist on strict

FIGURE 3.2

Regulations of Parent and Host Countries

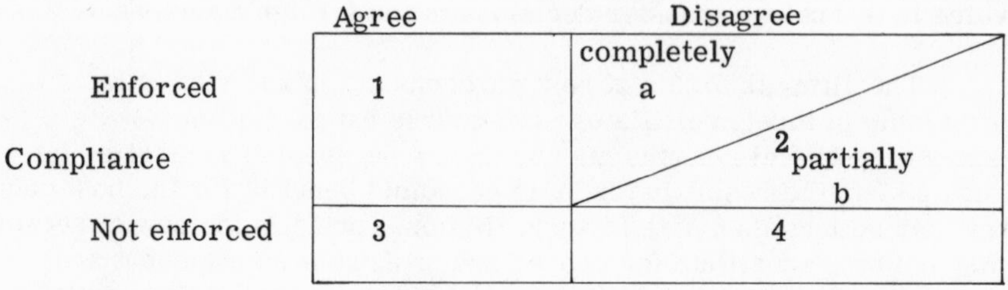

	Agree	Disagree
Enforced	1	completely a
Compliance		2 partially b
Not enforced	3	4

and damaging control. The situation is less difficult in situation 2b because the margin for avoidance of bothersome regulations is enlarged.

In situations 3 and 4 the companies have maximum leeway and therefore they may choose the strategies or activities which gain the most for their objectives. This is precisely what has been done by many multinational corporations and the more they are able to exercise their own choices in setting patterns of economic and commercial behavior, the more they are in a position to dictate the next step for the governments with which they deal. The governments then tend to play more the role of "reactors" rather than initiators or controllers.

It is obvious from the examination of parent and host government efforts to control the behavior of MNEs and their affiliates that domestic politics plays an influential role in the shaping of pertinent governmental decisions. Economic egoism and nationalistic forces support strong and extensive regulations and reinforce the suspicion of many governments, especially those in developing countries, that MNEs are acting in partnership with some foreign sovereign or are subservient to them. Certain private economic groups judging that their vested interests are threatened by MNE activities are pleased with the imposition of governmental controls and applaud openly or privately the efforts of their governments. On the other hand, extensive regulations may arouse apprehension also in domestic firms that in due time they may be subjected to similar supervision and then some internal counterpressures may well be generated. All this points up the domestic conflicts that MNEs can cause in various polities which are apt to magnify the drawbacks and may distort or shroud the genuine benefits that MNEs can bring to the governments and peoples of the countries in which they operate.

CONSEQUENCES FOR THE INTERNATIONAL SYSTEM

The final point in this discussion of the MNE as a nongovernmental force in world politics is an examination of the consequences for the international system and its subsystems flowing from the effects on national governments that have been and are being caused by transnational MNE initiatives. Are these effects promoting greater collaboration among governments or are they responsible for a wider range of conflicts? Do they produce greater interdependence between states or are they the cause for greater dependence of particular states on other governmental or nongovernmental actors? Are there indications that the world-wide net of relations created by MNEs is a factor for global political integration and how does it affect schemes for integration of international regions?

A growing number of authors have addressed themselves to these questions[59] but empirical data are scarce and therefore it is difficult to come up with anything but highly tentative answers. From the analysis of benefits and drawbacks for parent and host countries one general impression emerges. While from a rational point of view governmental decision-makers of both types of countries are fully aware of the benefits of MNE operations, their inability to control fully the continuity and direction of these benefits is highly frustrating and leads to many conflicts and tensions. For this reason the motivation for collaboration among these countries as might be evidenced by the harmonization of laws and policies is generally low despite the obvious need of MNEs with transnationally integrated production facilities for such harmonization and the clear benefits for governments and people springing from the results. Although the continued association of multinational executives and engineering staffs is likely to lead to the development of a transnationally rather than nationally centered elite—a development accelerated by the formation of transnational professional organizations—its power to induce governments to greater collaboration is apt to remain small until other, and often more influential, elites shift from their pursuit of mostly narrow national interests and objectives to those of a more world-wide or region-wide nature. Moreover, there is a salient question as to how much intergovernmental collaboration MNEs really want. Raymond Vernon suggests that they tend to support only limited selective intergovernmental agreements which in their view are particularly helpful.

Otherwise, many multinational corporations seem to have elected to present a low silhouette and to tone down previous emphases of the world-wide nature of their activities.60 While this new shyness may be primarily a tactical move, it may also reflect the recognition of certain domestic and global political realities adverse to many MNE objectives.

Without doubt, the sources for conflict introduced among national governments by MNE activities are substantial. They range from envy because of the uneven distribution of MNE benefits to fears of losing important national prerogatives. This fear is accentuated among the governments of smaller countries since they must reckon not only with the extensive power of larger states but also with that of giant, global enterprises disposing of enormous financial and technological resources. A good example of such confrontation is the earlier discussed case of the new Andean Investment Code which has not only aroused the strong displeasure and opposition of MNEs operating in the region, but which also seems to have prompted the U.S. government to delay the approval of a loan by the Inter-American Development Bank requested by Peru.61

The conflicts among governments generated by MNE activities are not likely to result in the outbreak of hostilities, but they can be responsible for dangerous suspicions and frictions damaging the climate of international relations. This situation can be aggravated when MNEs try to pit government against government either by seeking parent government support or by using the threat of moving investments from one country to another. Of course, MNE managers realize that for such actions they may have to pay a price in terms of ill will and retaliation, but nevertheless these are strategies that the particular nature of their operations makes available to them.

If a rising number of conflicts and tensions between governments are generated by MNE activities, one may raise the question of whether these effects are not moderated per force by the growing interdependence stemming from the expanding global network of MNE transnational activities such as investments, integrated production facilities, transfers of technology and managerial skills, and others. This proposition implies that the governments of the states of the world become so mutually dependent on each other because of the transnational interactions caused by MNEs that the high cost of disentanglement compels them to maintain a level of collaboration. However, as Kenneth Waltz has persuasively argued,62 this proposition is open to question or at least needs modification since interdependence is reduced by the immense disparity in the capabilities of states.

As a consequence, Waltz asserts that high inequality among states entails lowered interdependence. For example, a powerful country such as the United States can extricate itself from transnational business entanglements with much greater ease and impunity than economically weak countries for whose governments certain MNE activities including new exports may be an essential part of economic and perhaps political development and stability. For this reason governments of smaller countries are strongly constrained to make domestic economic and political decisions with an eye on their external environment and have difficulty in casting off transnational business ties even if its citizens vehemently object to the relationship of interdependence as in the case of Canada's fear of U.S. economic domination.[63] The imbalance in the interdependence relationship among some states can also be seen from Table 2.13 which relates investments to GNP and exports. Comparing the percentages of the investments of the United States and Britain to their GNPs, one can see that in Britain's case it is double that of the United States suggesting a higher degree of British interdependence with respect to the international environment than that of the United States. On the other hand, if one also takes international trade into account as an indicator of interdependence as Kenneth Waltz does, one finds that while Germany's level of interdependence is low as far as investments are concerned, it is very high in terms of export trade.

Considering that MNEs dispose of tremendous financial resources and are at times willing to use them to mold international regions together while national governments are reluctant to effectively take such action, multinational corporations can sometimes impose interdependence. An example can be found in Latin America, where multinational firms, in order to achieve economies of scale, have obliged two countries to cooperate by specializing production of components in each country.[64] Such instances are rare, however, although from a rational standpoint a proliferation of similar production arrangements in developing areas could have highly beneficial long-range consequences for the economic development of the Third World.

Waltz argues that the word "interdependence" is pleasing rhetoric inasmuch as it obscures the inequalities of national capability, points to reciprocal dependence, and suggests that all states are playing the same game.[65] If such perceptions are in fact conjured up in the minds of national decision-makers, this would be all to the good. It would induce governments to treat the acts of other governments as though they were events within its borders and this could lead to a feeling of at least converging interests. However, the

realistic recognition of the inequalities of states is more likely to
cause or increase perceptions of dependence rather than interdependence
and will tend to sharpen suspicion, envy, and tension thereby contri-
buting to greater conflict rather than collaboration in the international
system. The sentiments of frustration harbored by many Canadians
vis-à-vis the United States constitute a case in point. As a consequence,
governmental leaders may feel called upon to resort to national means
and solutions as a countervailing force against the real or imagined
threat of dependence on international business and other countries.
Such actions harm the prospects of useful collaboration among states
and are likely to undermine the fruitful performance of the transnational business network for the transfer of ideas, technology, know-
how, and capital.

A special dimension of interdependence and dependence pertains
to MNE activities in Communist countries where the multinational
firm can play the role of a transideological enterprise as discussed
earlier.[66] While an increasing number of MNEs such as Fiat undoubtedly have engaged in transideological enterprises, responding to
changing attitudes and needs in Communist countries and impelled by
new opportunities for markets and profits, the number of actual MNEs
involved remains small. Nevertheless, certain forces in the capitalist
and Communist worlds may be instrumental in expanding the transideological experiences of businesses. Socialism and capitalism are
not uniform in all countries where such systems exist, but assume a
number of forms, some of which come to resemble each other. Over
the years the importance of ideology has receded world-wide and
pragmatic approaches to the solution of problems are preferred. In
turn, common ways of looking at problems can produce the feeling
that common interests exist.[67] Finally, while competitive coexistence
may still be the order of the day, borrowing of beneficial elements
of the respective capitalist or socialist systems has become accepted.
For all the above reasons it is not at all inconceivable that transideological enterprises may contribute to a growing level of interdependence between Communist and Free World countries, but the
process of changing the pattern of transnational interaction is likely
to be slow and subject to political and military pressures on both
sides of the Iron Curtain. As Howard V. Perlmutter suggests, the
learning process along the East-West watershed is painful but in the
end it may result in the legitimization of what he calls "transideological
zones, mediated through transideological dialogues, and culminating in
a greater abundance of already existing transideological licensing,
subcontracting and co-production systems."[68]

In conclusion some observations will be made regarding the
impact which the transnational interaction process mobilized by MNEs

has now and in the future on global and regional integration. While
rational thinkers may recognize the need of the world economic
system to be a whole and the existence of true common economic
interests, this concept may be accepted by individual national decision-
makers only in theory and disregarded when it comes to specific
decisions for their country which may be governed by overriding
considerations of an entirely different nature. Moreover, while geocentric orientations of MNE executives and national decision-makers
could well be the wave of the future, this future could be far off if
one considers that at present only 2 percent of the top executives of
U.S.-based MNEs are non-American.[69] Thus, the evolvement of
a sizable, truly transnational elite in business stemming from multinational associations among executives with a global outlook may be
slow in coming and this elite's ability to influence other powerful
elites in the national decision-making processes is very limited at
this time.

Another argument in support of the MNE as contributor to global
political integration is essentially functionalist in nature. It states
that MNEs satisfy important needs of mankind by raising economic
levels, by reducing social disparities in the fields of education and
health, by narrowing the gap between the rich and poor countries, and
by fostering supporting transnational groups benefiting from the MNE
activities, i.e. consumers and workers. Even if one were to accept
these results as forthcoming, although full evidence at present is not
available, one must keep in mind that functionalist forces are inherently
weak and rarely are able to overcome ideologically and emotionally
inspired counterforces such as pervasive nationalism, strong ethnocentric orientation, and powerful political ideologies. Therefore,
although the author is most sympathetic with the forces of functionalism
and their direction, he has little faith in their ability to bring about
any rapid movement toward global political integration.

Finally, there is the institutional argument that the proliferation
of MNE activities requires international institutions for their regulation.[70] The clamor for such a regime may come from the national
governments, powerful labor unions, and the MNEs. The governments
may recognize that their interests would be safeguarded better through
such a regime which might control transnational movements of capital,
profits, and expense allocations. Labor would regard such a regime
as a possible protection against a loss of job opportunities in the
advanced countries and against the erosion of wages and benefits
through competition by low-wage workers in the Third World. The
MNEs might find that such a regime would bring greater security,
stability, and predictability for the management of their transnational
affairs. Such institutions could be incorporated in the United Nations

structure which might give this organization a new important function and needed lift of morale. At the same time, it might instill in the national governments an awareness that the world and mankind are indeed interdependent and that new problems can best be solved on a global basis. Again, however, a word of strong caution is in order. National bureaucracies, although accepting initially the establishment of the above institutions, may later perceive them as a threat to their own positions of power inasmuch as they will reduce contacts, functions, and administrative authority over MNEs regarded as important by high-ranking civil servants for their prestige and influence. National bureaucrats may also be fearful that a new layer of authority might be created which will lower their position in the overall hierarchical structure.[71] Similar apprehension may also be aroused in the minds of the national political leadership which may view the new institutions as competitors in the exercise of what previously were exclusive national prerogatives.

On balance, then, while the author sympathizes with the vista of a global industrial estate and favors the development of geocentric orientations in MNE and governmental leadership groups, he is very pessimistic about the short-range contribution MNE activities can make to global political integration. Although it is reasonable to assume that in a shrinking world and a rapidly expanding MNE net trends toward a global industrial estate and toward geocentric orientations are emerging, little empirical evidence can be offered at present to support this argument and much research needs to be done to determine their strengths and effects.

The situation is somewhat different when it comes to the contribution made by transnational MNE activities toward regional political integration. One reason is that in a number of regions, such as in Western Europe, a clearly defined institutional framework exists which influences both national governmental agencies and regional organs and provides channels for articulating and presenting coordinated demands of MNEs. If these demands have widespread utilitarian value for the people of the region, favorable responses by the national authorities may be delayed or may come only in small increments, but they cannot be completely denied no matter how strong the national opposition is. The slow harmonization of fiscal laws and technical standards in the EEC is at least in part the result of concerted MNE pressures.[72] Under these conditions the political socialization process among executive elites of the MNE may also receive a strong impetus. This process is accelerated as MNEs form or participate in functional and general interest group structures within the member states and the regional system.[73] These transnational groups operating within a regional context have the advantage that they can shift their identity and loyalties to a more specific target than is possible on a world-wide basis. Regional ideologies can then be fostered which may become stronger as the number of beneficiaries from these activities expands and the benefits assume greater viability. Politically speaking, what is being witnessed is the creation of a penetrative political system in which business elites and bureaucrats of different countries and the regional organization begin to make joint decisions affecting the distribution of resources and values within the region.

All in all, one may conclude that while the consequences of MNE initiatives and their affects on national governments are clearly visible, it is too early to render definite judgments as to enhanced collaboration or conflict in the global pattern of international interaction. The author is tempted to state that from a short-range view conflict is likely to increase, but that over the long run collaboration among governmental and nongovernmental actors may win the upper hand as the advantages and disadvantages flowing from growing interdependence will be seen in more rational and balancing terms. With respect to global integration, little hard evidence is available to suggest a meaningful contribution by MNE initiatives and activities at the present time. However, the prospects of regional political integration through MNE activities are better and this will become even more obvious when one turns to the phenomenon of transnational business collaboration which will be discussed in Chapter 4.

NOTES

1. See Harry G. Johnson, "The Efficiency and Welfare Implications of the International Corporation," in Charles P. Kindleberger, ed., The International Corporation: A Symposium (Cambridge. Mass.: M.I.T. Press, 1970), pp. 35-56.

2. Jack N. Behrman, National Interests and the Multinational Enterprise: Tensions Among the North Atlantic Countries (Englewood Cliffs, N.J.: Prentice-Hall, 1970), p. 23.

3. John H. Dunning, "Foreign Investment in the United Kingdom," in Isaiah A. Litvak and Christopher J. Maule, Foreign Investment and the Experience of Host Countries (New York: Praeger Publishers, 1970), pp. 205-55 on pp. 230-1.

4. Behrman, National Interests and the Multinational Enterprise, p. 22.

5. For other examples, see ibid., pp. 23-26.

6. John H. Dunning, American Investment in British Manu-facturing Industry (London: George Allen and Unwin, Ltd., 1958), p. 66.

7. Behrman, National Interests and the Multinational Enterprise, p. 17.

8. Dunning, American Investment, pp. 73 and 147-53.

9. Behrman, National Interests and the Multinational Enterprise, p. 20.

10. For additional details see Harry Magdoff, The Age of Imperialism: The Economics of U.S. Foreign Policy (New York: Monthly Review Press, 1969), pp. 32-54.

11. Marie T. Bradshaw, "U.S. Exports to Foreign Affiliates of U.S. Firms," Survey of Current Business, XLIX, (May 1969), 34-51.

12. Cf. also Elizabeth R. Jager, "The Conglomerate Goes Global," AFL-CIO American Federationist, January 1970.

13. See pp. 54-56.

14. See Howard V. Perlmutter, "Attitudinal Patterns in Joint Decision Making in Multinational Firms—Nation State Relationships," M. Radnor, and R. Chirchdm eds., International Decision Making (Chicago: Aldine Publishing Company, 1972)," pp. 44-45 and Figure 4.

15. Ibid.

16. See pp. 24-31.

17. See pp. 85-89.

18. Cf. The Multinational Company and National Development: A Lamp Anthology (New York: Standard Oil Company of New Jersey, 1970), passim.; and Neil H. Jacoby, "The Multinational Corporation," The Center Magazine, III, 3, (May 1970) 37-55. See also Harry G. Johnson, "The Multinational Corporation as Development Agent," and Paul Streeten, "Obstacles to Private Foreign Investment in the LDCs," Columbia Journal of World Business V, 3 (May-June 1970), pp. 25-30 and 31-39 respectively.

19. For a more detailed discussion of this subject see Deena R. Khatkhate, "Management in Development Countries," Finance and Development, No. 3, 1971, pp. 8-14. The author argues that in view of the large unemployment in the Third World the managerial approach should be qualitatively different from that in developed areas and that high labor intensity should be regarded a virtue rather than a vice when factories are planned in Third World Countries.

20. Cf. Jacoby, "The Multinational Corporation," p. 43 for details and sources.

21. Mauritius, 4-Year Plan for Social & Economic Development, 1971.

22. Harry Magdoff, "The Logic of Imperialism," Social Policy, September-October 1970, pp. 20-29.

23. Jacoby, "The Multinational Corporation," p. 44.

24. Gilles Y. Bertin, "Foreign Investment in France," in Litvak and Maule, Foreign Investment and Host Countries, p. 116.

25. For details see Behrman, National Interests and the Multi-national Enterprise, pp. 89-93.

26. Lawrence A. Mayer, "Into a Time of Stagflation," Fortune, August 1971, pp. 144-49. The original source of Eurodollars were foreign-owned balances with U.S. banks. As the owner deposited such funds in banks abroad, they took on a special status as a kind of international money, called Eurodollars.

27. Cf. Behrman, National Interests and the Multinational Enterprise, pp. 93-98. Another example that American controls are considered as direct interference in a host country's economy is the following: Cuba placed an important order for agricultural machinery with a Belgian firm in which an American company had taken a 60 percent investment. As a consequence of the American law com- pelling an embargo on Cuba, the American authorities forced the order to be cancelled. This aroused many angry remarks in the Belgian Parliament and labor unions were not only concerned about consequent unemployment, but also began to speak about "economic colonization of Belgium," (Roger Blanpain, "American Involvement in Belgium" in Alfred Kamin, ed., Western European Labor and the American Corporation (Washington, D.C.: The Bureau of National Affairs, 1970), pp. 455-65).

28. See Sanford Rose, "The Rewarding Strategies of Multi-nationalism," Fortune, September 15, 1968, especially p. 104 for details.

29. These categories are borrowed from Behrman, National Interests and the Multinational Enterprise, op cit., Chs. 3-5.

30. See pp. 31-37.

31. Berham, National Interests and the Multinational Enterprise, p. 33.

32. Ibid., pg. 34 Some observers place U.S. ownership at 67 percent, see, International Herald-Tribune, November 3, 1971. These figures depend on what is counted and what is meant by being "owned." It is also claimed that companies employing 5,000 workers or more are 90 percent owned or controlled by American firms.

33. For further details on foreign controlled firms in Canada see Thomas L. Powrie, "Foreign Investments in Canada," in Sidney E. Rolfe and Walter Damm, eds., The Multinational Corporation in the World Economy (New York: Praeger Publishers, 1970), pp. 86-106, especially pp. 93 and 94.

34. Communauté européene, No. 134, September 1969, p. 9. For further details, see Rainer Hellmann, The Challenge to U.S. Dominance of the International Corporation, translated by Peter Wouf (New York: University of Cambridge, Mass, Dunellen, 1970), p. 98. For detailed figures see Table 24 on p. 100. The percentage is less than 50 percent in Britain. For a full discussion of the West European situation with numerous tables see pp. 47-124.

35. Jacoby, The Multinational Corporation," p. 40.

36. This was done in Belgium on several occasions. See also Blanpain, "American Involvement in Belgium," pp. 455-65.

37. This is developed in greater detail by Behrman, National Interests and the Multinational Enterprise, pp. 57-58.

38. For additional details see ibid., pp. 62-67.

39. Cf. Dunning, American Investment, pp. 89, 164-74, 310; and Dunning, "Foreign Investment in the United Kingdom," in Litvak and Maule, Foreign Investment an Host Countries, p. 242.

40. Behrman, National Interests and Multinational Enterprise, p. 71.

41. For examples see Fortune, September 15, 1968, p. 104 and Business Week, November 30, 1968, p. 37.

42. For additional details see Behrman, National Interests and the Multinational Enterprise, pp. 73-82.

43. Khatkhate, "Management in Development Countries," pp. 10-12.

44. Perlmutter, "Attitudinal Patterns in Joint Decision Making," Table 6, p. 29.

45. By 1972 the Fiat plant in the Soviet Union is expected to reach its full capacity of 300,000 cars a year. (Berliner Morganpost, November 5, 1971).

46. Howard V. Perlmutter, "Emerging East-West Ventures: The Transideological Enterprise," Columbia Journal of World Politics, September-October 1969, pp. 39-50.

47. This topic will be discussed in more detail in Chapter 4.

48. See pp. 82-84.

49. Cf. Walter Damm, "The Economic Aspects of European Direct Investment in the United States," in Rolfe and Damm, eds., The Multinational Corporation, pp. 35-51.

50. See Behrman, National Interests and the Multinational Enterprise, pp. 133-36, and for general information W. H. Balekjian, Legal Aspects of Foreign Investment in the European Community (Manchester, England: Manchester University Press, 1967), passim. The French government has rejected a number of requests for investment authorization by MNEs. No statistical information is available on the number of rejections, but they are said to run between four and six a year. In important cases the rejections may find their way to the press, in others the principals involved may shun publicity.

51. Time, December 6, 1971, p. 94.

52. Walter Damm, "The Economic Aspects of European Direct Investment in the United States," pp. 37-38.

53. German plans are said to exist to introduce legislation in the <u>Bundestag</u> to levy higher taxes on dividends of firms in Germany whose ownership is more than 10 percent in foreign hands than on those of "German" companies (<u>Business Week</u>, October 23, 1971).

54. See <u>Times-Picayune</u> (New Orleans), September 21, 1971.

55. <u>Agence Europe Document</u>, #647, October 25, 1971.

56. Behrman, <u>National Interests and the Multinatational Enterprise</u> p. 141. However, European state-controlled companies are known to have not always supported the objectives of their own governments.

57. <u>Journal of Commerce</u>, April 20, 1971.

58. Adapted from Jack N. Behrman, "The Multinational Enterprise and Nation States: the Shifting Balance of Power," paper presented at the Conference on the Multinational Corporation, held at the Department of State, February 14, 1969, pp. 19-21.

59. See the various articles of Perlmutter cited earlier; Behrman, "National interests and the Multinational Enterprise"; Kenneth N. Waltz, "The Myth of Interdependence," and Raymond Vernon, "Future of the Multinational Enterprise" in Charles P. Kindleberger, ed., <u>The International Corporation</u> (Cambridge, Mass.: M.I.T. Press, 1970), pp. 205-223 and 373-400, respectively; J. S. Nye, "Multinational Enterprise and Prospects for Regional Global Integration," and Johnathan F. Galloway, "The Role of Multinational Enterprise in the integration of Western Europe and the North Atlantic Countries," papers presented for the Research Conference in the Multinational Corporation in the Global Political System, University of Pennsylvania April 22-23, 1971 (mimeo., 1971).

60. Vernon, "Future of the Multinational Enterprise, p. 395.

61. <u>Journal of Commerce</u>, April 20, 1971.

62. Waltz, "The Myth of Interdependence," pp. 207 and 214.

63. See also Litvak and Maule, <u>Foreign Investment and Host Countries</u>, p. 95.

64. The framework of such cooperation was set by the LAFTA Treaty which advocated the conclusion of so-called complimentarity agreements among member countries. See Sidney Dell, <u>A Latin American Common Market</u> (London: Oxford University Press, 1966), pp. 125-38 and 174-96.

65. Waltz, "The Myth of Interdependence."

66. pp. 95-97.

67. Perlmutter, "Emerging East-West Ventures," pp. 44-45.

68. Ibid., p. 50.

69. Nye, "Multinational Enterprise and Prospects," p.10.

70. See for example Paul M. Goldberg and C. P. Kindleberger, "Toward a GATT for Investment: A Proposal for Supervision of the International Corporation," Law and Policy in International Business, II, 2 (Summer 1970), pp. 295-325.

71. See Werner Feld, "National Bureaucracies of the EEC Member States and Political Integration: A Preliminary Inquiry," in Robert S. Jordan, ed. International Administration: Its Evolution and Contemporary Applications (London: Oxford University Press, 1971), pp. 228-244.

72. This subject is treated in greater detail in the next chapter. See also Eric Stein, Harmonization of European Company Laws, National Reform and Transnational Coordination (Indianapolis: Bobbs Merrill, 1971).

73. The European Movement, a group strongly promoting West European unification, has 102 corporate members including a number of American MNEs with affiliates in Britain. These MNEs have given their full support (financially and otherwise) to Britain's entry in the Common Market which has aroused bitter complaints from British labor unions opposed to British membership in the EEC.

4

TRANSNATIONAL
BUSINESS
COLLABORATION

NATURE AND FORM

Transnational business collaboration is an entrepreneurial scheme in which not only multinational corporations may be engaged, but also independent national enterprises of different countries. It may be defined as a long-term collaborative effort across national boundaries between two or more economic entities located in different countries. It goes beyond a mere export and import trade relationship under which orders are placed with different suppliers according to the most favorable terms available. Rather, it aims at partnership in a broad sense—ideally with a well-defined common interest—and suggests a border-crossing interlacement of efforts on the part of the entities involved in the collaboration. This interlacement must not be understood merely in terms of technical contributions to the cooperative efforts by the participating units and their staffs. As Wolfgang G. Friedmann and George Kalmanoff point out in their study of joint international business ventures, there is also an emotive side to such efforts which produces in the staff members and operating personnel directly concerned with the collaboration a distinct feeling of being involved in a "united or cooperative" endeavor.[1] This is an important dimension of transnational business collaboration because it points to the border-crossing human and social relations created by the collaboration schemes in addition to economic and administrative transactional flows.

Since the major concern of this chapter is with the political aspects of transnational business collaboration in the national and international spheres, such terms as "partnership" and "joint ventures" will be used in a broad, nontechnical sense. As such, these terms are understood to refer to organizational structures under which the top management is divided among several units, each located in a

different country. The tie between the units may be a collaboration
agreement which leaves the corporate structures of the participating
firms untouched and excludes any investment schemes among the
partners. A more intense collaboration is likely to be established
when the agreement includes the investment by one of the participating
firms in the enterprise of the other. In the latter case, the undertaking may be called an "equity" joint venture, while in the former
case, it is a "nonequity" joint venture.[2] Under some collaboration
agreements new corporate structures may be created, either in the
form of a holding company, a jointly-owned subsidiary or, in fact, two
corporations as in the case of Agfa-Gevaerts.[3] In all these cases
top management is distributed, though perhaps unevenly, among two
or more headquarters located in different countries and the collaboration venture functions more or less as an international coalition.
Finally, the partners need not be exclusively private firms; in fact,
it is the virtue of this scheme that transnational collaboration can be
created between private enterprises and state-owned or state-controlled enterprises and agencies such as the public development
corporations operating in many Third World countries.

MOTIVATIONS FOR INITIATIVES

The particular motivations for collaboration ventures and their
objectives vary. The closest kind of collaboration involves the joint
rationalization and specialization of production, either by assigning
the manufacture of whole products or the production of parts of a
particular item to the various plants of the partners. A third method
is the establishment of a jointly-owned subsidiary to which the manufacture of either one or several products is assigned. The advantages of the last method are the sharp delimitation of tasks and
responsibilities among the partners, a clear delineation of the risks
of the partners, a relatively easy accounting of costs and profits,
and a fairly uncomplicated evaluation of the success of the collaboration. The establishment of a jointly-owned production subsidiary in
an EEC country other than where the main plants of the partners are
located adds to the interlacement effect of the collaboration.

The overall advantages of collaboration and division of labor
in the field of manufacturing are not only opportunities for optimum
production runs (depending on the minimal optimum plant size for
a particular industry) but also shared development costs and risks
as well as shared know-how.[4] As a result of the specialization which
the partners undertake in the manufacture of their products it is
also possible to introduce a higher degree of automation in the

manufacturing process which is often essential for the effective mass production of certain goods and which, in turn, permits more competitive pricing. In the event that the collaboration partners have established a joint production subsidiary, collaboration may also lead to diversification of products and perhaps markets.

While production collaboration ventures undoubtedly engender the highest interlacement effect, another frequent objective sought is the establishment of joint marketing arrangements permitting the partner located in one country to use the sales and service facilities of the partner in the other country. But the motivation for transnational marketing arrangements may also be defensive. The management of a company may be afraid that competitors may get a head start in a particular market and thereby threaten their national market positions. Since the opening and penetration of markets often require considerable investments in new marketing organizations as well as considerable expenditures for advertising, transnational collaboration may be a means of avoiding at least part of these costs. Moreover, the counsel of the local partner may be useful in reducing the risks of psychologically unsuitable sales and advertising methods.

Transnational marketing collaboration among several manufacturers is often combined with production collaboration as described earlier or becomes the first step for such a collaboration. Each partner limits himself to the production of those items for which he has the most technical know-how or which he can produce at the lowest cost. The collaborating firms market then not only their own products, but also those of their partners, enabling them to offer an integrated range of well-balanced, highly competitive items. Depending on the specific legal provisions in the countries of the partners, this arrangement may make it possible to enter very competitive bids for purchases by their governments which stipulate preferences for domestic suppliers. Finally, this kind of collaboration may offer advantages for sales to Communist countries if the government of one of the partners maintains especially good relations with one or more Communist countries or has a particularly favorable commercial agreement with it.

Another frequent objective of border-crossing collaboration is the creation of joint research and development operations, an arrangement sometimes emanating from earlier agreements aimed mainly at the exchange or acquisition of licenses. Research and development play an essential role for the maintenance and improvement of the competitive positions of many companies in a highly innovation-oriented and technology-based economy. Since the cost of research is high, especially in such sectors as aerospace, electronics, and the chemical industry, joint ventures may bring high quality and extensive research within the reach of an expanded circle of smaller companies. Collaborative research efforts may also spill over in time to other functional areas of the firms involved, leading eventually to collaboration in production and marketing.

A final objective of transnational business collaboration deserving mention is the improvement of the credit position of one or the other partner in order to finance plant expansions or long-term delivery contracts. Sometimes one partner may guarantee the bank loans of the other. The objectives discussed should not be considered as representing an exhaustive list. Other possibilities may emerge. Moreover, any combination of objectives is conceivable when two or more companies negotiate a border-crossing collaboration agreement.

GEOGRAPHIC AREAS OF
COLLABORATION AGREEMENTS

Because of its flexibility, transnational business collaboration is a phenomonon that can be observed in many parts of the world. Among the developing countries it found early acceptance in India and Brazil, but today it can be found in many other countries of the Third World as well. The basic reason for these arrangements as pointed out in the preceding chapter is the apprehension of the governments of developing countries about full foreign ownership and control over industrial enterprises within their borders on the one hand, and yet on the other hand their desire to promote economic development through the use of the technological and financial resources possessed by firms in the advanced countries. At the same time, for foreign investors, joint ventures are often the only practicable way of investing in a developing country, an investment motivated either by the need for raw materials or the long-range recognition that in the not too distant future many developing countries will constitute important markets for a company's products. An example of a successful collaboration venture in the Third World is the Lamco joint venture for the exploitation of iron ore in the Nimba Mountains of Liberia. The company involved in the project, the Liberian American-Swedish Minerals Company (Lamco) is jointly owned by the Liberian government and Liberian Iron Ore, Ltd. The latter company, whose sole purpose is to hold Lamco stock, is in turn owned by a consortium of Swedish companies, an African-American corporation, and public stockholders.[5]

While the record of transnational business collaboration through joint ventures in the Third World is not unsullied because of governmental rigidities in Western and developing countries and the lack of capable managers, joint participation by foreign investors and national institutions has created a sense of partnership and has enhanced economic development in the countries where such ventures were set up.

Another area in which transnational business collaboration has been successful is the realm of East-West business relations as exemplified by the previously discussed "transideological enterprise." In these joint ventures it is not necessarily MNEs that might be involved, but individually owned, national firms that have also been successful participants. For example, IKEA, a Swedish furniture chain, supplies to associates in Poland machinery and designs under its technical control for the semi-manufacture of furniture which is then shipped to Sweden for finishing by IKEA.[6]

Of particular significance for East-West joint ventures is the Yugoslavian foreign investment law enacted in July 1967. It is an attempt to attract foreign investments from countries where private ownership is permitted to a country where private ownership of the "means of production" is prohibited. The law is specific about the rights and liabilities of the foreign investor including the repatriation of income and capital. However, there is room for bargaining and negotiation on the part of the foreign investing partner and Yugoslav authorities are known to be willing to interpret and administer the law to ease the entry of foreign partners who bring to the country much-needed technology.[7]

Only about 20 joint ventures with Western firms have been concluded so far under the new legislation, one of which involves an American and a Yugoslav printing firm.[8] A very far-reaching joint venture has been negotiated between a French MNE, Pechiney-St. Gobain, and Progress-Invest of Belgrade which aims at the construction of plants for fertilizer, fluoride chemicals, organic plastics, and plastics not only in Yugoslavia, but also in France and Third Countries.[9]

In 1971 Romania also passed a law dealing with "economic and technicoscientific cooperation activities." It permits the establishment of joint ventures with Western firms provided that foreign financial participation does not exceed 49 percent.[10] While it is too early to judge the impact of the new Romanian legislation, the fact alone that Romania has felt it expedient to follow the Yugoslavian example is significant in itself.

While the importance of transnational business collaboration ventures in developing countries and for East-West relations is undoubtedly considerable, perhaps their greatest significance in terms of impact on the international system may be in regions where a number of countries are pursuing an economic integration scheme as is the case in the European Economic Community, or the Latin American Free Trade Association. If under these circumstances a substantial number of enterprises in two or more countries should be involved in border-crossing collaboration, the resulting widespread pattern of interlacement may well have definitive effects upon the economic structures of the countries in the area, either in particular sectors or as a whole. In addition, it could give rise to a variety of political effects in the member countries and conceivably contribute to a gradual transformation of the existing political structures in the regional international subsystem.

It is indeed among the member countries of the EEC that a rising trend of transnational business collaboration has become manifest during the last decade. [11] Both very large enterprises as well as smaller firms have engaged in joint ventures. This is perhaps not surprising when one considers that the customs union upon which the EEC is predicated has been implemented ahead of the 12-year schedule of transition and the free movement of labor and business establishments is now being assured to an increasing degree. Transnational business collaboration ventures, therefore, can benefit from an expanded internal market, make use of the economies of scale wherever this should prove to be advantageous, and optimalize the allocation of resources. In the following pages the author will concentrate on the EEC because data and information regarding the effects of transnational collaboration on the national governments of the Member States and possible consequences for the international system and especially the Community subsystem are more plentiful than for other areas of the world, although the statistics are not always fully satisfactory. However, some observations will also be made about such effects and consequences stemming from transnational joint ventures in the Third World and those formed between Free World and Communist enterprises.

TWO BRIEF CASE STUDIES

Two examples involving principally German and French firms will serve to illustrate the far-ranging network of relations and

interactions created by transnational business collaboration. One
example is a collaboration without financial participation while the
other includes financial interests.

The first example is a collaboration agreement between MAN
of Germany and Saviem of France. The latter firm is part of the
state-owned Renault complex, which is the 19th largest company
outside the United States. [12] The agreement, concluded on February
21, 1968, has two major objectives: to strengthen the competitive
position of the partners and to share with their customers the benefits flowing from the rationalization of production and research. [13]
For the attainment of these objectives collaboration between the two
companies extends to research and development, a division of labor
in the manufacture of parts and certain types of trucks, and sales
and services for all trucks produced jointly or individually. MAN
assembles the trucks whose parts are produced jointly for the German
market, and Saviem is charged with assembly of these trucks for the
French market. [14] It should be noted that already before the conclusion of the collaboration agreement, MAN and Renault, Saviem's
parent company, were linked by a license agreement. Moreover,
since the spring of 1967 MAN has represented Saviem in Germany
as sales agent for trucks up to 7.5 tons.

The marketing arrangements of the collaboration agreement
provide that the sales and service organizations of the two companies
in Germany and France offer an integrated line of trucks manufactured
by them as well as services for their products. As a consequence,
750 service centers are available in both countries. In addition,
some elements of a collaboration venture between Renault and Alfa-
Romeo[15] dating back to 1959 are tied in with the MAN-Saviem arrangement. Alfa-Romeo produces certain motors for Saviem with
MAN patented carburation systems, but much more important is the
use of the Alfa-Romeo distribution net for the sale of Saviem and
MAN trucks. [16] As far as exports to other countries are concerned,
the marketing organization of either one or the other company is
used depending on which has proven itself most effective in a particular state. This method is especially beneficial for MAN in African
countries, which were former French colonies, but may also prove
advantageous for the partners in Eastern Europe where in some
countries French products are more welcome than German goods.
The good connections of Alfa-Romeo with Communist countries are
also useful for MAN and Saviem trucks.

Each company has appointed a staff coordinator who reports to
and works very closely with one or more top-level executives. Various
coordinating committees composed of members of both companies have

been established in different functional areas such as production and advertising. Engineering and administrative working groups operate under these committees. About 120 people from both partners are involved in the coordinating scheme.

The chief coordinators and key personnel of the committees meet once a month, either in Paris or in Munich. Attorneys are usually part of the delegation since the contract between the two companies requires continuous adaptation to changing production and marketing conditions. A bond of personal friendship has grown up between the two chief coordinators and their families and this bond, as one will see, is a significant element when it comes to solving problems that crop up between the partners.

The second example of a collaboration agreement with a financial participation is the joint venture between Farbwerke Hoechst of West Germany (one of the world's largest chemical concerns)[17] and Roussel-Uclaf (France's second largest pharmaceutical company). Hoechst acquired an indirect interest of about 20 percent in the French company through the purchase of about 40 percent of Compagnie Financière Chimio of Paris, a privately owned bolding company which controls Roussel-Uclaf.

The agreement, concluded for a ten-year period and renewable for similar periods, covers joint research, production, and marketing efforts throughout the world. All new products, developed by either firm, as well as revenue derived from licensing fees, will be shared between the two companies. Hoechst has been given two seats on the 12-man board of directors of Roussel-Uclaf and the president of the French firm has been elected to the board of Hoechst, [18] which is clear evidence that financial participation by its nature requires closer ties. Initially the negotiations between the two companies aimed merely at the conclusion of a license agreement, but their scope was expanded when it was discovered that there was a high degree of complementarity in the products of the two companies.

The channels of communications established by the cross appointments of high-ranking officials of both companies to their respective boards constitute an important instrument for top-echelon coordination. For operational coordination, Hoechst and Roussel-Uclaf have created four main committees dealing with research and development, sales, production, and economic policy. Below this level are a number of working groups concentrating on details. About 50 to 60 persons are involved in coordinating activities. Meetings of the committees alternate between Paris and Frankfurt and top executives also make frequent visits to the headquarters of their opposite numbers.

The collaboration with Roussel-Uclaf is not Hoechst's only transnational activity in France. Another collaboration agreement with the French firm Nobel-Bozel was announced in March 1969. In addition, four wholly-owned marketing subsidiaries were set up earlier and three jointly-owned marketing subsidiaries operate in which Hoechst owns shares ranging from 25 to 50 percent. To co-ordinate the various transnational ventures in France, Hoechst uses a special, wholly-owned subsidiary.[19] Other transnational collaboration ventures of Hoechst in the Common Market are found in the Netherlands where the German company has a wholly-owned and a jointly-owned subsidiary. Roussel-Uclaf also has a second collaboration venture with a German firm, C. F. Boehringer, an important manufacturer of pharmaceutical products. The objectives of this venture are joint production and the sale of the German products through Roussel-Uclaf marketing channels in a number of countries. Hoechst supports this collaboration in the field of research. The three companies form the largest European chemical and pharmaceutical group and are capable of offering strong competition to the American giants in these sectors.

THE GROWTH PATTERN OF
COLLABORATION VENTURES

To make judgments regarding the effects of transnational business collaboration ventures in the member governments and institutions of the EEC, one needs to examine first the growth, scope, and direction of these transnational initiatives. The statistical data available do not cover uniformly the full range of collaboration endeavors and are sometimes based on different sources. Moreover, data are lacking on the size of many of the entities involved, especially their sales records, capitalization, and employees, which can only be discovered with relative ease when rather large enterprises are participants in transnational ventures.[20] Nevertheless, the statistics available are at least suggestive and the data presented in Table 4.1 which cover collaboration ventures involving financial participations and the establishment of subsidiaries indicate a definite upward trend of border-crossing endeavors. It should be noted that wholly-owned subsidiaries of a parent company located in another member state and transnational mergers are included in the statistics. Although the terms "partnership" and "joint venture" may not be appropriate for these cases, their inclusion in the

TABLE 4.1

Growth of Transnational Business Collaboration
Within the European Common Market, 1961-1969

Year	Collaboration Ventures Including Financial Participations Without Assumption of Control and Jointly-Owned Sub- sidiaries Between Com- mon Market Enterprises	Mergers and Financial Participations with Assumption of Control Between Common Market Enterprises	Wholly-Owned Subsidiaries From Member State to Mem- ber State	Total
1961	104	19	241	364
1962	114	11	232	357
1963	61	28	195	284
1964	123	34	273	430
1965	140	17	247	404
1966	112	31	320	463
1967	104	32	328	464
1968	160	35	304	499
1969*	83	50	160	293
Total	1,001	257	2,300	3,558

Growth of Intranational Collaboration
Ventures 1961-69

Year	Collaboration Ventures Including Financial Participation Without Assumption of Control	Mergers and Financial Participation With Assumption of Control	Total
1961	100	131	231
1962	141	162	303
1963	55	157	212
1964	132	172	304
1965	177	228	405
1966	205	221	426
1967	166	253	419
1968	231	272	503
1969*	145	265	410
Total	1,352	1,861	3,213

*The first six months.

Source: Adapted from Commission des Communautés Europeéne, La Politique Industrielle de la Communauté (Brussels, 1970), p. 92.

TABLE 4.2

Distribution of Transnational Collaboration Ventures in the
Common Market by Type and Country, 1968, 1969, 1970

Receptor	Type	Initiator Germany 1968	Germany 1969	Germany 1970	France 1968	France 1969	France 1970	Italy 1968	Italy 1969	Italy 1970	Netherlands 1968	Netherlands 1969	Netherlands 1970	Belgium 1968	Belgium 1969	Belgium 1970	Luxembourg 1968	Luxembourg 1969	Luxembourg 1970	Total 1968	Total 1969	Total 1970
Germany	A	0	0	0	10	0	4	0	0	0	0	2	0	0	5	0	1	0	0	11	7	4
	B	0	0	0	4	2	4	1	1	0	4	5	1	1	1	0	0	1	0	10	10	5
	C	0	0		4	3		0	0		1	1		1	0		0	1		6	5	
	D	0	0	0	35	17	25	5	7	4	27	7	4	11	2	3	0	0	0	78	33	36
	E	0	0	0	4	4	3	1	2	1	0	4	1	0	1	0	0	1	0	5	12	5
	F	0	0	0	1	1	1	0	1	0	1	0	4	1	1	1	0	0	0	3	3	6
	G	0	0	0	0	0	0	0	0	0	0	0	0	0	0	0	0	0	0	0	0	0
	Total	0	0	0	58	27	37	7	11	5	33	19	10	14	10	4	1	3	0	113	70	56
France	A	5	11	3	0	0	0	1	2	0	0	0	0	0	1	2	0	0	0	6	14	5
	B	10	9	5	0	0	0	5	1	0	4	1	0	7	2	1	1	4	1	27	17	7
	C	4	4		0	0		0	0		1	1		3	0		0	0		8	5	
	D	34	21	20	0	0	0	14	0	4	7	6	4	4	7	4	0	2	0	59	36	32
	E	8	10	4	0	0	0	0	0	1	2	3	3	4	5	0	0	0	0	14	18	8
	F	0	2	5	0	0	0	1	0	0	0	3	0	1	0	3	0	0	6	2	5	14
	G	0	0	0	0	0	0	0	0	0	0	0	0	0	0	1	0	0	1	0	0	2
	Total	61	57	37	0	0	0	21	3	5	14	14	7	19	15	11	1	6	8	116	95	68

(Continued)

Table 4. 2 (Continued)

Receptor	Type	Germany 1968	Germany 1969	Germany 1970	France 1968	France 1969	France 1970	Italy 1968	Italy 1969	Italy 1970	Netherlands 1968	Netherlands 1969	Netherlands 1970	Belgium 1968	Belgium 1969	Belgium 1970	Luxembourg 1968	Luxembourg 1969	Luxembourg 1970	Total 1968	Total 1969	Total 1970
Italy	A	4	6	0	3	1	1	0	0	0	0	0	1	0	0	0	0	0	0	7	7	2
	B	3	4	1	2	3	1	0	0	0	0	0	0	1	1	1	0	2	0	6	10	3
	C	3	1	1	2	1		0	0		0	1		1	0		0	0		6	2	
	D	15	17	6	17	9	9	0	0	0	5	1	1	4	0	1	0	0	0	41	27	17
	E	0	3	0	1	2	1	0	0	0	0	0	0	0	2	0	0	0	0	1	7	1
	F	1	1	0	2	0	0	0	0	0	0	2	1	0	0	0	1	0	0	4	3	1
	G	0	0	0	0	0	0	0	0	0	0	0	0	0	0	0	0	0	0	0	0	0
	Σ	26	32	7	27	16	12	0	0	0	5	3	3	6	3	2	1	2	0	65	56	24
Netherlands	A	4	6	1	5	1	1	0	0	1	0	0	0	1	2	0	0	0	0	10	9	3
	B	1	4	5	1	3	0	0	0	0	0	0	0	2	0	0	0	0	0	4	7	5
	C	2	2		0	3		0	0		0	0		2	4		0	0		4	9	
	D	14	18	12	4	4	7	1	3	3	0	0	0	6	8	1	0	1	2	25	34	25
	E	2	7	4	2	3	1	1	1	0	0	0	0	1	2	3	0	0	0	5	13	8
	F	0	1	2	0	0	2	0	0	0	0	0	0	0	1	2	0	0	0	0	2	6
	G	0	0	0	1	0	0	0	0	1	0	0	0	0	0	0	0	0	1	1	0	2
	Σ	23	38	24	13	14	11	1	4	5	0	0	0	12	17	6	0	1	3	49	74	49

128

Belgium

	1	2	3	4	5	6	7	8	9	10	11	12	13	14	15	16	17	18	1968	1969	1970
A	5	3	0	1	2	2	1	1	1	0	1	0	0	0	0	0	0	0	7	7	2
B	3	9	2	12	11	9	1	1	0	10	14	0	0	0	0	1	2	2	27	37	14
C	2	5	19	2	4	31	0	2	8	0	12	51	0	0	0	0	2	0	4	25	110
D	11	10	15	19	17	18	3	0	0	27	24	24	0	0	0	0	1	1	60	52	58
E	4	4	1	4	7	4	3	1	0	4	9	0	0	0	0	0	0	1	15	21	6
F	0	0	0	0	0	0	1	0	0	1	2	0	0	0	0	0	0	0	2	2	0
G	0	0	0	0	0	0	0	0	0	0	0	0	0	0	0	0	0	0	0	0	0
	25	31	37	38	41	64	9	5	9	42	62	75	0	0	0	1	5	4	115	144	190

Luxembourg

	1	2	3	4	5	6	7	8	9	10	11	12	13	14	15	16	17	18	1968	1969	1970
A	1	1	0	0	1	1	0	1	0	0	0	0	0	4	0	0	0	0	1	7	0
B	3	4	2	3	4	0	3	2	2	3	0	0	0	2	0	0	0	0	12	12	6
C	0	0	0	0	1	0	0	0	0	0	0	0	0	0	3	0	0	0	0	1	17
D	2	1	8	2	2	3	2	1	3	0	0	2	1	1	2	0	0	0	6	5	11
E	0	1	1	0	1	4	0	1	0	0	0	2	0	1	0	0	0	0	1	4	3
F	1	0	0	0	0	0	0	0	1	0	0	0	0	0	0	0	0	0	1	0	0
G	2	5	5	3	7	6	6	9	6	3	2	2	2	9	9	0	0	0	14	32	27
	9	12	16	8	16	14	11	14	12	6	2	6	3	17	14	0	0	0	35	61	64

	1	2	3	4	5	6	7	8	9	10	11	12	13	14	15	16	17	18	1968	1969	1970
Total Initiations	144	170	121	144	114	138	49	37	38	98	100	101	54	62	37	4	17	16	493	500	451
Total Receptions	113	70	56	116	95	68	65	56	24	49	74	49	115	144	190	35	61	64	493	500	451

SUMMARY

Type of Collaboration

A – No Financial Participation
B – Financial Participation, no control
C – Controlling Financial Part
D – Wholly Owned Subsidiary
E – Joint Subsidiary
F – Merger
G – Holding Company

	1968	1969	1970
A	42	51	16
B	86	93	40
C	28	47	237
D	269	187	91
E	41	75	36
F	12	15	31
G	15	32	
	493	500	451

Source: Information on business interpenetration reported in the daily bulletin of Agence Europe.

statistics seems warranted as far as this study is concerned because of interest in the effects which the border-crossing flow of human, social, administrative, and economic relations and transactions generated by such transnational initiatives and their consequent inter-lacement might have on the perceptions and decisions of national decision-makers. It must be pointed out, however, that over the years there have also been failures of collaboration ventures and some wholly-owned subsidiaries may have been abandoned. Since failures are rarely publicized widely, it is difficult to estimate their numbers.

If the figures for the growth of transnational business collabora-tions are compared with those of the intranational collaboration ven-tures in the Common Market, also shown on Table 4.1, it is found that the latter have enjoyed a substantial increase as well. In fact, in 1968 and the first six months of 1969 the number of intranational ventures was greater than that of transnational collaboration under-takings. Two major reasons may account for this. First, the absence of a uniform European company law and other legal and fiscal obstacles have made it difficult to negotiate transnational mergers. Second, the spreading virus of nationalism caused by de Gaulle's aversion to political unity in Western Europe has had its effect on business decision-making in all EEC countries but some change can be expected here in the post-de Gaulle period.

An overview of the distribution of newly established collabora-tion ventures within the EEC by type and country during 1968, 1969, and 1970 can be seen in Table 4.2. These data stem from another source than those of the preceding table and for this reason do not fully agree with the total of 1968 as recorded in Table 4.1. However, the comparison between 1968 and 1969 reveals a continuing upward trend of transnational ventures, but a slight decrease of 10 percent in 1970 which may not be significant but on the other hand could sug-gest dissatisfaction with the effectiveness and success of the trans-national collaboration arrangements.[21]

The distribution of these ventures during the three years sug-gests a strong though declining German interest in the French market and an increasing interest in the Belgian and Luxembourg markets. The French show a growing interest (1970) in the German, and espe-cially the Belgian and Luxembourg markets, while their interest in Italy appears to be waning. The Dutch show a pronounced predilec-tion for Belgium and Luxembourg but seem to have lost interest in the Germans as partners. The Italians have mounted relatively few initiatives in any of the EEC Member States, considering the size of their country.

The most forceful initiators of transnational collaboration ventures clearly are the Germans, French, and Dutch, while the country on the receiving end of the largest number of initiatives is Belgium. In addition, Luxembourg also has a net balance in favor of receptions of border-crossing initiatives. Italy, which in 1968 and 1969 was more often a receptor than originator of these initiatives, reversed its position in 1970 although its total number of initiatives was not large.

As for the form of transnational business penetration, Tables 4.1 and 4.2 indicate that the wholly-owned subsidiary is the most popular and obviously the most easily managed arrangement. Collaborations involving financial participations which fall short of outright control are next in terms of attractiveness, followed by jointly-owned subsidiaries. Mergers are becoming increasingly popular despite the fiscal and legal impediments to corporate structural changes currently prevailing in the EEC.

THE EFFECTS AND CONSEQUENCES OF
TRANSNATIONAL VENTURES

Political Objectives and
Goal Attainment

While the statistics presented clearly indicate that the incidence of transnational business collaboration in the Common Market is increasing, it is not easy to determine and to measure the effects of this development on the international subsystem represented by the EEC and perhaps on the international system as a whole. It is fair to assume that the enterprises through their participation in transnational undertakings are likely to enhance the progress of economic integration in the EEC. However, what kind of political effect can be achieved in terms of changes in the attitudes and policies of the member governments and EEC institutions may well depend on the specific political objectives of these entities and on their capacity for goal attainment.

From interviews conducted during 1968 and 1969[22] with executives of enterprises engaged in transnational business collaboration in the Common Market it is apparent that the following objectives have high priority with firms engaged in border-crossing collaboration:

1. The elimination of restrictions on foreign investments and capital movements;

2. The complete elimination of border customs check points within the Common Market;

3. The harmonization of fiscal laws;

4. The harmonization of national laws setting technical standards for industrial products;

5. The creation of a European patent law;

6. The enactment of a "European company" statute either through Community regulation or the promulgation of identical national laws; and

7. The liberal application of the EEC anti-trust laws.

These objectives are also supported by many firms not engaged in transnational ventures. However, they are especially significant for the collaborating firms because of the very direct effect that their attainment would have on the initiation of collaboration agreements and on their economic results.

Collaborating firms are naturally also interested in promoting the coordination of economic and monetary policies of the member governments since such coordination would have beneficial effects on the joint ventures. However, the attainment of these goals did not seem to have the priority as the other objectives listed when the interviews were conducted, but the monetary crisis during the fall of 1971 may have led to a shift of priorities.

Clearly, the attainment of all of the above objectives with the exception of the liberal application of the EEC anti-trust laws depends mainly on the favorable actions taken by the member governments of the EEC, although the Commission of course plays a vital role by making the necessary proposals to the Council of Ministers. If the objectives were attained, implying the full harmonization of pertinent national laws and policies, the member governments must be understood to have assumed the explicit or implicit obligation of no future unilateral changes in these laws and policies. As a consequence, the autonomy of the national governments would have been reduced, while the power of the EEC institutions would have been enlarged correspondingly.

In Table 4.3 a scorecard is presented of how far the above objectives have been achieved. Since favorable actions and support

TABLE 4.3

Goal Attainment of Transnationally Collaborating Enterprises in the EEC

	Pertinent Industrial Interest Groups	SCORES Commission	Council of Ministers	National Governments	Total
1. Elimination of restrictions on foreign investment and capital movements	10	10	0	0	20
2. Harmonization of national customs regulations	10	7	6	2	25
3. Harmonization of fiscal laws (TVA, corp. taxes, excise tax)	8	8	5	2	23
4. Harmonization of laws on technical standards	10	8	3	1	22
5. European patent law	10	10	5	0	25
6. The "European Company" Statute	10	5	0	0	15
7. Liberal application of EEC anti-trust law	10	6	NA	NA	(16)*
8. Harmonization of economic policies	10	8	4	1	23
9. Harmonization of monetary policies	10	8	3	1	22

*Optimum score would be 20.

133

by interest groups (national and European), the Commission, the
Council of Ministers, and the national governments are required for
full goal attainment, the responses of these units are scored on a
scale of 0 to 10 depending on the scope and extent of their approval.
The maximum score suggesting full attainment of the major objective
would be 40.

The table reveals that the full attainment of the major political
objectives pursued by enterprises engaged in transnational collaboration is still elusive. There is strong support on the part of European
and national industrial interest groups for these objectives, and the
Commission also has provided substantial support and initiative for
most of the goals. However, favorable action by the Council of Ministers has been lagging behind the Commission proposals. In addition,
the member governments, key actors for the harmonization process
of laws, procedures, and policies, have not shown as yet very much
enthusiasm for the implementation of what the pertinent ministers in
the Council have agreed upon. An exception is the introduction of the
TVA taxes where only Italy remains a temporary holdout.

Effects of Transnational Staff
Association and Clienteles

An important factor with potentially favorable implications for
the goal attainment of transnational business collaboration ventures
is the interaction of management and technical staff between collaborating companies and the resultant border-crossing flows of
administrative, technical, social, and human transactions. As the
examples have shown, the coordination of the joint activities is
usually carried out through a network of committees and working
groups composed of an equal number of officials from the collaborating
firms. Depending on the size of the firms and the range of the joint
activities, 50 to 200 officials may be involved in the coordinating
operation. Although frictions and frustrations are not infrequent,
especially because of diverging viewpoints on technical matters and
insufficient preparation of executives to cope with the influences of
particularistic cultures, traditions, and habits, many problems have
been overcome ultimately through the use of thoughtful guidance and
effective communications channels. Especially where positions in
the committee systems have been held by younger men, the collaborative activities have moved along quite smoothly despite differing
mentalities and professional jealousies. Conceptual differences have
been side-stepped by tolerance and understanding of the cultural
background and temperament of collorators of other nationalities.

A desire to be flexible and to engage in true give-and-take has often produced genuine camaraderie among the members of a committee or working group. It has created the feeling amongst them of belonging to a multinational, if not "European," group with shared goals and opened up between them communications going beyond those usual among co-workers. The continuous interaction necessitated by the transnational collaboration ventures have provided opportunities not only to understand better the traits peculiar to other nationalities in the Common Market countries, but also to appreciate the values attached to these traits. In some cases highly personal ties have been established between members of the coordinating groups and visits between families of committee members in their respective houses are not uncommon.

If one considers that in each coordinating system of a transnational collaboration venture up to 200 individuals may be active, it would not be unjustified to assume that a subtle political socialization process is operating through which a very gradual adoption of "European" values and beliefs may take place. Of course, the experiences flowing from coordinating activities are not intended to have political effects nor are these effects immediately recognized. Nevertheless, they have political implications because the individuals involved in this process may relate these experiences to their political environment. To a great extent, committee and working group members participating in the coordination activities of a border-crossing collaboration may "socialize themselves"[23] However, a positive though subtle influence toward the adoption of "European" values and norms may also be exerted by leaders of companies engaged in joint ventures who are outspoken in their support for European integration. Such leaders may take on the role of "socializing agents." An example is Giovanni Agnelli, the chairman of the board of Fiat, who not only has expressed himself on many occasions with great vigor for moving European unification forward, but who also has explicitly stated that the collaboration with Citroen was motivated strongly by this goal.[24] Another example is Karl Winnacker, former president of Hoechst, who was equally interested in the pursuit of this goal and who was surrounded by a remarkably Europe-oriented top leadership group.[25]

The particular significance of the socializing process stemming from transnational business collaboration within the EEC is the presence of a clearly identifiable rallying point which in geographic, cultural, and ideological terms is fully recognizable: Europe. It therefore provides a convenient handle to which shifting loyalties, new identity, and emerging expectation can be attached and thereby strengthens the effectiveness of this socializing process. An additional stimulus may be the feeling that transnational collaboration is part of the European answer to the "demi-American."

Some of the elements operative in the socialization process among staffs of collaborating enterprises in the Common Market which spring from the typical European environment are likely to be absent from the joint ventures in Third World countries or East-West enterprises. However, some of the regions of the world such as Latin America could provide for transnational business collaboration the cultural and ideological homogeneity to foster the political socialization process among multinational staff. The effectiveness of this factor is likely to be weakened if the multinational staff includes many nationals of the advanced country where one of the partners in the joint venture is headquartered. In East-West ventures practical results are apt to count most for collaborating firms and staffs; as a consequence ideological differences are likely to be pushed in the background, turn out to be irrelevant, and become easy to ignore. The relationships between Western and Communist managers and technicians therefore tend to cross and cut through ideologies and, as Howard V. Perlmutter put it, "transideological thinking is beginning to blossom."[26] If the East-West joint enterprise is based on the principles of equality and mutual benefit, the socialist workers are likely to become convinced that they are not being exploited by foreign capitalists. New political values may then slowly be adopted by the workers and a climate of confidence and trust generated among the collaborating partners and their staffs which will be beneficial not only for this particular venture but also for subsequent initiatives by different enterprises.

Some kind of socialization process toward the adoption of new political values may also be operative among the multinational staffs of MNEs as suggested in the preceding chapter. However, unless the activities of the MNEs are mainly concentrated in a particular region of the world,[27] the process may not function effectively. While polycentric and geocentric attitudes of top management of MNEs may enhance the socialization process somewhat, the target for new loyalties and identity may be too diffuse or abstract to offer definite directions for this process.

Whenever the political socialization process results in a perceptible shift of identity, loyalties, and expectations of multinational staff as appears to be the case among executives of transnationally collaborating enterprises in the EEC, some effects on the national decision-makers in countries affected by the collaboration can be anticipated. This group of executives, which is bound to grow in members as the number of joint transnational ventures expands, may develop into a special type of Europe-oriented business elite whose future behavior will be of increasing consequence for the operation of the political systems in which they live. Since many members of this group are relatively young, their positions of power are likely to be still on the rise and therefore their outlook and influence may in time further enhance the impact they are apt to have on national decision-makers. Moreover, the intensity of their efforts may deepen as they perceive of having a growing vested interest in the maintenance of the integration level achieved. Finally, the members of the elites may be influential through intracountry and transnational cross communications with other elites in soliciting increased support for harmonization measures by the member governments as well as for the Community system in general and thereby could evolve as a significant pro-integration force.

Another group of people in the EEC member countries which might be motivated to exert pressures on national decision-makers in support of the political objectives of joint transnational business ventures consists of the workers of the enterprises involved and their customers. Studies made in Europe suggest that the larger the enterprises, the higher is likely to be the wage level of their employees.[28] Thus, one could argue that the more transnational business collaboration ventures are established, the greater will be the circle of beneficiaries[29] with strong economic interests to see the operating conditions for transnationally collaborating enterprises improved. (See Table 4.4.) However, despite the possible rise in wages that is likely to be engendered by the expansion of transnational business collaboration, the attitudes of the labor unions toward this activity are complex and, as will be discussed in Chapter 4, often more unfavorable than favorable. Nevertheless, it may be in the unions' interest to support, at least on a selective basis, some of the political objectives of collaborating enterprises and thus organized labor in the member States may eventually emerge as a potent, although perhaps reluctant, ally. In fact, a coalition between a Europe-oriented business elite and a less parochially-oriented labor elite would not be inconceivable and would constitute most likely a powerful force for gathering support for the Community system and overcoming the nationalistic tendencies of many political and administrative elites.

The second segment of potential supporters of the objectives of transnational business collaboration is the circle of customers. One could argue that customers can become direct beneficiaries of

TABLE 4.4

Number of Employees of 15 Largest Firms
Engaged in Transnational Collaboration

Company	Employees
Philips' Gloeilampenfabriken	359,000
Montecatini Edison	163,000
Fiat	185,000
Siemens	301,000
Farbwerke Hoechst	139,000
Renault	155,000
Farbenfabriken Bayer	102,000
Cie Francaise des Petroles	24,000
BASF (Badische Anilin-& Soda-Fabrik)	107,000
Pechiney	62,000
Citroen	91,000
Rhone-Poulenc	121,000
Dunlop	107,000
Mannesmann	69,000
Gutehoffnugshutte	68,000
Hoesch	76,000
Pirelli	81,000
AKZO	101,000
Michelin	80,000
Ugine Kuhlmann	47,000
Saint-Gobain	115,000
Agfa-Gevaert Group	34,000
Alfa Romeo	18,000
Total	2,605,000

Source: Fortune, August 15, 1971.

such collaboration if savings in the cost of production and marketing resulting from the elimination of border check points and the harmonization of fiscal and other laws were passed on to the consumers in the form of lower prices. However, whether these cost savings would lead to price reductions is not certain. Some doubt for such a development arises from the insistence of the collaborating firms on a liberal application of the Community antitrust provisions. Moreover, the European studies referred to above suggest that despite expected cost savings no correlation exists between increased industrial concentration and the formation of prices. But even though it may be difficult to produce concrete evidence of price benefits from transnational business collaboration, customers nevertheless may receive this impression when they associate the advertising of lowered prices of firms involved in collaboration ventures with news items regarding the conclusion of such ventures which often have received wide publicity. Of course, consumer groups are rarely organized very effectively and therefore the potency of their influence, if attempts were made to exert it in support of the political objectives of transnational ventures, is open to considerable question.

CONSEQUENCES FOR THE INTERNATIONAL SYSTEM

From the foregoing analysis one may conclude that while the increasing rate of transnational business collaboration in the Common Market over the last ten years has produced a more intensive degree of economic integration, the responses of national decision-makers to demands for more favorable conditions for the transnational ventures have been hesitant and unenthusiastic. Despite strongly motivated assistance by collaborating firms and perhaps even leadership for bringing about the initial steps toward fiscal and legal harmonization, progress has been slow and the process of political integration as measured by a rise in the powers of the EEC institutions has benefited only slightly up to now.

The immediate effect of the emergence of a "Europe"-oriented transnational business elite and the widening circle of potential beneficiaries from transnational business collaboration seems to have been minimal. If the harmonization process is permitted to move forward, the autonomy of the member governments is likely to be whittled down and larger increments of political integration can be expected. As has already been observed, legal harmonization and perhaps also policy coordination by the member governments carries with it at least the implicit obligation of no further unilateral changes and as a consequence, the powers of the EEC authorities would be gradually strengthened as the process of harmonization and coordination progresses. In addition, the development of a European patent law may result in the assignment of new functions and powers to the EEC institutions either de facto or through multilateral conventions among the Member States. Under such circumstances the political activities of an increasing number of political actors would, in all likelihood, shift toward the central EEC authorities and with it increasingly their expectations and perhaps even their loyalties. This shift may also engender a rise in the European Community support level of politically powerful elites and enhance the legitimacy of the central authorities as appropriate political institutions in the eyes of the public of the Community.

As the conditions for transnational business collaboration improve as a result of greater fiscal and other harmonization measures and the eventual disappearance of border control points, the trend toward border-crossing collaboration within the Common Market is apt to receive additional impetus. In turn, the clamor for full implementation of these measures is likely to rise further. Eventually, however, a plateau of satisfactory conditions for transnational collaboration ventures may be reached. At that time the stimulus of this activity for political integration will cease to operate and the main concern will be the maintenance of the level of integration attained. However, although the incentive for integration growth will have disappeared, certain effects such as the increased legitimacy level of the EEC institutions and procedures and the greater commitment of business and perhaps other elites to European values would probably persist and remain influential for possible further progress of political integration in the future. Moreover, the acquisition of vested interests in a certain level of integration would constitute a bulwark against regression or dismantlement of the Community system and enhance its stability. If such a sequence of events were to unfold, it would suggest that Paul Reuter's prediction, that "it is the industrial leaders who will build Europe"[30] contains indeed a measure of truth, although other potential forces promoting political integration obviously must be considered as well.

The chain of events sketched above suggests that transnational business collaboration within an international region can indeed constitute a potent nongovernmental force which may contribute materially to the transformation of an international subsystem by changing the patterns of political interaction within that system. In turn, the transformation of this subsystem is bound to modify the global pattern of political interactions. The growing economic and political force of the EEC as reflected by the common stand taken by the six member governments in the face of the international monetary and trade crisis which had been unleashed by the American currency and trade measures of August 15, 1971, clearly illustrates the gradual change in the present and future distribution of power in the global international system.

While transnational business collaboration in Europe offers us at least some kind of fuzzy blueprint of the long-range consequences which a nongovernmental force can produce for the changes in the pattern of interactions in the international system, the impact on the global system of transnational ventures involving either Third World or Communist countries can only be judged on the basis of more or less informed speculation.

While the regional rationalization of production is acceptable, if not desired, in the EEC countries, Third World governments often object to it on the grounds that plants in their countries may be assigned the production of less profitable items and that they will lose control over the sale price of the total product and over the management of the local facilities. If the partner in the advanced country seeks to overcome this problem by buying out the local partner, this usually can only be done at great cost if at all, because the local government will attempt to prevent it. It is also doubtful, as has already been noted, whether joint ventures in the Third World can stimulate the same kind of political socialization process as was possible in Europe. The reason is that operational and policy disputes often are very serious and that their resolution, which by necessity has to be based in most cases on the expertise of the partner from the industrialized country, leaves deep psychological scars. These scars are all the more serious because of the wide cultural and conceptual gaps that exist between the nationals of the developed and developing countries.

Having said this, it should be stressed that some of the benefits of these joint ventures may have long-range benefits in terms of changing the pattern of interaction in the international system. The motivation of many companies in industrialized countries to seek new ventures is the exploration for new markets and consequently many new consumer goods can be made available to developing countries at reasonable prices. This may lead to a rise in the technical capabilities of developing countries and to greater uniformity of consumer tastes, both factors with favorable implications for bridging the schism between the developing and advanced countries. Another benefit of joint ventures may be the building of

new entrepreneurial and managerial classes as well as fostering the
development of a variety of auxiliary services and manufacturing
enterprises through the transfer of new technological and management
skills. As a result, the climate of dependence prevailing among the
people of the Third World may be reduced, the transition to the economic emancipation of developing countries eased, the prospects of
a continuing "North-South" conflict reduced, and the basis built for a
more equitable, congenial world of the future.

Toward reaching this goal East-West joint ventures can also
contribute. Some of the benefits of these ventures have already been
discussed in evaluating the contribution which the MNE can make
toward changes in the pattern of interaction in the international
system. It should be added here that these ventures may contribute
to changes not only in the global system, but also the transformation
of the East European regional system as represented by Comecon.[31]
These ventures demonstrate that it is harmful for Comecon and its
member states to depend exclusively on an international division of
labor confined to East Europe's Communist countries. Rather, for
the development of their economies, especially those of the smaller
Comecon countries, the financial and technological resources of the
West are needed and these can be provided through joint ventures.
Cooperating with foreign economic entities whose structures, skills,
and business policies are completely different from their own, provides a learning process for the Communist partners demonstrating
to them how a socialist society of self-management might operate.
The interaction between the domestic and foreign partners will not
only have an impact on the internal economic life of the East European
Communist countries, but may also bring about a gradual political
awareness that economic cooperation with Western countries will
result in fuller integration of Communist economies into the World-
wide division of labor and thereby promote a policy of genuine peaceful coexistence.[32] Thus, the joint ventures can be seen as slowly
expanding windows of the East toward the West and vice versa. In
addition, they may well help to substantiate what has long been
suspected in many circles on both sides of the Iron Curtain, namely
that the Communist economic system has been moving toward the
adoption of many concepts and methods traditionally associated with
capitalistic economic methods while the West has been moving
toward the modification of the market forces, given an increasing
role to government planning in industry, and has greatly expanded
the public sector in the national economies. What the final result
for the constellation of the international system will be, of course
cannot be predicted, but a guess that greater harmony will eventually
reign does not seem to be unreasonable.

NOTES

1. Wolfgang G. Friedmann and George Kalmanoff, Joint International Business Ventures (New York: Columbia University Press, 1961), pp. 5-6. It should be note that the two authors have focused their study mainly on joint ventures in developing countries with the partnerships organized between firms from advanced countries and local enterprises. However, some of the principles evolved by Friedmann and Kalmanoff are also applicable to joint ventures and other forms of transnational collaboration in developed countries.

2. E. J. Kolde, International Business Enterprise (Englewood Cliffs, N.J.: Prentice-Hall, 1968), p. 260. If capital is needed for a joint venture, it is raised from whichever capital market provides the best source for a particular undertaking. See also Kolde's discussion of the "transnational" company on p. 251.

3. In this venture, the most prominent producers of photographic equipment in Germany and Belgium, AGFA A.G. and Photo Produits Gevaerts, established in each country in 1964 two new corporations, the Agfa-Gevaerts A.G. in Germany and the Gevaerts-Agfa N.V. in Belgium, each of which has the same capitalization and is owned equally by the founding companies.

4. The local partner can also contribute his knowledge about the labor market and labor conditions and local financing possibilities.

5. For details and additional examples see Johannes Meynen, Wolfgang Friedmann, and Kenneth Weg, "Joint Ventures Revisited," Columbia Journal of World Business I, 2 (Spring 1966), pp. 19-29.

6. For other examples see Howard V. Perlmutter, "Emerging East-West Ventures: The Transideological Enterprise," Columbia Journal of World Politics, September-October 1969, pp. 39-50.

7. For details see Miodrag Sukijasovic, "Foreign Investment in Yugoslavia," in Isaiah A. Litvak and Christopher J. Maule, Foreign Investment and the Experience of Host Countries (New York: Praeger Publishers, 1970), pp. 385-406.

8. Printing Developments International (New York) and Beogradski Graficki Zavod (Belgrad).

9. Perlmutter, "Emerging East-West Ventures," p. 40.

10. Journal of Commerce, April 20, 1971.

11. LAFTA has sought to stimulate consciously transnational collaboration among member country industrial enterprises by the use of so-called complementarity agreements. However, the success of efforts in that direction has been very limited. See Sidney Dell, A Latin American Common Market (London: Oxford University Press, 1966), pp. 120-145.

12. MAN is controlled by Gutehoffnungshuette, a German holding company with interests in machinery, engineering and metal products. According to Fortune (August 15, 1971) it is the 56th largest industrial group outside the United States.

13. The agreement runs until December 31, 1982. Unless notice for termination is given by December 31, 1979, it continues in force but can be cancelled after three years' notice. It took nearly five years to negotiate this agreement.

14. The trucks whose parts are produced jointly range from 7.5 to 19 tons. Smaller trucks are manufactured exclusively by Saviem, larger ones by MAN. For additional details see the special edition of the Handlesblatt on German-French Commerce (June 1968), p. 15.

15. The agreement with Renault had some joint production features, but it was mainly focused on the rationalization of marketing. However, today Renault and Alfa-Romeo have separate distribution networks for their passenger cars in France and Italy.

16. Saviem also has its own distribution subsidiary in Italy, Saviem-Italiana.

17. This company occupies rank number 11 among non-U.S. firms.

18. International Herald-Tribune, October 2, 1968.

19. Le Monde, October 22, 1968, and Agence Europe, March 28, 1969.

20. Fortune's annual listing of the top 200 industrial companies outside the U.S. since 1963.

21. See Paul M. Goldberg, The Evolution of Transnational companies in Europe (unpublished Ph.D. dissertation, Sloan School of Management, M.I.T., June 1971), pp. 208-258.

22. See Werner J. Feld, Transnational Business Collaboration Among Common Market Countries (New York: Praeger Publishers, 1970), pp. 58-80.

23. See Richard E. Dawson and Kenneth Prewitt, Political Soc- ialization (Boston: Little, Brown and Company, 1969), pp. 38-39; and Gabriel A. Almond and Sidney Verba, Civic Culture (Boston: Little, Brown and Company, 1965), pp. 266-306. Individuals so- cializing themselves adopt, there, new values and beliefs of a political nature.

24. International Herald-Tribune, January 17, 1969.

25. Express (France), December 9-15, 1968.

26. Perlmutter, "Emerging East-West Ventures," p. 47.

27. See Bernard Mennis and Karl P. Sauvant, Multinational Corporations and the Prospects for Regional Integration, paper pre- sented for the Research Conference on the Multinational Corporation in the Global Political System, University of Pennsylvania, April 22- 23, 1971 (Mimeo., 1971).

28. See Louis Phlips, "Effets economiques de la concentration industrielle: Essai d'analyse empirique" (Mimeo, 1969); and H. W. de Jong "De Concentratiebeweging in de Westeuropese Economie," Economisch-Statistische Berichten (January 22 and 29 and February 5 and 12, 1969), especially Table 3.

29. The number of employees of 15 EEC-based enterprises engaged in transnational ventures of different types that are listed among the 50 largest corporations outside the United States totals a respectable 2,605,000. Fortune, LXXX, 3 (August 15, 1971), 107. See Table 4.4 for this list. The total civilian labor force in the EEC is nearly 74 million.

30. A similar function was performed by business interests in America and Switzerland. Charles A. Beard points out that support for the adoption of the U.S. Constitution came principally from the cities and the regions where the commercial, financial, and manufacturing interests were concentrated. These interests had been adversely affected by the system of government under the Articles of Confederation and they therefore sought to secure greater protection through a "revision" of the Articles which culminated in the present Constitution. (Economic Origins of Jeffersonian Democracy [New York: Macmillan, 1915] p. 464; and An Economic Interpretation of the Constitution of the United States [New York: Macmillan, 1960],

p. 63 and passim.) For the Swiss experience in 1815 see Charlotte Muret, "The Swiss Pattern for a Federated Europe," in International Political Communities, An Anthology (Garden City, N.Y.: Doubleday, 1966), pp. 149-73.

31. See Werner Feld, "The Utility of the EEC Experience for the People's Democracies in Eastern Europe," in J. Lukaskewski, ed., The People's Democracies After Prague (Bruges, Belgium: De Tempel, 1970).

32. Sukijasovic, "Foreign Investment in Yugoslavia," pp. 403, 404.

5

THE TRANSNATIONAL
ACTIVITIES
OF ORGANIZED LABOR

The ability of MNEs to "export" jobs from one country to another and similar, though less frequent, opportunities of transnationally collaborating firms have aroused the ire of national and international labor organizations despite the advantages that may be presented by the multinational production facilities of these entities to bargain up wages and improve other conditions normally included in a labor contract on a cross-national scale. An economist of the AFL-CIO, Elizabeth R. Jager, observed early in 1970 that the fear of working people all over the world is heightened by the operation of the multinational firms.[1] The basic reason for this fear is that search for cheaper labor is generally accepted as a rational decision for the management of MNEs to make. A similar opinion has been expressed by the Chairman of the German Federation of Trade Unions, Heinz O. Vetter. He declared that "the industrial giants which reach beyond national borders will ruthlessly exploit the international working cost differential for the purpose of increasing their profit."[2]

The apprehension of organized labor concerning MNEs and transnationally operating joint business ventures, however, is only one of many concerns trade unions have in the international arena. In fact, the transnational interests of organized labor are far reaching, extending from the desire of eventually bargaining with multinational corporations on an international basis to helping fledgling labor unions in the developing countries. The instruments for obtaining these objectives also show a great variety. This chapter will first provide data on the membership and geographic distribution of the international labor movement, then examine the initiatives in which national and international labor organizations have engaged when seeking to promote their world-wide interests, attempt to evaluate the effects which these initiatives have on national decision-makers and IGO institutions, and finally assess the consequences, present and future, for the international system and its subsystems.

GROWTH AND DISTRIBUTION PATTERNS OF
INTERNATIONAL LABOR FEDERATIONS

Three world-wide labor federations are at present preeminent on the international labor scene. They are the International Confederation of Free Trade Unions (ICFTU), the World Confederation of Labor (WCL, formerly the International Federation of Christian Trade Unions—IFCTU), and the Communist-controlled World Federation of Trade Unions (WFTU). The three federations are basically umbrella organizations; their constituent or subordinate units are functional, regional, or national labor federations which in turn have national or local member unions. Examples of the functional and regional units are the influential International Metalworkers Federation (IMF), affiliated with the ICFTU, and the strong Latin American Federation of Christian Trade Unions, which is part of the WCL. Among powerful national labor federations are the German Federation of Trade Unions (DGB); the major British trade unions, all belonging to the ICFTU; the WFTU-affiliated French General Confederation of Labor (CGT); and the Italian Confederation of Labor (CGIL).

The WFTU is more tightly organized than the other two international labor federations. As George C. Lodge points out, it is a tool of the Communist parties around the world, financed, organized, and staffed by them, and a major agency to promote the Communist cause.[3] However, it would be an error to assume that all WFTU member unions follow slavishly the dictates of the WFTU leadership. A case in point is the CGIL which often pursues policies somewhat at variance with the official WFTU line.

Table 5.1 shows the growth of the three international federations of labor from 1956 to 1970. The strongest group is the WFTU. However, it should be noted that many labor unions in the Communist countries do not reflect really the spirit of trade unionism and collective bargaining but are primarily organizations serving as political tools for the Communist governments of these countries. The WCL is the smallest federation but has shown the highest rate increase.[4]

With respect to geographical distribution the ICFTU is represented more equally around the world and in more countries than either of the other organizations. It is interesting to observe that all three federations have fairly widespread representation in the

TABLE 5.1

Growth and Geographic Distribution of International Labor Federations

Membership Growth

	1956	1962	1970
WFTU	88,600,000	107,000,000	138,000,000
ICFTU	54,525,288	56,477,000	63,412,228*
WCL	4,000,000	5,500,000	6,801,000 (est.)

Distribution by Number of Countries, 1970

	WCL	ICFTU	WFTU
Africa	24	17	13
Asia	9	16	15
South Africa and Caribbean (except Mexico)	28	34	18
Australia and New Zealand	—	3	1
Europe	12	21	15
North America (including Mexico)	2	3	1

Growth and Distribution—ICFTU

	1962		1970	
	Number of Countries	Number of Members	Number of Countries	Number of Members
Africa	29	1,978,000	17	631,864
South America and Caribbean (except Mexico)	34	6,081,000	34	7,941,093
Asia	20	7,345,000	16	8,227,674
Australia and New Zealand	3	1,050,000	3	1,547,685
Europe	20	25,907,000	21	30,373,416
North America	3	14,110,000	3	3,700,000

*With the withdrawal of the AFL-CIO from the ICFTU, 15,000,000 should be deducted at present from the figure listed. However, since some of the member unions of the AFL-CIO remain members of such federations as the IMF which in turn is a member organization of the ICFTU, it is difficult to calculate directly the loss of ICFTU membership caused by the AFL-CIO action.

Source: Yearbook of International Organizations (13th edition, 1970-71); and Hans Gottfurcht, Die Internationale Gewerkschaftsbewegung im Weltgeschehen (Cologne: Bund-Verlag, 1962).

developing countries, but this picture is somewhat misleading because in tropical Africa only 5 percent of the total population are wage earners and only 10 percent are union members.[5]

Although basically a national organization, the AFL-CIO has been active in international affairs since the early days of World War II. In 1944 it established a Free Trade Union Committee as an instrument to revive aggressively the Free Trade Union Movement all over the world. Opposed strongly to the Communist orientation of the WFTU, the American Federation of Labor (prior to its merger in 1955 with the CIO) participated in the formation of the ICFTU. In addition it helped organize a regional Federation of Trade Unions in Latin America known as CIT to combat efforts by Communist-dominated labor organizations to control the labor movement in that area of the world.

With the merger of the AFL and CIO the Free Trade Union Committee and its far-flung operations were terminated. The functions of this committee were assigned to the International Affairs Department of the AFL-CIO which attempted to channel most of its international efforts through the ICFTU. It should be added that some of the member unions of the AFL-CIO such as the United Steel Workers (USW) and the United Auto Workers (UAW) have their own extensive international activities.

During 1960-61 the AFL-CIO expended about $1.5 million for international activities which was roughly 8 percent of the federation's income. The AFL-CIO has continued its efforts in the international field and today constitutes one of the most potent nongovernmental forces in labor activities throughout the world. Because of differences in 1969 between the leadership of the AFL-CIO and that of the ICFTU regarding the latter's political views which are oriented toward mild socialist concepts, the AFL-CIO has withdrawn from the ICFTU. This means that at least temporarily the membership of the ICFTU has been reduced by 15 million, but there are strong sentiments within the AFL-CIO to return to the ICFTU. Moreover, some of the subordinate unions of the AFL-CIO such as the USW and the UAW continue their membership in the International Metalworkers Federation, a member unit of the ICFTU.

THE INITIATIVES OF ORGANIZED LABOR

Responses to MNE Challenges

Since during the last few years the problems presented by the
MNEs have been particularly troubling to the trade unions the author
will first examine the major issues involved in this relationship.
The existence of an MNE with headquarters in a country different
from where a union represents workers in a production affiliate and
where therefore management personnel dealing with union officials
are subject to pressures or control from a foreign source, is the
basic challenge presented by the MNE to organized labor. Aggravating
this situation are several additional factors. The headquarters of the
MNE may insist that affiliates reflect the broader international or
domestic objectives and policies of the parent company whose industrial relations practices may be at variance with the local conditions.
Job security may be more or less dependent on the global operation
and performance of the MNE which means that unprofitable operations
in one country may have serious effects on the stability and conditions
in another one. Finally, nationalistic, cultural, and ideological influences may impair a rational approach of union leaders and members
in dealing with the affiliate of an MNE.[6]

Under the operational conditions enjoyed by MNEs, the ultimate
weapon available to unions against a local affiliate, the strike, may
not be useful. Measures to reduce production and to apply economic
sanctions such as slowdowns may also be ineffective. To the extent
that products affected by such measures can be readily imported
from facilities in other countries, the union weapons can be blunted.
An example is the eight and one-half month-long strike by the United
Steel Workers of America (USWA) against the U.S. copper, lead,
and zinc companies in the 1960s. Because of the multinational nature
of the major producers, production was intensified in Chile and other
countries where the struck companies had mines and their products
were imported into the United States. Closing down the American
mines drove the world price for the metals sky high. Thus, the
losses suffered by the MNEs involved in the United States were

more than made up by their increased profits from their operations abroad. The result was that the companies could have remained on strike indefinitely.

Two additional factors may be responsible for materially re- ducing the effectiveness of a strike against a local MNE affiliate. The particular item produced in the affiliate might be only a small part of the MNE's global business and therefore the damage which may be suffered by the entire enterprise may be relatively minor. Moreover, the threat of "exporting" the production facilities them- selves is always present and may constitute an alternative option of MNE management to union harrassment and unfavorable labor climate. In fact, the governments of third countries and their labor organizations may seek to exploit such situations and induce the MNE through various incentives to shift their production facili- ties to their own territories. Such a shift is facilitated if it can be carried out within a region in which an economic integration scheme is pursued.

This problem is highlighted by testimony given during the 1970 Hearings of the Subcommittee on Foreign Economic Policy in the Multinational Corporation and International Investment. Paul Jen- nings, president of the International Union of Electrical, Radio and Machine Workers stated:

> About a year ago, General Instrument Corp. transferred
> TV tuner and other component production to its Taiwan
> and Portuguese plants, shutting down two New England
> plants and most of a third. Between 3, 000 and 4, 000
> workers were permanently laid off. General Instrument
> increased its employment in Taiwan from 7, 200 to over
> 12, 000. General Instrument is that nation's largest em-
> ployer, with more workers employed there than in all
> its U.S. operations combined.

> A few months ago, Motorola shut down its picture
> plant, selling its machinery and equipment to a General
> Telephone and Electronics subsidiary in Hong Kong. A
> second picture tube firm commenced operations in Mexi-
> co, taking advantage of item 807 of the Tariff Schedules.
> Friden, a division of Singer Corp., and Burroughs, both
> discontinued production of electronic desk calculators.
> Their desk calculators are now made for them in Japan
> by Hitachi and other Japanese firms. The calculators
> are sold in the United States by their former

manufacturers under the latter's label. So, here we have
another growth industry that U.S. based multinational firms
have abandoned as producers—becoming importers of the
products they once made.[7]

The responses of the larger labor unions and union associations
in the United States and Europe to these problems have been to organize
transnational cooperation of unions wherever plants of MNEs are
located. David H. Blake observes[8] that this is a rather new phenomenon
which has neither deep nor wide-ranging roots. Most of the efforts
toward transnational cooperation date from the 1960s although the
International Metalworkers Federation with a membership exceeding
10 million had established world autoworker company councils for
Ford and General Motors as early as 1956.

While inter-union cooperation is now growing more extensive
and intensive as the reader will later see, the use of the strike as a
weapon on an international basis to force acceptance of union demands
remains highly questionable. Only where the technology of an MNE is
vertically integrated to a point where interruption would be very
costly despite possible alternative technical facilities, can a strike
directed at the proper plant succeed in checkmating the entire enterprise. MNEs falling into this category are found in the petroleum and
aluminum industries and labor relations in these industries are likely
to be designed by management to avoid such trouble.

While it is evidently difficult to organize comprehensive strike
action against all production affiliates of MNEs, what other measures
are available for organized labor to meet the challenges of the multinational corporation? The first task is to ensure having viable
cooperative partners in the countries where MNE affiliates are
located. This does not present any great difficulty in most advanced
countries of the Free World where unions are recognized as legitimate
bargaining agents for the interests of the workers and have the
necessary experience in performing this function. Problems, however,
exist in many developing countries in which unions are extremely
weak and are subordinated to the national political leadership as
instruments of control. R. W. Cox calls these organizations "political
front" unions which may be the downgraded residue of former revolutionary movements or a protective device engineered by a conser-
vative leadership.[9] These unions operate under governmental and
political pressures and do not always understand either the advantages
or mechanics of collective bargaining nor the advantages that may
flow from increasing productivity and adhering to agreed-upon rules.

Union Strategies

In order to help these unions grow and develop if governmental policy permits this, American and European unions have established training and exchange programs, provided staff and research facilities, offered financial and equipment support, and provided information on comparative wages and fringe benefits of MNE affiliates in advanced countries as well as on the companies' profits, dividends, executive pay, etc.[10]

An interesting example of transnational union cooperation in which the success of a local strike was at stake involved the USWA, a union of bauxite miners in Jamaica, and the Aluminum Company of America. When the bauxite miners, with the advice of USWA officials, went on strike against Alcoa in order to obtain higher wages and other benefits, the first reaction of Alcoa and the Jamaican government was to throw the American union advisers out of the country. However, USWA is an international union representing steelworkers and unions not only in the United States, but also in Canada. Using its office in Toronto, the USWA leadership asked to have three experienced Canadian strike leaders sent to Jamaica. Since they held Commonwealth passports, the Jamaican government could not deny their admission. With their help the strike was settled resulting in substantial benefits to the Jamaican workers.[11]

In some cases the net of union cooperation spreads beyond the two partners in the advanced and the developing country and includes additional union organizations. This happened when the USWA and the IMF attempted to assist in 1970 a union of nickel workers in New Caledonia to face a joint venture of the International Nickel Company of Canada and the Societé Le Nickel of France for the purpose of expanding nickel production on that island. Special seminars were scheduled introducing the Caledonians to modern trade union organization and financing. Other objectives were the training of union officials to negotiate complicated agreements and to counter employer arguments by knowing comparative wages and fringe benefits in affiliates in advanced countries and the economics of the international nickel industry. However, the seminars could not be held because the two Canadian USWA men sent to New Caledonia to conduct the training sessions were denied admittance by French government officials. This action by the French government was taken despite vigorous protests by the IMF affiliates in France, Force Ouvrière de la Metallurgie and CFDT Metallurgie, the socialist and democratic unions respectively.[12]

A second measure of transnational union collaboration consists
of the coordination of objectives, policies, and strategies with respect
to MNEs. The process of coordination takes place mainly among
unions and union federations of specific industries, but at times
exceeds these confines. The major vehicle for the automobile industry has been the IMF whose councils have been expanded to include
union representation of Chrysler, Fiat, Simca, Rootes, Volkswagen,
Mercedes-Benz, and Japanese firms. The United Automobile Workers
(UAW) spearheaded many of the coordinating activities; a high point
was the Declaration of Detroit of June 3, 1966, which was issued at
the end of the First World Automotive Conference in which union
delegates from 14 countries participated.[13] At the Third World
Automotive Conference held in Turin, Italy, in 1968 delegates from
30 countries, representing more than 2 million workers, came together to discuss common problems and to strengthen their working
solidarity in an effort to find answers to these problems, many of
which arose from the multinational operations of their employers.[14]
Similar coordination attempts have also been made in other industries
such as the production of agricultural implements. In addition, smaller
annual meetings between pertinent unions in two countries have also
been initiated to coordinate international bargaining. For example,
in the summer of 1969, two British unions, the Transport and General
Workers Union (membership, 1.5 million) and the Amalgamated Union
of Engineering and Foundry Workers (membership, 1.1 million) met
with a delegation from the UAW led by Leonard Woodcock, then Vice
President and now President of the union. Commenting on the talks,
Woodcock said, "These were but the first of a series. We have much
to learn from each other. And we have much accommodating to do to
each other. But the rise of internationally-flung corporations operating
beyond the reach of any laws dictates that we work out ways to make
binding agreements for the protection of all workers with our brother
and sister unions all over the world."[15]

On a more informal level some unions representing workers of
Philips have also engaged in coordination talks with respect to bargaining with various affiliates of the MNE. For example a meeting
was held between the European Committee of the Christian Metal
Workers Union joined by other national organizations of the same
union, and management staff members of Philips. The topics of the
meeting included a comparative assessment of the labor costs in the
EEC and the effect of automation and production rationalization on
labor. The Socialist Labor Unions also held a meeting with the Philips
management in 1969[16] during which similar topics were discussed.
Another example of transnational union coordination in Europe has

been the attempt to work out common strategies for dealing with the management of Fiat and Citroen after the two firms had concluded their transnational collaboration agreement in 1968. These coordination meetings have been put on a continuing basis and include Italian and French unions representing the workers of both firms, including the Communist-controlled unions, but at least initially, excluding the Force Ouvrière.[17] Finally, the recent rebuilding and expansion of the European labor organization of the Christian and Socialist Unions in the EEC countries have not only activated a more detailed program of coordination among their national and local member unions, but have also attempted to come to some form of organized and structured cooperation among themselves.[18]

Union Objectives

What are the major objectives which the transnational union coalition pursues with respect to MNEs? According to Leonard Woodcock, a long-range goal is to "eliminate labor as a competitive factor in the international sphere, just as we have eliminated labor as a competitive factor in the national sphere."[19] This implies transnational bargaining, perhaps negotiating with an MNE giant such as GM on contracts in world-wide terms. It also implies leveling up wage rates in all countries where MNE affiliates are on the basis of a standard rate for a particular job. The European union federations basically support these goals, but because of the regionally limited nature of their activities demand only that employers be persuaded "to negotiate on the European level."[20]

The near-term specific world-wide objectives leading toward international bargaining include:

1. Full recognition of the right to organize, to bargain collectively on wages, working conditions and social benefits, and to negotiate grievances;

2. Upward harmonization of real wages and social benefits to the maximum extent;

3. Coordinating the terminal dates of collective agreements in the various foreign operations of the corporation;

4. Humanization of the industrial process by providing adequate relief as well as healthy and safe working conditions;

5. Reduction of working time through a shorter work week without loss of pay, more paid holidays, longer vacations, vocational training and early retirement, in the light of technological progress and increased dehumanization of industrial employment;

6. Adherence to the principle of the contractually or legally stipulated work week by a manpower policy which is designed to eliminate overtime;

7. Adequate implementation throughout the world of the vacation bonus principle, already conceded by some companies in certain countries;

8. Pensions sufficient to assure the security and dignity of workers, while keeping up with the rising living standards;

9. Guaranteed annual income for all workers and protection of income of those workers who are victims of production fluctuations and technological change;

10. Organizing consumer boycott of corporation products in cases of employer intransigence.

Some results of the coordinated pursuit of global and regional objectives by unions and union federations have already emerged. Carefully coordinated pressures applied on headquarters and affiliates of MNEs have resulted in wage rises both in advanced countries such as Australia and Japan as well as in many developing countries. Wages in the United States and Canadian automobile factories have been equalized. In one case Venezuelan union organizers fired by a Ford affiliate in that country were reinstated. And the first EEC-wide collective bargaining agreement was signed in June 1968 between agricultural unions affiliated with the ICFTU and the WCL, on the one hand, and Community farmers organizations on the other.[21] In addition, the existence of international labor union coordination in the Community has helped to narrow the gap in living standards between workers in different member countries. Ten years ago the working population of Italy and the Netherlands had the lowest per capita income in the Community. By 1966 these countries had increased their average income per wage or salary earner by 118 percent and 110 percent respectively—while the average Community increase was only 97 percent.

Appeals to Governments

A final set of measures employed by unions to meet the challenge of MNEs consists of appeals to national governments and IGOs. Some union spokesmen also call for economic and political control of MNEs.[22] Such control could be exercised by the national governments which inter alia could insist on the enforcement of anti-trust laws in order to prevent the giants of the industrial world from abusing their economic power. Another solution would be to entrust such regulation to regional institutions or the United Nations, whose powers of enforcement however may well be insufficient.[23]

The exportation of jobs by MNEs is fought in the United States also by union demands to the government to institute a careful control of the flow of American capital to build foreign plants which would compete unfairly against domestic wages. In addition the union leadership advocates a much higher tax on earnings of foreign affiliates of American MNEs. Some unions also propose import quotas on those items whose production has been shifted to low cost labor areas such as the manufacture of TV's to Mexico and Taiwan.[24] Specifically the AFL-CIO has urged the rescission of U.S. Tariff Schedule 807 which confines tariffs to the value added abroad for components shipped from the United States and assembled in foreign plants. Finally, the UAW has urged the government to require U.S. foreign affiliates to increase wage standards in their plants as fast as productivity of individual workers rises.

Some unions in Italy have also appealed to the government to halt or control the outflow of capital because of the detrimental impact on national economic development. The leftist unions opposed the 1968 collaboration agreement between Fiat and Citroen on the specific grounds that the massive outflow of capital resulting from it would harm future Italian employment prospects, especially in the south. Moreover, some of the labor unions in the EEC sought to delay in a subtle way the possibility of creating a unified "European" company law which would facilitate transnational mergers within the Common Market. The tactic of the Italian unions was to oppose suggested provisions for labor participation in the boards of directors of these companies upon which especially the German Federation of Trade Unions insisted. The Italians argued that sitting "on both sides of the fence" would reduce their bargaining power. At the same time, all unions in the Common Market appealed to the national governments and the Community institutions to enforce strongly the national and Community anti-trust provisions to prevent the emerging industrial giants from using their position of power.[25] However, not all unions

in industrially advanced countries oppose the exportation of jobs.
When Swedish textile manufacturers transferred production facilities
to Portugal, a low wage country, Swedish trade unions did not oppose
the move—in fact, this move was seemingly welcomed by the unions
for removing a low wage industry from Sweden and at the same time
benefiting a developing country.[26]

Non-MNE Related Initiatives

Some of the union initiatives with transnational effects that are
not related to the challenges of the MNE are quite similar to the activities which were discussed in the preceding section. For example,
both large national unions and international union federations help
fledgling unions in the developing countries to grow stronger. This
is being done by providing staff assistance, aid in setting up the
proper administrative framework, logistical support in the form of
typewriters and other office equipment, and furnishing comparative
data on wages and other benefits to workers in other countries. These
activities normally center around occasional visits by union officials
from industrially advanced countries or from the headquarters of
union federations often located in Geneva. For example, to help the
agricultural workers in Mauritius, the International Federation of
Plantation, Agricultural and Allied Workers sent a field official to
Mauritius who assisted in setting up a recruitment organization for
expanding the membership of the union among the sugar industry
workers and training recruitment supervisors. At the same time,
the union federation provided $800 to finance the reorganization of
the local union.[27] Another kind of assistance provided to all the
unions in Mauritius was a week-long seminar organized by a German
foundation dealing with labor problems and the organization of unions.[28]
In Guyana, South America, the USW lent a boat and a jeep to a small
union in order to help them to organize workers in their little country.
In India the same union helped democratic unions to organize the steel
workers. In some cases the socialist and democratic unions and union
federations battle the Communist-oriented WFTU in order to bring
the budding labor unions under its own wing rather than see them
fall under the domination of their Communist-oriented competitors.[29]

Of course, the efforts to aid foreign unions is not confined to
the developing countries although there the need is undoubtedly greatest
for establishing viable labor organizations. An example of assistance
to a union in an industrially advanced country is the close friendship
and collaboration which has developed between the Japanese Steel
Workers Union, Tekko Roren, and the USW. The latter has made

available to the Japanese its know-how on strike tactics, collective bargaining, job evaluation, and similar needed information. The USW also has been instrumental in creating in Japan a single metal workers federation representing approximately 600, 000 members in the steel, electrical, machine, automotive and shipbuilding industries. The long-range objective of this federation is to make possible effective collective bargaining on the national scale and substantially raise the living standards of all metal workers of Japan. The organization of a labor federation undertaken by the highly organized national unions in the United States and Western Europe has in some cases been expanded to the creation and enlargement of international federations. For example, German union officials were responsible for organizing the miners in various developed and developing countries and then later banding them together in the International Miners Association which now has affiliates in 33 countries.[30]

While all these activities, especially in the developing world, will assist the individual workers to operate in a more desirable environment in economic, social, and health terms, one must not forget that one long-range objective of these transnational initiatives of unions in the advanced countries is to protect, if not enlarge, their own power and influence. However, if in the long run the world-wide activities of these unions serve to raise the standard of living all over the globe, the end result certainly more than justifies the motivations lying behind many transnational union initiatives.

Beyond organizational and informational assistance given by unions in advanced countries to their counterparts in the Third World, another of their activities deserves to be mentioned. In many cases unions in the advanced countries have engaged in technical assistance in the developing world. For example, the UAW has shipped needed medicine, medical supplies, and reconditioned surgical and hospital equipment to hospitals in Brazil, India, and Viet Nam. The union also has transformed busses into mobile medical clinics for use in the Philippines. It has repaired and refurbished office equipment for institutions in the Dominican Republic and Indonesia. It has provided tools and equipment for vocational skills in many developing nations. Finally, it has provided vocational training programs for young people in developing countries by making available retired union members and has helped recruit and train mechanics for the American Peace Corps. While these examples highlight activities of the UAW, many other unions in the United States and Europe have provided similar services and equipment to the developing world.[31]

Finally, a few words need to be said about the efforts of national and international labor organizations to ensure the enactment of labor laws favorable to union organization. This is a particularly important activity in the developing world, because most of the unions in the industrially advanced countries have been in existence for a long time and have gained a high degree of skill and experience in lobbying for their particular interests and goals. On the other hand, unions in many developing countries are often beholden to the government and are used by them as instruments of control or as a protective device. One of the main political objectives of the unions therefore is to ensure that national legislation does not restrict legitimate union objectives and that a body of law be produced which provides for proper health standards and working conditions to upgrade the fate of indigenous workers.

Unions and union federations may also have objectives that might bear directly on the international system. For example, during the recent monetary crisis the ICFTU asked for the immediate convening of a world conference to seek out the cause of the present economic and monetary difficulties and to find remedies for them. It rejected solving the problems on a purely national basis as the United States was accused of doing. The ICFTU also attempted to solidify sentiments among its members to oppose the 10 percent American surcharge.[32]

Relationships Between Free World and
Communist Labor Organizations

During the last decade we have witnessed increased relations and interactions between Communist labor organizations and Free World unions and union federations. An interesting example relates to the efforts of the Communist unions in Italy (CGIL) and France (CGT) to be represented on the Common Market institutions. Although the WFTU at first opposed this project because it contravened Soviet policy toward the Common Market and although it succeeded at first in persuading the CGT not to become involved, both the French and Italian Communist unions eventually launched a strong offensive in 1966 to be recognized on the Community level as participants in the EEC decision-making process. The European organizations of the Free and Christian labor unions strongly opposed the initiatives of their Communist counterparts, but eventually softened their stand when the European Communities resolved to take up contacts with the liaison committee established by the two Communist union federations. The Christian union federation more than the Free unions declared themselves to be prepared to work with the Communist unions but made this cooperation contingent on the concrete behavior of the latter regarding the specific subjects under consideration.[33]

The WFTU has persistently pursued the policy of asking for international trade union unity. However, the ICFTU and WCL have usually rejected the overtures of the WFTU everywhere in the world; in fact, they frequently compete for the organization of workers in developing countries.

Recently there have been exchanges of visits between Communist unions belonging to the WFTU and American unions. For example, a three-man delegation from the Metal and Engineering Workers' Union of the Romanian General Trade Union Federation was received as guests of the UAW in October 1969. During the ten-day visit the delegation inspected production lines of automobile, tractor, and agricultural implement plants and were introduced to the way the American worker lives, plays, and learns.[34]

The German Federation of Trade Unions (DGB) has also established contacts with workers' organizations in East Europe including those of the Soviet Union. In most of the East European Communist countries these organizations do not behave as trade unions in the Western sense as far as collective bargaining is concerned. Exceptions are Hungary and Yugoslavia where the unions make specific demands on the state officials in charge of various plants and industries for the improvements of wages and working conditions. Moreover, in Yugoslavia, workers' committees play an important role in the management of industrial and commercial enterprises. The DGB seeks to instill in the workers' organizations of the other East European countries the spirit of true trade unionism in their relations to the plant managers. However, only in Czechoslovakia does there seem to be signs of a timid response to these efforts, a surprising development considering the pervasive control exercised by the post-Dubceck government. The DGB has gained special influence with the Yugoslav Trade Union Federation by requesting equal treatment of the 500,000 Yugoslav workers employed in West Germany with their German colleagues.[35] In view of the declining job market from which Germany suffered at the time of the request, the position taken by the DGB reflected considerable courage in domestic political terms.

THE EFFECTS OF UNION ACTIVITIES ON
NATIONAL GOVERNMENTS

While the fight of American unions to narrow the wage differential between workers in the United States and those of the other countries of the world may indeed produce benefits in terms of raising the standard of living, governmental decision-makers of the developing nations in particular may perceive the effects of these initiatives more as drawbacks. The reason is that one of the major problems of developing countries is large-scale unemployment which may not be remedied by higher wages. The International Labor Organization (ILO) estimates that perhaps 75 million people in the Third World are unemployed and many millions more underemployed. This problem has been accentuated by the growing urbanization in many of these countries. But even this is only the tip of an iceberg. Under the pressure of the population explosion, at least 170 million additional workers will require jobs in the non-Communist developing countries in the 1970s. These figures constitute the equivalent of providing jobs for the entire U.S. labor force twice over in the course of ten years.[36] Obviously the high estimate of present and potential unemployment has important political implications inasmuch as it seriously effects the stability of many governments in the Third World. The results have been extreme swings in governments such as Uganda, Chile, and Peru. In many of these countries the reduction of unemployment constitutes the core of planning for the next decade. For example, in the Four-Year and Ten-Year Plans for Mauritius every aspect is considered in terms of bringing about a higher level of employment.[37]

As wage rates rise in some of the developing countries the incentives for MNEs and other foreign firms to establish production facilities in the developing countries are lowered. Up to now, the ratios of U.S. hourly earnings including fringe benefits to those in foreign affiliates in 1969, for example for the assembly of office machines, were as follows:

Mexico	6.2:1
Taiwan	9.8:1
Korea	10.1:1
U.K.	2.3:1

Of course the productivity differentials are also significant but nevertheless not as great as the differences in wage costs. This has been the reason that such countries as Korea, Taiwan, and Mexico which have relatively well-educated and adaptable labor forces have attracted large numbers of American plants and are increasingly attracting investments from European companies as well. Wage rates in these plants range from 15 cents to 35 cents an hour. They are matched by the general wage rates in that part of the world ranging from 10 cents an hour in Hong Kong to $1 an hour in Japan. Obviously, the American worker, with an average hourly rate in the electrical industry of $3.75 an hour, cannot compete against these wage scales.[38]

An example of the importance of the foreign firms for developing countries occurred in Mauritius. This small island has no domestic market and therefore must attract firms which already have established export markets in different parts of the world. The wage rates in Mauritius run from 36 cents a day for trainees to 50 cents a day minimum wage for experienced workers. When in early 1971 a foreign company working jointly with a local entrepreneur opened up an assembly plant for precision parts and the management advertised openings for 50 women trainees, over 1,000 women descended on the offices of the new company, breaking windows and damaging furniture, to get a job for 36 cents a day. This highlights the precarious situation in these countries.

On the other hand, as wage rates go up, foreign companies are likely to close their plants and move away. For example, a few years ago an electronics company opened a TV manufacturing plant in South Korea. After a couple of years the workers organized and went on strike for higher wages. They could not live on the 15 cents an hour they were being paid. The American corporation closed the plant down and moved it to Taiwan. Despite the fact that the poor countries are anxious to attract foreign firms to establish production facilities, the spread effect may be limited and may not reach the population at large. Thus even increased wages may have limited benefits. For example, in Colombia real wages for workers in modern industry doubled between 1955 and 1965. However, the poorest half of the rural population has seen virtually no improvement in their position over the last 40 years. Another example is found in Zambia where a semi-skilled worker on the copper belt averages about $60 a week in pay. This amount is earned by much of the population in a year. Since, however, a major part of the income of these highly paid workers is either spent on imported goods or semi-luxury merchandise the increased earning power of the copper workers does not create much employment elsewhere in the economy.[39]

As a result of the exodus of plants caused by drives for increased wages, some of the governmental decision-makers in the developing world have passed legislation either forbidding strikes in general or prohibiting strikes against American corporations as was done in Korea. In Singapore labor legislation has also been enacted recently which is designed to keep union activity and wages down. It is not inconceivable that other developing countries which have begun to benefit from the influx of industry into their territories may follow the example of Singapore in order to protect the benefits they are now receiving in terms of higher employment. Since on the other hand some of the union activities aim at influencing the legislative

process in the developing countries to obtain favorable laws for organizing workers and protecting their rights, tension arises in these
countries. In some cases labor laws have been enacted which give
lip service to the freedom of action by trade unions and are vague
with respect to collective bargaining. At the same time, government
control remains pervasive and unions are used for the mobilization
of support for the government. The governmental elites are often
fearful that unions, if successful in their aims, will create new positions of power competing with those which the new leadership in the
developing countries has established only fairly recently.[40] This is
likely to induce the governmental elites to fall back on rekindling the
fires of nationalism and branding the activities of international labor
as a disturbing foreign element for the development of the newly independent countries. In many cases, the governmental elites in these
countries want to avoid the projection of a favorable image created by
the activities of the foreign unions. For this reason some of the clearly
beneficial technical assistance furnished by some of these unions may
be downgraded by the national governments in order to prevent the
local population from looking upon foreign unions as their savior.[41]

The governmental leaders in developing countries may also
seek alliances with national businessmen who are concerned that the
higher wages paid by foreign employers will disrupt their traditional
mode of doing business. National employers may give aid to the
interests of the political leadership by stimulating frictions between
the labor employed by themselves and the workers of foreign companies. Thus national employers together with their workers (and
workers trade unions where they exist) could become allies of the
indigenous political leadership in a nationalist opposition to foreign
or multinational business and foreign trade union penetration.[42]
However, national businessmen may also see advantages in foreign
investment if the new plants stimulate the growth of locally owned
industries without competing with them. The assembly of automobiles
is a case in point. Under such circumstances they will welcome the
newly established business and even tolerate the unions provided they
do not drive up too much the wages of indigenous labor.

In the developed countries the drive of American unions to raise
the wage levels of workers has not always been received favorably by
governmental leaders either. In such countries as Italy and Japan
the governments are apprehensive that rises in wages would eventually
undermine the competitive position of their exports and would unfavorably affect their trade balance and balance of payments. Of course,
in the industrially advanced countries the unions are much more
powerful than in the developing countries and consequently governmental

elites have to be much more circumspect in expressing their views or taking actions which would hold wages down. Italy, beset by a continuing series of strikes in practically all industries, is the obvious example.

There is no question that Japan already has suffered from increases in wages. Some foreign companies in the electronics industry which initiated overseas assembly in Japan earlier now have transferred this work to Taiwan in search of lower and more stable wages. There is some fear about a "reverse multiplier effect" by which a reduction in manufacturing jobs would ricochet through the rest of the economy destroying more jobs in other industries. The implications of increasing wage levels and exportation of jobs for the developed countries cannot be predicted at present with any kind of accuracy. Robert d'A. Shaw quotes Herman Kahn who predicts that neither the United States nor Japan will be producing automobiles by 1985 because production facilities will have moved to cheaper wage areas such as Southeast Asia.[43] This may be an exaggerated prediction, but it highlights the employment problems from which the developed countries may suffer in the future. Full employment in all advanced countries will require the creation of additional jobs every year. In fact, in the United States it is estimated that on the basis of 4 percent unemployment, 12 million additional jobs will be needed by 1976.

Even more difficult is it to make a judgment regarding the effects of transnational union activities on Communist countries. Clearly, meetings between Communist and Free World unions and collaboration between them as might occur within the European context, may suggest some transideological effects. However, one must keep in mind that Communist unions have primarily the purpose to mobilize the active population in the service of revolutionary national goals defined by the political leadership.[44] Thus they may be poor vehicles to produce ideological modifications in their governments although this situation may slowly change. But, as R. W. Cox points out, it is more likely that such unions adopt nationalist attitudes hostile to foreign economic penetration and that they may perceive meetings with Free World unions to be a tool for such penetration.[45]

In summary, one may say that while from a purely rational point of view many governments have benefited from transnational union initiatives in terms of higher incomes and better working and social conditions for their citizens, increased union strength has been frequently perceived as a drawback. In some cases the effects of the union initiatives cannot be determined as yet inasmuch as it is impossible to appraise at this time the long-term attitude changes among people and governmental elites produced by the various activities not directly related to increases of wages.

CONSEQUENCES FOR THE INTERNATIONAL SYSTEM

From the foregoing analysis it is evident that the net of transnational union activities has been spreading over the globe. In terms of collaboration and conflict affecting the global pattern of interaction in the international system, it seems that transnational union activities produce considerably more tension than collaboration. The protectionist tendencies manifested by some of the American labor unions are likely to be disruptive to the trend of expanding international trade manifested during the last decades. They are bound to arouse reactions in developed as well as developing countries to move toward protectionism in order to protect what is perceived to be the national interests of those countries. In fact, it may well stimulate unions to propose foreign economic policies in other countries similar to those which the USW and AFL-CIO espouse in the United States.

While many unions in the developed countries and the global union federations attempt to help the fledgling unions in the Third World to become stronger and more effective in the performance of their functions, the peculiar relationships which the latter have with many of their governments may create long-range internal conflicts which could have deleterious consequences for the international system. The unemployment problems in many of the developing countries and the rising power of local unions may produce domestic political upheavals which cannot but reverberate into the international arena. Such upheavals may affect the prospects for trade, for investment, and most important, for political alliances. At the same time, the solution to the unemployment problem in the developing countries will depend in part on increased levels of exports and greater private investment from the advanced nations of the world.

Of course one must not overlook the favorable consequences for the international system that could flow from the rising level of wages in the Third World. However, unless the rise in living standards can be spread among the population as a whole thereby strengthening the policies of the governmental leadership toward achieving greater political stability, uneven and explosive wage rises are negative rather than positive factors.

Another element exacerbating the propensity for conflict among

nation-states stems from the continuous efforts of the WFTU to per-
suade other unions, especially the ICFTU, to join in "united action"
on a world-wide basis. Tensions are created by the inability of the
other unions to respond positively to these seemingly reasonable
requests which as the leadership of the non-Communist unions realize,
are primarily politically motivated efforts to promote WFTU political
goals.[46]

    In what respect do the attempts of unions to challenge the world-
wide operations of multinational enterprises influence the processes
of regional and world-wide integration? It has been argued that the
implications of the development of international cooperation among
labor organizations to meet this challenge furthers the processes of
integration.[47] It has been asserted that as specific multinational
corporations become more geocentric and as business in general
becomes more international, the increasing international character
of union activities will help to provide a positive environment to
further spill-over of integration efforts on the part of other units of
a social, cultural, economic, and political character.

    The validity of these arguments is highly questionable. While
in a regional context, such as Western Europe, an appropriate climate may exist for the unions to regard transnational bargaining as
a benefit for themselves and the workers they represent, the effects
upon the process of political integration may only be minor. Even
within the European Community salaries cannot be equated without
taking into consideration the different benefits available in each
country through social legislation. This in itself impairs the thrust
of transnational bargaining as a prop for political integration. In
addition, unions have traditionally confined operations to particular
EEC Member States and remain basically oriented toward the national
governmental process with which they have long-standing and well-
operating contacts. The tendency, therefore, persists to use national
governments rather than regional institutions for improving the lot
of workers. Although the European Federation of Free Trade Unions
(a regional unit of the ICFTU) and the European Secretariat of the
WCL have expressed their support for European integration many times
and although transnational coordination among national unions has increased as was indicated earlier,[48] the impact on the process of integration remains weak for the time being. Only when cross-national
collective bargaining will produce tangible benefits for organized
labor in Western Europe and when the central institutions of the
European Community are in a position to make a substantial contribution to this result, is it likely that the labor unions will use their
full resources unreservedly to back the program of political integration
and the integration process may then receive a significant impetus.

On a world-wide basis, such an effect may be practically non-existent. While for example the automotive councils of the IMF do indeed focus on a particular corporation on an international basis, and while they have been successful in leveling up the wages of a particular corporation, the unions fully recognize that they do not want to lose the countervailing power of nation-states as a necessary aid to eventually controlling the growing power of MNEs. Although one could argue that in the long run the interests of MNEs, international unions, and nation-states are converging inasmuch as all of them would like to see the economic levels of the world rise, the vested positions of power within the nation-states of elites other than business and labor and the reliance of unions on the national decision-making process make it doubtful for the foreseeable future at least that multinational labor activities can be regarded as an effective instrument for promoting global integration.[49] Moreover, many unions have interests beyond expanding wages such as social goals of improved housing, educational benefits for children, and a higher level of medical services from cradle to grave. For the time being, only governments can allocate values to enhance these goals, again strengthening the national orientation of unions. The ability of unions to influence domestic and foreign policies of states and the difficulty of imposing their concepts on MNEs also casts doubt on the effective forces of union activities to enhance global integration. These prospects are darkened further because the MNE has numerous choices at its disposal to obtain its objectives, whereas the options for the unions are considerably more limited. This creates a sense of inferiority and dependence on the part of the unions which is an aggravating element of the relationship[50] and does not bode well for a partnership to enhance global integration.

NOTES

1. Elizabeth R. Jager, "The Conglomerate Goes Global," AFL-CIO American Federationist, January 1970.

2. Heinz O. Vetter, "The Lessons of the ICFTU Congress," DGB Report, III, 4 (1969), 38.

3. George C. Lodge, Spearheads of Democracy (New York: Harper & Row Publishers, 1962), p. 55.

4. For an excellent history of the international labor movement see Hans Gottfurcht, Die Internationale Gewerkschaftsbewegung im Weltgeschehen (Cologne: Bund-Verlag, 1962).

5. Rudolf Maerker and Christian Uhlig, Tasks, Organizations, and Aims of Trade Unions (Stuttgart: BZ-Druck, 1967), p. 45.

6. Cf. David H. Blake, "Multinational Corporations, International Unionism, and Global Integration," Paper presented at the Research Conference on the Multinational Corporation in the Global Political System at the University of Pennsylvania, April 22-23, 1971 (mimeo., 1971).

7. Paul Jennings, July 27-20, 1970, p. 815.

8. Blake, "Multinational Corporations, International Unionism, and Integration," p. 16.

9. R. W. Cox, "Labor and Transnational Relations," International Organization, XXV, 3 (Summer 1971), 573. Cox contrasts this type of union to social reform labor movements and interest group unions in the advanced countries of the Free World. The former are found for example in Britain and Scandinavia and can, because of their historical background, subordinate the interests of workers to general objectives of social reform for the benefit of the working class and other low status social groups. The latter are not likely to recognize any conflict between the interests of the workers they represent and broader social objectives and will act without inhibition in their members' particular interests. American unions fall into this category. A final category consists of mobilization unions which, following the Soviet pattern, serve to mobilize, in concert with other groups, the active population in support of revolutionary national goals defined by the political leadership. Each of these types of unions may be found occasionally outside their customary habitat. (See pp. 573-74).

10. James P. Gannon, "More U.S. Mining Help Foreign Workers to Pressure American Company Overseas," The Wall Street Journal, December 7, 1970, p. 30.

11. USW, Report of Officers, 15th Constitutional Convention (September 28-October 2), pp. 109-110.

12. USWA News Release March 29, 1971. For other examples involving different unions see Gannon, "More U.S. Mining Help Foreign Workers."

13. Belgium, France, Germany, Britain, Italy, Turkey, United States, Canada, Argentina, Brazil, Mexico, Venezuela, Japan, Australia. For a detailed account see Labor Free World, July-August 1966.

14. For details see UAW-Solidarity Report, July 1968.

15. UAW-Solidarity Report, October, 1969.

16. Agence Europe Bulletin, July 4, 1969.

17. Agence Europe Document, No. 528, May 30, 1969.

18. For additional examples see Cox, "Labor and Transnational Relations," p. 556.

19. Journal of Commerce, May 12, 1971.

20. Agence Europe Document, No. 528, May 30, 1969, p. 4.

21. European Community, June 1969, p. 18.

22. Elizabeth R. Jager, "The Conglomerate Goes Global," AFL-CIO American Federationist, January 1970; and Agence Europe Bulletin, July 9 and 25, 1969.

23. William Bywater, "Why Free Trade is Unfair to U.S. Workers," New York Times, January 3, 1971, p. 12F. Bywater is an official of The International Union of Electrical, Radio, and Machine Workers.

24. Cf. the statement by Heribert Maier, ICFTU, in U.S. Congress, Joint Economic Committee, Subcommittee on Foreign Economic Policy, "Foreign Economic Policy for the 1970's." 91st Cong., 2nd Sess., July 27-30, 1970, Part IV, pp. 821-33.

25. Cf. Werner J. Feld, Transnational Business Collaboration Among Common Market Countries (New York: Praeger Publishers, 1970), pp. 80, 81, 93-95.

26. Cox, "Labor and Transnational Relations," p. 567.

27. L'Express (Mauritius), August 6, 1971.

28. Le Mauriciène, August 12, 1971.

29. See for example John Norman, Labor and Politics in Libya and Arab Africa (New York: Bookman Associates, 1965). See also Heinz O. Vetter, "The Trade Unions as a Link Between the Nations," DGB Report IV, 7/8, (1970), p. 65.

30. DGB Report, March 1971, p. 16.

31. Cf. UAW, Solidarity Social, Technical Educational Programs (STEP) regarding social, technical, educational programs and Rudolf Maerker and Christian Uhlig, Tasks, Organization, and Aims of Trade Unions (Bonn: Friedrich-Ebert-Stiftung, 1967), pp. 44-51.

32. Agence Europe Bulletin, August 27, 1971.

33. Werner Feld, "The French and Italian Communists and the Common Market: The Request for Representation in the Community Institutions," Journal of Common Market Studies, VI, 3 (March 1968) 250-266, see especially pp. 255-258. Also see Agence Europe Documents, April 29 and May 30, 1969.

34. UAW-Solidarity Report, October, 1969.

35. Cf. Die Welt, November 1, 1971. See also DGB Report, No. 9/10, October 1971.

36. Robert d'A. Shaw, "Foreign Investment and Global Labor," Columbia Journal of World Business, VI, 4 (July-August 1971), 52-62.

37. Mauritius, 4-Year Plan for Social & Economic Development.

38. See Bywater, "Why Free Trade Is Unfair to U.S. Workers."

39. Cf. Shaw, "Foreign Investment and Global Labor."

40. Cox, "Labor and Transnational Relations," p. 572, suggests that under certain circumstances local unions when screening job applications for political orthodoxy can make political pay-offs to local authorities by providing jobs for the latter's supporters.

41. For details see Lodge, Spearheads of Democracy, pp. 37-38.

42. Cox, "Labor and Transnational Relations," pp. 573-74.

43. Shaw, "Foreign Investment and Global Labor," p. 54.

44. See note 4 supra.

45. Cox, "Labor and Transnational Relations," p. 574.

46. Lodge, Spearheads of Democracy, pp. 52-87.

47. Blake, "Multinational Corporations, International Unionism, and Integration."

48. See also the editorial in Agence Europe Bulletin, November 22, 1971, regarding the strikes in the metal manufacturing industry in Germany and those of other EEC countries.

49. It has been suggested that an international organization such as the General Agreement on Tariffs and Trade (GATT) be formed in which MNEs, labor, and governments would be represented in tripartite fashion and which somehow would control MNEs and reconcile conflicting interests. See Hearings cited on p. 5-8, fn. 7, pp. 844 and 927. While such an arrangement may benefit organized labor in terms of higher wages and the MNEs in terms of higher administered prices, consumers all over the world and unorganized labor are likely to suffer. Governments as representatives of the interests of the latter groups would be outvoted and the bulk of the 4 billion people would be governed by the MNEs and a few large trade union federations, obviously an unacceptable proposition for the majority of the people.

50. Raymond Vernon, Sovereignty at Bay: The Multinational Spread of U.S. Enterprises, Harvard Multinational Enterprise Series (New York: Basic Books Publishers, 1971), p. 191.

6

Pursuing interests in almost every segment of human life, the traditional NGOs have become ever more numerous. Included in this category of nongovernmental entities are the international labor federations discussed in Chapter 5. The Union of International Associations has set up a number of criteria for international NGOs covering aims, membership, governance, and financing of these organizations. The aims of these organizations must be genuinely international in character and manifest the intention to engage in activities in at least three countries. The membership must be drawn from individuals or collective entities of at least three countries and must be open to any appropriately qualified individual or entity in the organization's area of operations. The constitution must provide for a permanent headquarters and make provisions for the members to periodically elect the governing body and officers. The headquarters and the officers should be rotated among the various member countries at designated intervals. The voting procedure must be structured in such a way as to prevent control of the organization by one national group. Substantial financial contributions to the budget must come from at least three countries. As a consequence many "international" societies and unions in North America are excluded since their funds are usually derived wholly from U.S. members. No attempt must be made to make profits for direct distribution to the members of the NGOs, but this does not mean that members may not be helped to

---

This chapter has been prepared with the cooperation of John K. Wildgen, Department of Political Science, Louisiana State University in New Orleans.

increase their profits or better their economic organization through
the activities of the NGOs.1

NGO INITIATIVES

The objectives of transnational NGO initiatives can be broken
down into three groups:

1. To promote their own interests in the international and
national arenas;

2. To promote, modify, or oppose the goals of the U.N., its
specialized agencies and bodies, and regional IGOs, and;

3. To support, modify, or oppose the goals of national governments.

The objectives under groups 2 and 3 are likely to be functions
of the specific objectives in the first category, but this is not necessarily the case when it comes to general, often ideological goals. It is
also quite conceivable that a particular NGO will support specific
IGO goals, but oppose national goals of a particular government.
Therefore, IGOs and national governments may perceive an individual
NGO as either friendly or hostile and these perceptions may differ
from case to case.

The capability of NGOs to mount transnational initiatives depends
on the strength and distribution of their membership, their organizational effectiveness and financial resources, and their institutionalized
and informal contacts with governmental and IGO agencies. The
growing strength and geographic distribution of NGOs will be examined
first.

The Growth of NGOs

International NGOs as delineated above are generally assumed
to date back to 1846 when the World's Evangelical Alliance was founded.[2]
The dramatic growth of international NGOs from 1860 to 1970 is
illustrated in Figure 6.1. The increases in the number of NGOs
founded are especially pronounced in the time period during which
major wars (for example the Russo-Japanese War and World Wars

FIGURE 6.1

Growth Pattern of International NGOs
Compared with IGOs, 1860-1968

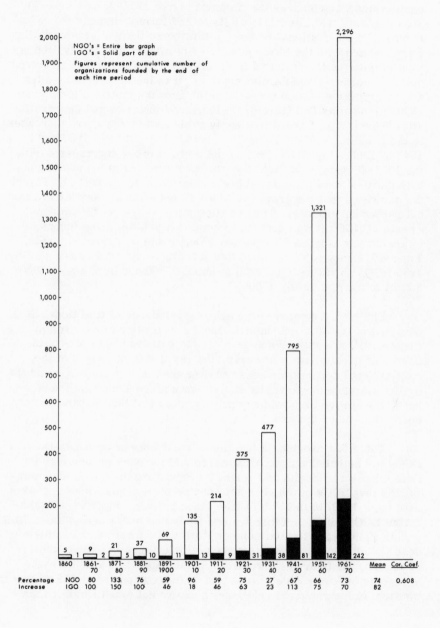

NGO's = Entire bar graph
IGO 's = Solid part of bar

Figures represent cumulative number of organizations founded by the end of each time period

		1860	1861-70	1871-80	1881-90	1891-1900	1901-10	1911-20	1921-30	1931-40	1941-50	1951-60	1961-70	Mean	Cor. Coef.
Percentage	NGO	80	133	76	59	96	59	75	27	67	66	73	74	0.608
Increase	IGO	100	150	100	46	18	46	63	23	113	75	70	82	

177

I and II) were ended or which immediately followed the end of hostilities, and they showed decided dips during periods of rising international conflict and wars such as the time span from 1911-20 and 1931-40. This suggests that international strife and turmoil impede the establishment of international NGOs, [3] while the settlement of devastating wars coupled with the bitter memories of misery and deprivation seem to stimulate the formation of international NGOs reflecting a revived spirit of border-crossing cooperation. It is interesting to note that a very similar situation prevails in the growth pattern of IGOs since 1860, also shown in Figure 6.1. Expanded international cooperation after World Wars I and II is clearly evidenced by the sharp increases in the founding of IGOs during the periods from 1921 to 1930 and from 1941 to 1960. Equally visible is the distinct dip in increases during the 1931-40 span. [4] In fact, the overall increases in the number of both entities show a respectable correlation with r being .61. Figure 6.1 indicates that the growth of NGOs is not a linear function of time but rather curvilinear. Thus in attempting to project the future growth of NGOs it was decided to employ a least squares technique to arrive at a polynomial equation which would fit the data closely. Figure 6.2 shows the result of this investigation and suggests that by 1980 NGOs should reach a total of about 2,600 and by the year 2000 a total of approximately 4,000. [5]

Figure 6.3 compares the growing incidence of traditional NGOs with that of the 187 U.S. multinational corporations discussed in Chapter 2. [6] Clearly, the growth of both entities shows a certain degree of parallelism. However, the rapid rate of growth of the multinational corporation began earlier than that of the NGOs and the parent system expansion has slowed down since 1955. On the other hand, the curves of subsidiary proliferation and NGO expansion continue to move upward.

Table 6.1 provides a functional breakdown of international NGOs for selected years. Commerce and industry groups lead the field followed by health and scientific organizations. It is also noteworthy that NGOs in the economic sector show a much higher growth rate from 1909/10 to 1970/71 than other groups. In addition to the active NGOs listed in Table 6.1 one finds that according to the 1970/71 compilations a substantial number (676) were inactive or completely dead. While not all disappearances of NGOs may become a matter of record, the figures shown are at least suggestive and it may be a syndrome of our troubled times that in this category fall 102 groups in the field of international relations, a figure not much smaller than

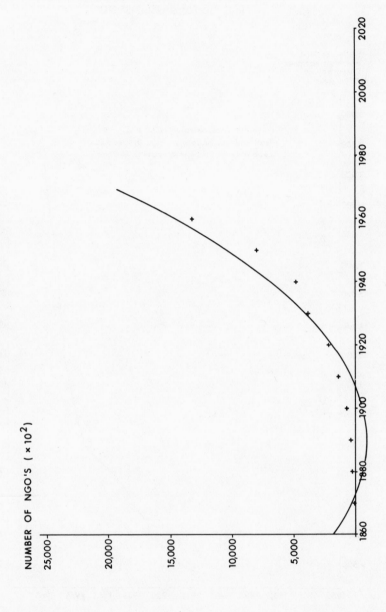

FIGURE 6.2

The Growth of NGOs, 1860–1970

FIGURE 6.3

Comparison Between the Growth
of Selected U. S. Multinational Corporations
and the Expansion of NGOs

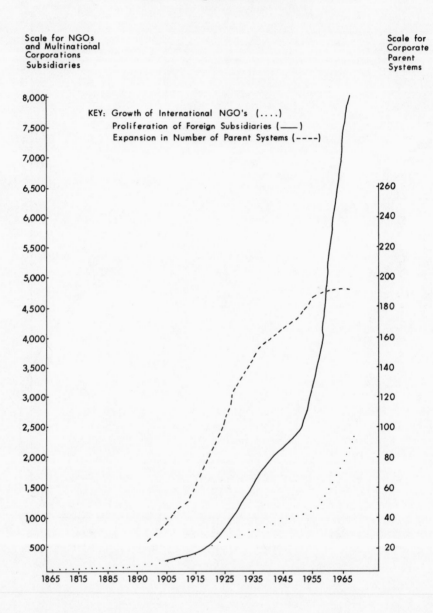

Scale for NGOs
and Multinational
Corporations
Subsidiaries

Scale for
Corporate
Parent
Systems

KEY: Growth of International NGO's (....)
Proliferation of Foreign Subsidiaries (——)
Expansion in Number of Parent Systems (————)

TABLE 6.1

Functional Breakdown of International NGOs

Category	1909/10	1956/57	1966/67	1970/71	Dead or Inactive 1966/67	1970/71
Bibliography, press	19	26	58	63	28	31
Religion, ethics	21	70	93	109	60	62
Social sciences	10	57	80	95	34	35
International relations	12	61	111	127	101	102
Politics	3	13	15	22	21	30
Law, administration	13	28	48	54	31	29
Social welfare	10	52	76	95	50	51
Professions, employers	2	67	93	112	34	34
Trade unions	1	48	63	70	21	22
Economics, finance	3	15	35	45	15	15
Commerce, industry	5	123	211	239	31	34
Agriculture	5	27	76	83	24	26
Transport, travel	5	40	72	82	15	15
Technology	8	36	83	113	26	28
Science	21	69	137	174	49	53
Health, medicine	16	100	173	225	35	37
Education, youth	10	56	91	106	31	35
Arts, literature, radio	6	34	70	80	28	27
Sport, recreation	6	51	90	99	16	18
European Common Market and EFTA business and professional groups	—	—	245	286	—	2
National organizations in consultative status with U.N.	—	12	15	15	—	—
TOTAL NGO	176	985	1,935	2,296	650	676

Note: The compilers of the 1909-10 edition defined "international" in a more restricted sense than is customary today. After discussions with ECOSOC officials in 1950 the UIA adopted criteria allowing the inclusion of regional bodies (involving three countries or more) which had been excluded in 1909-10.

Source: Yearbook of International Organizations (1st, 6th, 11th, and 13th editions).

181

those which are active (127). Even worse is the situation with organizations concerned with politics where inactive organizations outnumber
the active ones. The high percentage of inactive NGOs in these two
fields and the much smaller percentage of inactive NGOs in all other
fields may offer some indirect evidence for the argument that the
dynamics of functionalism are more effective when pragmatic, "low
politics," interests, and objectives are pursued and less effective
when the pursuit is concerned with "high politics" and strongly opposed
ideological commitments.[7]

Table 6.2 furnishes data regarding the number of states from
which members are drawn and the geographical distribution of NGOs
by continents and international regions. A substantial majority
(1,123) of NGOs draw their members from 25 or fewer states while
only a small number (70) have members from 76 or more states in
the world.[8] As to distribution by continent, 1,604 NGOs draw members
from Europe while only 722 have memberships in Australia. Of
course, many NGOs have members on more than one continent and
this distribution is found in the second section of Table 6.2. Roughly
one-quarter of the NGOs (550) cover all five continents, and may
therefore be considered as truly universal. At the other end of the
scale are NGOs limiting themselves to only one continent and in view
of the large number of European IGOs it is not astonishing that 454 of
this category of NGOs are operating exclusively in Europe. On the
other hand, only very few NGOs have confined their activities to
Australia, Asia, and Africa. Most of the organizations operating
there have links with other continents; in fact, a large majority of
them are in the four- or five-continent category, attesting perhaps
to the need for international linkages which the economic and other
sectors of the society on these continents have for the pursuit of their
overall goals.

Instead of using continents as units of geographic distribution
of NGOs, Kjell Skjelsbaek has focused on international regions whose
boundaries are determined on the basis of economic and political
similarity rather than territorial contiguity or geographic proximity.
He distinguishes eight distinctive regions: North West (North America,
Western Europe, Israel, Cyprus, Australia, New Zealand, Japan, and
South Africa), Latin America, the Arab World, Western (non-Communist) Asia, Communist Asia, Eastern Europe, Black Africa, plus
assorted remaining countries. The fourth Section of Table 6.2 shows
the number of countries with representation in international NGOs in
percentages per region from 1951 to 1966. The most striking features
of the data are the marked percentage decreases of the advanced

industrialized countries of the West and a slow ascendancy of the
Third World regions, with the exception of Black Africa which takes
a dramatic jump forward. Communist Eastern Europe, on the other
hand, exhibits remarkable stability.[9] It should be pointed out that
continental or regional distribution of representation in NGOs by
citizens of various countries says nothing about the strength of this
representation which may be very small or very large in individual
countries. The fifth section of Table 6.2 provides some insights into
membership strengths of international NGOs by region. From the
figures presented one can observe that most NGOs have a very small
membership roll and that only in the North West region and among the
Communist and neutral[10] countries are there a significant number of
NGOs with large membership (10,000+).

Table 6.3 shows the location of headquarters of international
NGOs. In keeping with the distribution of NGOs by continent, Europe
is the undisputed leader in the number of headquarters locations.
France heads the list followed by Belgium and the United Kingdom.
The Soviet Union is the headquarters for only four nongovernmental
organizations, but its citizens are members in about 200 NGOs.
The second section of the table shows that since 1954 a number of
countries in Black Africa have become hosts of NGO headquarters
which is not surprising in view of the sharply rising African representation in NGOs. Also, there are small increases in headquarters
in Latin America, the Arab countries, Western Asia, and East Europe,
with a corresponding percentage decline in Western Europe and North
America.

In view of the important roles that the European Common
Market business, agricultural, and professional groups play in the
decision-making process of the EEC, the pattern of their growth over
the last ten years and a breakdown of the interests represented by
these groups are given in Figure 6.4 and Table 6.4. Following
generally the correlation between the establishment of IGOs and NGOs
observed in Figure 6.1, one finds that the creation of European Community NGOs clusters around the establishment of the Common
Market. It is interesting to note that during the period from 1966 to
1968 the establishment of NGOs has again increased. The reason
may well be that business and agricultural interests in the Common
Market recognized that the EEC had passed the point of no return and
that more intensive representation of interests on the European level
would be beneficial. With respect to the distribution of interests
represented by those NGOs it must be pointed out that some groups
represent more than one of the interests listed and therefore the

TABLE 6.2

NGO Membership Distribution by Number of States, Continents, and Regions

Number of States From Which NGO Members are Drawn (1968)*

	0-25	26-50	51-75	76 and more
Number of NGOs	1,123	394	137	70

Distribution of NGO Membership by Individual Continents (1968)*

	Europe	America	Asia	Africa	Australia
Number of NGO's	1,604	1,160	1,021	830	722

Distribution of NGO's by Membership Coverage of One or Several Continents*

Africa-America-Asia-Australia-Europe	550
Africa-America-Asia-Europe	167
America-Asia-Australia-Europe	103
Africa-America-Australia-Europe	23
Africa-America-Asia-Australia	7
Africa-Asia-Australia-Europe	4
America-Asia-Europe	105
Africa-America-Europe	29
America-Australia-Europe	16
Africa-Asia-Europe	14
America-Asia-Australia	4
Africa-America-Asia	4
Africa-Australia-Europe	2
Asia-Australia-Europe	1
America-Europe	80
Asia-Europe	39
Africa-Europe	15
Asia-Australia	9
Africa-Asia	5
Australia-Europe	2
America-Asia	1
Europe	454
America	71
Africa	10
Asia	8
Australia	1

*Note that the data in the Yearbook for individual NGOs are not always complete and therefore the figures given in the first and last sections of the Table do not add up to the total in Table 6.1. Of course, the figures in the middle section cannot be added since individual NGOs may have members on several continents.

Source: Yearbook of International Organizations (12th edition 1968-69) pp. 52-240.

Table 6.2 (Continued)

Number of National Representations in International NGOs in Percentages
per Region, 1951-66

Region	1951	1956	1960	1962	1964	1966
North West	66.2	63.5	58.3	57.8	54.5	53.5
Latin America	15.5	17.2	16.4	15.9	16.5	16.6
Arab World	3.5	5.4	4.8	5.2	5.2	5.3
Western Asia	6.6	6.7	8.5	7.4	7.7	8.3
Communist Asia	.1	.4	.3	.3	.5	.5
Eastern Europe	7.9	6.6	7.5	7.7	8.0	7.9
Black Africa	.2	.3	3.5	4.8	6.7	6.8
Rest	0	0	.9	1.0	.9	1.1
Sum	100.0	100.1	100.2	100.1	100.0	100.1

Source: Kjell Skjelsbaek, "The Growth of International Non-Governmental Organization in the Twentieth Century", International Organization, XXV, 3, Summer 1971), 420-425.

NGOs Distribution by Numbers of Members and Regions, 1964

Number	Africa	Arab World	Asia & Oceania	Latin America	North West	Communist Countries	Neutral* Countries	Total	Percent
less than 100	21	11	54	62	1,155	19	192	1,514	84.0
100,999	2	0	4	4	84	1	9	104	5.8
1,000-9,999	0	0	0	0	42	0	8	50	2.8
10,000-99,999	0	0	1	1	18	0	9	29	1.6
100,000-999,999	0	0	1	2	36	0	3	42	2.3
1,000,000-9,999,999	0	0	1	0	23	5	11	40	2.2
10,000,000 +	0	0	2	1	10	7	3	23	1.3
	23	11	63	70	1,368	32	235	1,802	100.0

*Austria, Finland, Ireland, Sweden, Switzerland, Vatican, Yugoslavia.

Source: Yearbook of International Organizations (10th edition, 1964-65).

TABLE 6.3

Location of Headquarters of International NGO's, 1956

Africa, French West	1	Japan	1
Africa, North	3	Luxembourg	14
Argentina	10	Mexico	15
Australia	2	Monaco	3
Austria	26	Netherlands	85
Belgian Congo	1	Norway	3
Belgium	245	Pakistan	2
Bolivia	1	Panama	2
Brazil	8	Peru	7
Bulgaria	1	Philippines	3
Canada	4	Poland	9
Chile	6	Portugal	1
Colombia	5	Roumania	2
Crete	1	Salvador	3
Cuba	14	Silesia	1
Czechoslovakia	13	Spain	9
Denmark	18	Sweden	23
Egypt	3	Switzerland	184
Finland	1	Turkey	3
France	428	Union of South Africa	1
Germany	110	United Kingdom	189
Greece	2	United States	129
Guatemala	2	U.S.S.R.	4
Hungary	10	Uruguay	5
Iceland	1	Venezuela	1
India	8	Yugoslavia	2
Iran	1		
Italy	84	Total	1,710

Source: J. J. Lador-Lederer, International Non-Governmental Organizations: and Economic Entities (Leyden: A. W. Sythoff, 1963), p. 74.

Locations of Headquarters in Percentages per Region, 1954-68

	1954	1958	1962	1964	1966	1968
Western Europe and North America	93.2	92.0	90.8	89.4	88.7	87.1
Latin America	3.1	3.7	3.7	4.4	4.8	5.4
Arab Countries	.4	.5	.5	1.1	.9	1.1
"Western" Asia	1.3	1.5	1.8	1.7	1.7	2.1
Communist Asia	0	0	0	0	.0	.0
Eastern Europe	1.3	1.6	1.8	1.8	2.1	2.1
Black Africa	.5	1.6	1.2	1.4	1.5	1.9
Rest	.3	.1	.1	.1	.1	.2
TOTAL	100.1	100.0	99.9	99.9	99.8	99.9
N	1,198	1,257	1,549	1,758	2,207	2,663

Note: This table includes IGOs, but since their number is so very small compared with NGOs the trend visible in the table remains significant.

Sources: Adapted from International Associations, no. 11, 1954, pp. 548-549; no. 6, 1959, pp. 446; no. 2, 1965, pp. 86-89; no. 2, 1967, pp. 166-169; Yearbook of International Organizations, 12th edition.

figures cannot be added in order to obtain the total numbers of NGOs. However, the total figures given for business and economic groups in 1968 and 1970 which are found in the footnote to Table 6.4 and which have been collected from other sources than the Yearbook of International Organizations suggest a close correlation with the distribution of interests shown in Table 6.4.

Organizational Effectiveness and
Financial Revenues

While it is obviously difficult to make a comprehensive judgment on the organizational effectiveness of individual NGOs or of the totality of NGOs compared with other nongovernmental forces, one can hypothesize with justification that the larger the paid staff, the greater the annual budget, the larger the number of secondary offices, the more numerous the membership meetings, and the more numerous the publications issued, the higher is the organizational effectiveness. Data on these variables are often unavailable and it goes without saying that they differ greatly with respect to individual NGOs. For example, the International Chamber of Commerce, headquartered in Paris, has a paid staff of 50, an annual budget of $500,000, three secondary offices, holds biannual Congresses and has Council, Committee, and Commission meetings several times a year, and publishes a periodical and many specialized studies. On the other hand, the International Judicial Organization for Developing Countries, headquartered in Rome, has a paid staff of only 4, a budget of $20,000, no secondary offices, no regularly scheduled meetings, and no publication.[11] Many NGOs do not have any paid staff, only volunteers, and their finances are extremely precarious.

An overall view of paid staffs and annual budgets of NGOs is presented in Table 6.5 which provides fragmentary data on the mean size of paid staffs and of the budget for all NGOs that responded to inquiries made on these subjects. As can be seen, the number of paid staff employed by NGOs who provided the information declined from 1958 to 1960 and showed only small increases since then. The average number was nine, which suggests that a few large NGOs have an extensive paid staff, but most of the paid staffs are small. The budget figures increased materially from 1951 to 1954, but from then on did not change very much. The regional distribution of paid staff shown in Table 6.6 indicates that only in the North West do an appreciable number of NGOs have paid employees numbering more than 100. As far as budgetary prowess is concerned, again only in the North West have a number of NGOs relatively large financial resources, followed

TABLE 6.4

Interest Patterns of European Community NGOs

	March 1961	November 1965
Industry	88	135
Commerce	40	69
Artisans	7	11
Professions	19	22
Services	—	4
Transportation	7	7
Agriculture	81	124
Miscellaneous	3	3

Sources: Karlheinz Neunreither, "Wirtschaftsverbaende im Prozess der europaeischen Integration" in C. J. Friedrich, Politische Dimensionen der europaeischen Gemeinschaftsbildung (Koeln and Opladen: Westdeutscher Verlag, 1968), p. 401, Table 3. The CEE, Reportoire des organismes communs crees dans le cadre des Communautes europeenes, 1960 and 1970, basing itself on broader criteria than the Yearbook, furnishes the following figures for the total number of Community NGOs:

	1960	1970
Business	140	266
Agriculture	106	129
	246	495

by less affluence in the neutral countries and Latin America. NGOs in the remaining regions clearly suffer from budgetary woes and this applies also to many NGOs in the North West. The sources of funds are dues in the majority of cases; grants and publications provide financial support in relatively few instances. When one speculates about the origin of funds listed as unknown which represents a high percentage, one might suspect that in many instances the indirect donors might be the national governments using some kind of concealed form of contributions.

Increase or decrease in the NGO bureaucracy and budgets does not imply corresponding changes in the activity at grass roots level. The frequency of general membership meetings of international NGOs

FIGURE 6.4

Growth of European Community NGOs
(total 278)

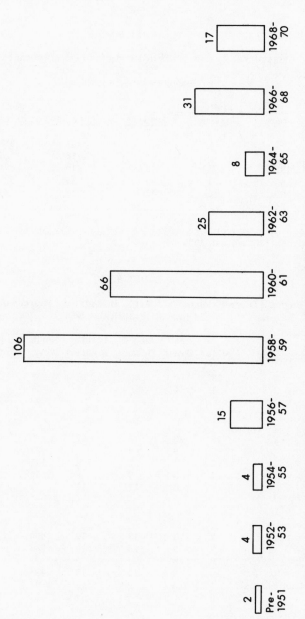

Source: Adapted from Donald J. Puchala, "Patterns in West European Integration," Journal of Common Market Studies, IX, 2 (December 1970), pp. 117–42; Yearbook of International Organizations (12th edition, 1968–69), p. 13.

TABLE 6.5

Average Size of Paid Staffs and Budgets of International NGOs
1951-64
(Budgets in U.S. $1,000)

	Staffs			Budgets		
Year	Average	No. Org.	% Answers	Average	No. Org.	% Answers
1951				134	315	38
1954				710	327	32
1958	12.5	478	45	610	477	45
1960	8.3	491	39	587	521	42
1964	9.0	615	42	629	417	28

Source: Adapted from International Associations and Yearbook of International Organizations, (12th edition, 1968-69).

TABLE 6.6

Regional Distribution of Paid Staffs, Budgets, and Sources of Funds
of International NGOs, 1964

Staff	Africa	Arab World	Asia & Oceania	Latin America	North West	Communist World	Neutral Countries
Less than 100	22	10	60	69	1,352	32	233
More than 100	1	1	3	1	16	0	2
Budget							
Unknown	19	10	48	47	1,029	30	152
$100-999	0	0	0	1	27	0	5
$1,000-9,999	2	1	2	9	148	1	24
$10,000-99,999	1	0	7	9	56	0	12
$100,00 +	1	0	11	11	71	0	2
Source of Funds							
Unknown	9	4	17	19	400	16	33
Dues	7	3	25	29	585	7	115
Grants	0	0	5	3	73	0	13
Dues & Grants	3	4	13	17	185	5	45
Dues, Grants & Publications	2	0	2	0	64	1	16
Others	2	0	1	2	61	3	13

Source: Yearbook of International Organizations (10th edition, 1964-65).

are shown on Table 6.7 and suggest slightly increased activity inasmuch
as the percentage of annual meetings rose from 1960 to 1964 while
the number of NGOs which held meetings every four years or less
often declined. The decrease in the percentage of North West meetings
compared to the total number of meetings may suggest a greater NGO
activity in other areas although the regional breakdown is not con-
clusive as to the regions especially involved. Fifty-two percent of
the international NGOs are not known to have regular meetings.
Again, the percentages of responses by NGOs must be taken into consideration when interpreting these statistics.

Another possible indicator of the effectiveness of NGOs is the
number of periodicals these organizations issue. Forty-nine percent
of NGOs publish one or more periodicals, while 38 percent issue
occasional studies and reports. Only 4 percent publish historical
accounts. For example, the International Cooperative Alliance
publishes six periodicals in four different languages plus a large
number of individual studies. However, many NGOs publish only a
periodical bulletin. It is fair to assume that a large number of
periodicals and publications are useful tools for influencing the views
of national governments and IGOs regarding the validity of the objectives individual NGOs are pursuing. A breakdown of publications in
terms of periodicals, nonperiodicals, and historical accounts by
region is furnished in Table 6.8. Obviously the new countries are
not represented in the category of historical publications, but periodicals and nonperiodicals are published by some NGOs in all regions.
It is interesting to note that international NGOs headquartered and
active in the neutral countries are very prolific in the field of publication. From the foregoing analysis it is evident that while the number
of international NGOs has been growing steadily, their overall
effectiveness may not have changed much over the years. Moreover,
this data suggest that the effectiveness of the majority of international
NGOs is limited and only a relatively small number of NGOs possess
the means to pursue their aims with good prospects for success.
Among the latter may well be the international NGOs headquartered
in neutral countries which seem to show considerable strength in terms
of numbers, financial resources, scheduled meetings, and publications.
This may suggest that leadership groups in these countries, by
definition opposed to military means, seek to influence other national
governments, IGOs, and the international system as a whole through
various kinds of extensive NGO activity.

Contacts and Coalitions

The major vehicles for achieving success in attaining NGO
objectives are formal and informal contacts with IGOs and governmental

TABLE 6.7

Membership Meetings of International NGOs

Frequency of Meetings, 1960-64

Frequency	1960	1962	1964
Annual and more often	40.9	41.6	43.2
Every two years	22.8	22.4	22.9
Every three years	20.5	21.7	21.7
Every four years	9.4	9.6	8.8
Every five years	5.8	4.1	2.8

Percentages of North West Meetings of Total Meetings

1951	1954	1956	1958	1960	1962	1964	1966
87.0	83.3	83.3	84.3	77.5	76.8	78.6	75.5

Source: Kjell Skjelsbaek, Development of the System of International Organization, paper presented at the third conference of the International Peace Research Association, Karlovy Vary, September 21-23, 1969 (mimeo., 1969).

Frequency of Meetings by Regions, 1964

Frequency	Africa	Arab World	Asia	Latin America	North West	Communist Countries	Neutral Countries
No regular meetings known	11	4	24	24	598	15	72
Annual and more often	6	5	13	10	320	2	68
Every two years	2	1	11	18	189	5	37
Every three years	2	1	7	11	153	4	42
Every four years	1	0	4	5	81	6	10
Every five years	1	0	3	2	24	0	4
Every six years and less	0	0	1	0	3	0	2
Total	23	11	63	70	1,368	32	235

Source: Yearbook of International Organizations (10th edition, 1964-65).

TABLE 6.8

Publications of International NGOs
by Type and Region, 1964

Number of Periodicals	Africa	Arab World	Asia	Latin America	North West	Communist Countries	Neutrals
0	14	4	31	30	728	12	94
1	7	5	19	22	465	9	90
2	0	1	10	10	101	10	35
3	2	1	1	4	49	0	12
4	0	0	1	1	16	1	1
5 and more	0	0	1	3	9	0	3
	23	11	63	70	1,368	32	235
Number of Nonperiodicals							
0	13	8	35	43	860	25	126
1	7	1	13	16	251	2	49
2	3	0	4	2	110	5	24
3	0	1	5	6	59	0	15
4	0	0	2	0	35	0	12
5 or more	0	1	4	3	53	0	9
	23	11	63	70	1,368	32	235
Historical Publications							
0	22	11	61	69	1,314	31	216
1	0	0	2	1	44	1	15
2	1	0	0	0	4	0	4
3 and more	0	0	0	0	6	0	0
	23	11	63	70	1,368	32	235

Source: Yearbook of International Organizations (10th edition, 1964-65).

193

agencies. In this endeavor the formation of coalitions among NGOs
has also proven to be beneficial. As a consequence, access to the
decision-making process of intergovernmental organizations is valued
highly and regarded as very important by the NGOs in the pursuit of
their international objectives. The remarkable increase in the number
of NGOs which have been accorded some kind of consultative status
with different universal and regional IGOs (shown in Table 6.9)
testifies to the efforts of these organizations to obtain this access.
It should be noted that not only international but also a few national
NGOs have been admitted as consultants.[12] The largest increases of
consultation relationships with NGOs have been recorded by the ILO
and the Food and Agriculture Organization (FAO).

Some observers consider the instrumental value of the consultative status for NGOs to be exaggerated, especially given the
continuing rise in the quantity of the consulting arrangements.[13]
Nevertheless, the importance of this access is also recognized, although
at times reluctantly, by the IGOs which often display an attitude of
reserve toward NGOs that has grown more intense over the years as
the number of these groups has multiplied. To appear hospitable
without making the job of consultation unmanageable, some of the intergovernmental organizations such as the Economic and Social Council
(ECOSOC), the ILO, and others have set up different classes of
consultative status for the NGOs. For example, ECOSOC has three
classes: I, for NGOs concerned with most of the activities of the
Council; II, for organizations with special competence in a few ECOSOC
activities; and R, for ad hoc consultations of certain groups. Similar
triple categories are used by FAO and the United Nations Educational,
Scientific, and Cultural Organization (UNESCO). The ILO and the
United Nations Conference on Trade and Development (UNCTAD) have
two classes, one for groups with "important interest" (ILO) or falling
in a "general category" (UNCTAD), and the other for special interests.

Applications for consultative status are decided upon by a
special NGO Committee of ECOSOC. Considerable political log-
rolling has characterized this process and inter-NGO coalitions may
be helpful. The Committee, after scrutinizing available data on size,
spread of membership, operating budget, and range and kind of
activities, recommends whether the NGO in question should be admitted
and to which category it should be assigned. From 1947 to 1951
NGOs with legally constituted branches in Spain were excluded from
consultative status. During the Cold War, a long-standing battle was
waged by the Soviet Union for admission of certain groups which,
according to Western countries, did not support the "purposes and
principles" of the United Nations. Complaints were registered in the

TABLE 6.9

NGO's Accorded Consultative Status by Intergovernmental Organizations[a]

International Organization	1951/52	1958/59	1962/63	1966/67	1970/71	Growth[b]
ECOSOC	212	302	332	360	352	166
ILO	5	47	58	81	92	1,840
FAO	10	40	51	79	106	1,060
UNESCO	99	125	200	250	264	266
WHO	26	46	57	68	82	315
ICAO	17	26	27	28	28	164
ITU	18	23	28	30	31	172
WMO		11	11	15	15	136
IMCO			11	11	21	190
IAEA			19	19	19	100
UNICEF		57	70	75	77	135
IRO	9					
UNCTAD				17	35	205
UNIDO					16	NA
CL of E				76	106	139
OAS				48	46	95
Total	396	677	864	1,157	1,290	

[a]Most of these NGOs are of the international kind, but a few national NGOs have also been granted consultative status: 12 in 1956/57, increased to 16 in 1968/69. They include some important American organizations, for example the Chamber of Commerce of the U.S., the Committee for Economic Development, and the Carnegie Endowment for International Peace.

[b]Base = 100 for first year organization appears on this chart.

Source: Adapted from the Yearbook of International Organizations of the years shown.

Committee that some NGOs received government subsidies and consequently were subject to undue influence.

The financing of NGOs has produced a number of problems. On the one hand the basic principle of NGOs requires that these organizations should be independent of any government influence. Clearly if secret governmental finances are furnished, this may imply that these organizations are to be induced to undertake actions which might be contrary to the purposes and principles of the Charter of the United Nations.[14] On the other hand, most of the NGOs are strapped for money and consequently any kind of financial support may be most appealing to the management of NGOs.[15] As a consequence, efforts have been made by IGO agencies (ECOSOC) to require periodic disclosures of sources of funds. Voluntary contributions by amounts and donors are to be revealed faithfully and financing from sources other than individual members or national nongovernmental affiliates must be explained, especially those which suggest direct or indirect governmental support. If an NGO cannot furnish a satisfactory explanation its consultative status may be terminated.

There has been criticism by delegates of some developing countries against NGOs currently enjoying consultative status that they were predominantly "Western oriented." On the other hand, Committee members from the Third World have shown a tendency to vote admission on the basis of the policies and capabilities of consultative status-seeking NGOs with respect to providing assistance to developing countries.[16]

It is obvious that the various types of consultative relations with intergovernmental organizations give the NGOs opportunities to exert influences for the attainment of their goals. Moreover, United Nations bodies make available to NGO representatives reports of special studies, notices of forthcoming events, and summary records of debates and decisions which, although it may be a time-consuming task to select relevant materials, provide an important source of information necessary for the lobbying activities of NGOs and for the statements of NGO representatives before IGO bodies. It should be noted that the overwhelming majority of NGOs do not have special U.N. representatives but dispatch ad hoc representatives to the IGO sessions pertinent to their interests.[17] It is fair to assume that the higher the consultative status, and the more special U.N. representatives an NGO has, the closer the relations with intergovernmental organizations, and the more effective the exertion of influence on decisions affecting the international system. But an important caveat must be stated. Although ideas and information

offered to delegates of IGO bodies with which NGOs have consultative
status are considered carefully, the delegates often wait for specific
instructions from their governments before taking actions on NGO
proposals. Therefore, in order to influence effectively the policies
of United Nations and other IGO bodies, it is necessary to exert pressures at the national as well as the international level.[18] In this
connection, another aspect of the consultative relationship must be
mentioned. NGOs may often become the instruments of implementation
which stand at the disposal of IGOs. Such action can add power to the
NGOs' goal attainment potential. Moreover, because of sometimes
close NGO relations to national authorities which use NGOs occasionally for carrying out technical and administrative matters, IGOs may
gain special means of influencing national governmental agencies.[19]
All this points up the importance for NGOs to have good connections
to the governmental decision-makers and other elites in the countries
where they have offices and members and the usefulness of contacts
with other NGOs.

Despite some of the reservations stated above, it seems logical
that in general the larger the number of intergovernmental organizations
with which NGOs have consultative status and the higher the category
of this status, the greater the latter's capability to influence the
international environment. Table 6.10 shows the NGOs having consultative status with at least six of the intergovernmental organizations
listed in Table 6.9. Looking over Table 6.10 one finds that the assumption that a positive correlation may exist between the quantity and
quality of institutionalized consultative relations enjoyed by NGOs
and their influence on the international system and environment is
confirmed to a substantial degree. In the business sector the International Chamber of Commerce is undoubtedly the most influential
group which has greatly advanced economic intercourse in the international field and has influenced appropriate national legislation in
different countries for this purpose as well. Perhaps one of its most
outstanding contributions was the establishment of a Court of Arbitration which has dealt with over a thousand commercial cases and which
filled a need that perhaps no official agency could meet.[20] While
less prestigious than the ICC, and representing institutions of little
wealth, the International Co-operative Alliance has seen a substantial
rise in its international influence and now represents several million
consumers in the world. Politically, it opposes totalitarian regimes
and sympathizes with the international objectives of the Free and
Christian Trade Unions. The International Organization for Standardization, holding one of the top honors in Table 6.10, operates in a very
pedestrian field, but its long-range contribution to international
cooperation by breaking down the barriers resulting from differing

TABLE 6.10

NGOs with Consultative Relations to Six or More Intergovernmental Organizations

Organization	ECOSOC	ILO	FAO	UNESCO	WHO	ICAO	ITU	WMO	IMCO	IAEA	UNICEF	UNCTAD	UNIDO	CL of E	OAS
International Organization of Standardization	II	S	L	A		x	x	x	x	x		S			
ICFTU	I	x	C	A					x	x	x	G	x	x	
World Confederation of Labor	I	x	C	A					x	x	x	G	x	x	
World Federation of U.N. Associations	I	S	C	A	X			x		x	x	G			
International Chamber of Commerce	I		C	C		x	x		x	x		G	x		
International Federation of Agricultural Producers	I	x	C	C				x			x	G		x	
International Co-operative Alliance	I	x	C	A						x	x	G			
International Federation for Documentation	R		L	A		x	x			x				x	
Catholic International Union for Social Service	II	S	L	B							x			x	x
World Federation of Trade Unions	I	x	C	A							x	G	x		
European Confederation of Agriculture	R	S	S	C						x				x	
International Council of Nurses	R	S		C	x						x			x	
International Council of Scientific Unions	R		S	A	x		x			x					
International Society for Rehabilitation of Disabled	II	S		B	x						x				x
International Union for Child Welfare	II	S	C	B	x						x				
International Union of Family Organization	II	S	C	B							x			x	
League of Red Cross Societies	I	S	C	B	x						x				
World Assembly of Youth	II	S	S	B							x			x	
World Jewish Congress	II	S		B							x			x	x

Explanation of special letter symbols other than x:

    ECOSOC - Economic and Social Council of the UN
          I "concerned with most of the activities of the Council"
          II "special competence in . . . only a few of the fields of activity covered by the Council"
          R (= Ros) "can make occasional and useful contributions to the work of the council"

    ILO   - International Labor Organization
          S "Special List of NGOs interested in some particular sector"

    FAO   - Food and Agriculture Organization of the U.N.
          C consultative status
          S specialized consultative status
          L liaison status

    UNESCO - United Nations Educational, Scientific and Cultural Organization
          A "proven competence in an important field of Unesco's work"
          B "able to advise in a particular field"
          C "able to contribute to achievement of Unesco's objectives"

    UNCTAD - United Nations Conference on Trade and Development
          G general category
          S special category

technical standards may be substantial. In the agricultural sector, the International Federation of Agricultural Producers occupies a prominent place in the table. Of post-World War II origin, it does not enjoy the international influence of its industrial counterparts nor does it possess the political prowess of the national farm organizations. The reason may well be that farm problems in most cases depend on national structures and conditions. Moreover, for domestic political reasons, the national governments are intent to exercise maximum control over agricultural questions.[21] Only when a number of countries seek to regionalize their agricultural activities, as in the EEC, do farm NGOs seem to be able to exert substantial influence beyond the national confines.

In the field of labor all three major international union associations are represented on Table 6.10; in fact the ICFTU and WCL share top honors with the International Organization for Standardization. The legislative and political actions of the ICFTU in the international arena have been perhaps the most important, but as has been seen in the preceding chapter, the WCL and WFTU also play significant roles in transnational activities. In the pursuit of their overall activities, the international trade union organizations and their powerful national counterparts such as the AFL-CIO seek to influence the politics developed within the complex United Nations system in such a way as to keep any increase in private investment in developing countries from infringing on their specific goals. Thus, the conflict of special interests characteristic of domestic politics exists also at the international level. At the same time, one finds organizational rivalry playing an important role on both the international and national levels.[22]

The remaining NGOs on Table 6.10 have primarily a social and technical character. Because of their multiple consultative status they are in a position to make themselves felt in the international arena, but their actual influence, without doubt of an undramatic nature in most cases, is difficult to gauge.

As mentioned earlier, the European Community also has institutionalized contacts with certain NGOs. The main organ for this purpose is the Economic and Social Committee (ESC) composed of representatives of the various categories of economic and social life. The distribution of the membership representing major NGO categories during the 1966-70 period is shown in Table 6.11.

It should be noted that the total of the NGOs listed is less than the total number of representatives authorized in Article 195 of the

TABLE 6.11

Distribution of NGO Categories
in the Economic and Social
Committee of the EEC

NGO Category	Number
Industry	16
Commerce and Banking	15
Agriculture	15
Labor	27
Education	5
Handicraft	4
Misc. Political	7
Total	89

Source: CEE, Comité Economique et Social, Liste Alphabetique des Membres (May 17, 1966-May 16, 1970).

EEC Treaty, which is 101.[23] This discrepancy is due to the fact that not all of the ESC members represent NGOs since some are private individuals. It should also be pointed out that the groups represented on the ESC constitute powerful national groups although they in turn are members of the pertinent European associations shown in Tables 6.1 and 6.4 for the European Community. Finally, it must be recognized that the ESC enjoys only limited power in the decision-making process of the Community and therefore the influence exerted in and through this body may not be very effective in advancing the desired objectives of the NGOs with respect to Community system policies and pattern changes.

More important for the NGOs, both European and national, are the institutionalized contacts in a variety of committees which are especially numerous and significant in the evolvement and management of agricultural policy in the Community and which draw not only on agricultural groups, but also have representatives of labor, consumers, and industry.[24] Beyond these formal consultations, the Commission leadership engages also in frequent informal contacts with the major European NGOs in the industrial and agricultural fields, especially UNICE and COPA, thus permitting these and smaller groups to present their viewpoints regarding the future direction of Community evolution.

International and national NGOs may also form coalitions for the pursuit of their international objectives, thereby enhancing their goal attainment potentials. These coalitions may be on a horizontal basis whereby for example NGOs pursuing goals in the field of law may form an alliance with NGOs in the fields of economies and finance or technology. It is also possible that NGOs form vertical coalitions that may lead to the creation of umbrella type NGOs in a particular field which seek to coordinate and promote in a more effective manner the interests and objectives of similarly situated NGOs. Thus the interconnections between NGOs as well as overlapping memberships of individual members in various NGOs produce an ever expanding network on a world-wide basis, whose growth is likely to continue in the future.

Of particular interest is the possibility that certain NGOs may form alliances with multinational enterprises—a relationship already mentioned in discussing the MNEs. Common interests are likely to exist, especially between the MNEs and professional NGOs binding together organizations of employers, business executives, economists, financial experts, and perhaps those working in technological fields. It is interesting to note that since 1909 these groups have manifested a generally higher growth rate than other categories of NGOs. For example, the category of professionals and employers (see Table 6.1) showed an average annual percentage increase of 86 percent since 1909 and 11 percent since 1951. Economics and finance showed an increase of 21 and 10 percent respectively and technology 20 and 10 percent respectively. The future implications of such coalitions are difficult to assess at this time, but if managed effectively they are likely to aid in the promotion of objectives and common interests which both these NGOs and MNEs have. It is interesting to note the rank order correlation of the number of multinational firms by nationality of corporate headquarters and the number of principal officials of international professional associations by nationality. Table 6.12 furnishes pertinent data and shows that the correlation is quite high, R_S being .84.

Although in many cases the objectives and interests of NGOs are conflicting and antithetical, international NGOs have found it useful to form an umbrella group of their own, the NGO Conference. This groups seeks to coordinate the activities of all NGOs, promote interaction among NGOs, facilitate the contacts between IGO bodies and NGOs, and seeks ways by which the NGOs might give more "collective" as distinctive from "individual" advice on matters relating to the consultative process. The Conference meets triennially in Geneva and elects a president and vice president and an executive

TABLE 6.12

Rank Order Correlation of Number of Multinational
Firms by Nationality of Corporate Headquarters
and Number of Principal Officials of
International Professional
Associations by Nationality

Country	Number of Multinational Firms	Rank Order	Number of Principal Officials of International Professional Associations	Rank Order
United States	2,816	1	133	3
United Kingdom	1,651	2	138	2
Germany (West)	801	3	50	8
France	471	4	202	1
Switzerland	349	5	105	5
Netherlands	222	6	74	6
Sweden	219	7	31	9
Belgium	197	8	106	4
Italy	101	9	53	7
Denmark	82	10	30	10
Norway	78	11	13	11
Austria	38	12	12	12
Spain	9	13	11	13

R_s = .84, significant at .01.

Sources: Union of International Associations, Yearbook of
International Organizations (12th ed., 1969), p. 1189; International
Associations, 19 (May 1967), pp. 354-55. Adopted from William M.
Evan, "Multinational Corporations and International Professional
Associations as Mechanisms for Integration of the International
System," paper presented at ISA Convention, Puerto Rico, March
1971.

bureau of 15 members. The hope is to create a more functional and efficient relationship in particular areas of concern to NGOs and to improve the representation of NGOs in the United Nations.[25]

EFFECTS ON GOVERNMENTS AND IGOs

The diverse nature of international NGOs and the great difference in their effectiveness make it difficult to assess their transnational impact on national governmental decision-makers. Clearly, NGOs generally do not possess the financial resources available to MNEs and therefore their effects on national governments are bound to be much less dramatic and more of the "pin-prick" variety. Nevertheless, as the Soviet delegation during an ECOSOC review of the human rights organizations observed, governments at times perceive NGO activities as an "infringement of national sovereignty."[26] However, they are not faced with the same dilemmas which MNE activities pose.

For the evaluation of the effects which NGO activities have on governmental leaders it is, perhaps, well to make several distinctions among NGOs. The first distinction refers to the nature of the group's action. One category of NGOs bases its capabilities on technical expertise, such as the International Organization for Standardization; while others exert influence by leading and representing large segments of the public in various societies. In the latter category fall trade union federations and religious organizations which pursue objectives based on widespread interests. Another useful distinction flows from the fields in which the NGOs are active. One group operates in the fields of activity that are of major concern to national governments such as the economy, industry, commerce, finance, and technology; a second category of NGOs is concerned with essentially noneconomic matters such as sports, religious affairs, etc. Since the first group affects much more the politics of individual countries, their impact on national governmental decision-makers is likely to be greater than that of the second group and the reactions of the governments more severe. It is also significant that the first group is growing much more rapidly in numbers than the second as can be seen from Table 6.1. As Kjell Skjelsbaek points out, some of the NGOs falling in the first group may have more influence in their respective fields than some of the smaller nation-states.[27] A third distinction that should be made refers to the countries in which international NGOs carry out their transnational activities. As Table 6.2 shows, economically developed, pluralistic countries have a greater multitude of international NGOs operating within their midst than do the developing countries. In fact, among developed countries it appears that those espousing a pluralistic ideology have a higher incidence of international NGO membership than those following a more totalitarian orientation.[28]

From the foregoing one may conclude that in general terms at least the effects of international NGOs on national government decision-makers are more pronounced in the industrially advanced countries with pluralistic orientations and that the interest groups in economic fields are likely to have a greater impact than those in other fields. It should be recalled that coalitions between professional organizations of various kinds and MNEs may reinforce their respective effects on national governments as long as they pursue common objectives. Whether national governmental decision-makers and political elites will perceive these effects as benefits or drawbacks is impossible to judge. In some cases the effects may be of the indeterminate type and perceptions regarding their value may depend on long-run attitude changes of the public and elites. However, since concern with national autonomy remains an overriding consideration in most nation-states of today, one may speculate that drawbacks rather than benefits may be perceived in many instances.

There is another aspect of transnational NGO activity which deserves to be mentioned, particularly inasmuch as it has a minimum of political implications for national governments. This aspect relates to NGO activity which may bring much needed aid outside the normal realm of governmental concern and without suggestion of any kind of patronage. This has occurred on many occasions when activity at government level might have been impossible in the context of existing relations. A hospital built from the efforts of an NGO on the edge of a desert in Africa can bring comfort and health to the surrounding villages without the government of the country having to sacrifice any of its declared positions in its international relationships. For this reason alone, international NGOs have been able to operate and achieve outstanding successes in the fields of child care, medical aid, in stilling the pangs of hunger and quickening dormant minds in countries which as a result have obtained benefits without having to abandon their independence and freedom of action in the international community.

What has been the impact of international NGOs on intergovernmental organizations? No systematic study exists so far dealing

with the effect of the NGO consultative relationship on United Nations
policies and programs. In order to come up with some kind of
evaluation it might be helpful to consider views expressed by various
member states and by the staff of the United Nations Secretariat. The
Secretary General, addressing a Conference of NGOs in May 1969,
stated that he wanted to express his:

> very sincere thanks to all of you, not only for your magnifi-
> cent work for the United Nations and the peoples of the
> United Nations but also for your consistent understanding,
> cooperation and support, and your very sincere spirit of
> dedication and devotion to the principles of the Charter. As
> a matter of fact, the United Nations owes all of you a deep
> debt of gratitude.

A different aspect of NGO activity was expressed by President Kenneth
Kaunda of Zambia in 1968 at a NGO-sponsored conference on human
rights. He said:

> We are still too national in our thinking and outlook . . .
> the efforts of NGOs . . . must be directed towards
> strengthening the world body and increasing its capa-
> bility to solve problems which continue to bedevil human
> development . . .

He also expressed the "sincere hope that NGOs will continue to assist
in whatever way to shed more light on possible solutions to current problems facing the United Nations and the world. . . ."[29] Finally, during
an ECOSOC debate of 1969 a delegate of Norway said it was certain
that in the future the Economic and Social Council would have to rely
more on cooperation with NGOs having consultative status. These
optimistic and euphemistic statements must be juxtaposed to the
actual attitudes in the United Nations vis-à-vis NGOs. Walter R. Sharp
reports that few of the speeches delievered before ECOSOC by NGO
representatives appear to be taken very seriously. For the most
part they are considered dull, while some have a definitely propogan-
distic flavor. As a consequence, according to Sharp, delegates of
national governments may be seen frequently reading newspapers, or
absenting themselves, during NGO presentations. At times the representatives of closely related NGOs seem to insist on all of them holding
forth on the same issue, instead of authorizing one of their colleagues
to speak in behalf of the group. This tendency might suggest vanity
or the need of each to justify his presence as an NGO representative.[30]

While Sharp's comments may reflect the views of many observers
of NGO activities in New York and Geneva, his judgement may be

overly critical. The fact that delegates may not always listen to the statements of NGO representatives might not, in fact, be convincing evidence that these statements are not being taken seriously. Certainly in every national legislature of the world as well as in the state legislatures in the United States, statements by interest groups may not arouse on the floor the greatest enthusiasm, yet behind the scene contacts based on the statements made officially might well produce an impact. Moreover, United Nations officials and delegates are showing an increasing interest in the value of cooperation with NGOs who can and are willing to help inform the public of the activities and goals of United Nations agencies and are able to exert influence on both the public and national governments in support of these goals. As a consequence, greater emphasis is being placed on liaison between United Nations Agencies and NGOs which suggests a greater acceptance of the value of the NGOs. An example is the major effort being made to accommodate 200 to 300 observers from NGOs at the UN Conference on Human Environment to be held in June 1972 in Stockholm to insure maximum participation in the proceedings of the meeting.[31] Another example is the cooperation between United Nations officials and NGOs to promote the goals and achieve the targets of the Second Development Decade. A number of NGOs are taking steps to schedule seminars, initiate training programs, and provide fellowships in order to assist the United Nations efforts.

On a regional level mention must be made of the leadership provided by the Action Committee for a United States of Europe, headed by Jean Monnet, to further European political unification. Composed of 50 representatives of trade unions and political parties in the Common Market countries the Committee has used Monnet's prestige and connections as well as the contacts of the Committee members to open doors to influential elites within and outside the EEC for generating active and potent support for its objectives. Although the Committee has made a contribution to advancing the progress of political integration, its efforts so far have not been crowned with success despite its impressive human and material resources. An important reason for this failure may well have been a misreading of the political realities in the EEC Member States and the use of erroneous strategies to engender acceptance of the Committee's views.[32]

THE CONSEQUENCES FOR THE INTERNATIONAL SYSTEM

What can one say about the consequences of NGO activity for the global interaction process in the international system? In terms

of collaboration and conflict, the transnational contacts of NGOs in
the technical field have promoted and are likely to promote in the
future an increasing amount of collaboration among states. In this
field, NGO activity is mostly unobtrusive and governmental decision-
makers do not consider such activity as building a competing base of
power. However, when NGOs pursue primarily economic goals, the
results in terms of collaboration are more difficult to discern as the
activities of these NGOs might run counter to the declared objectives
of national governments.

It was mentioned earlier that some NGO activities in the human
rights field may be viewed as infringements on sovereignty, especially,
but not exclusively, by totalitarian governments. However even these
infringements produce only very gentle waves of conflict and are not
very significant for changing the global interaction pattern. Of course,
the more ideological the goals of NGOs are, the greater the conflict
which may be caused among individual governments. But since the
majority of NGOs recruit members and operate according to functional needs, political and ideological barriers may be overcome and
a contribution made to collaboration.[33] A further favorable factor
is the fact that memberships of individuals in various organizations
are frequently overlapping and therefore, as Kjell Skjelsbaek points
out,[34] adversaries and competitors in one connection might be allies
and collaborators in another.

In view of the clear tendencies toward regional clusters among
international NGOs, one may speculate that the collaboration generally is greater within regional contexts than on a world-wide basis.
Moreover, since the data show that NGOs are concentrated in developed
areas of the world, collaboration is likely to occur with greater
frequency among industrially advanced countries. This tendency may
be heightened by the fact that headquarters of NGOs are more often
found in the developed countries than in the poor countries which may
indicate that the leadership of these NGOs is also concentrated in the
advanced world. An overriding factor in all cases may be how equal
the distribution of benefits is that flows from NGO activities. This
factor has already been pointed to in discussing the consequences
of MNEs for the international system. It seems fair to assume that
the more equal the benefits for different countries, the greater the
propensity for collaboration.

An interesting question to conjecture upon is whether the growing
net of international NGOs has consequences for bringing about better
prospects for international peace. Skjelsbaek reports[35] that an analysis of international NGO representation of the divided countries of the
world—Germany, China, Korea, and Viet Nam—shows that in each

case there were more co-memberships among them than expected
on the basis of each country's total number of co-memberships. This
is particularly significant inasmuch as IGO co-memberships are
almost nonexistent. Especially pronounced was the relationship between the two Germanies: in 1964, West Germany was represented
in 93 percent of the international NGOs in which East Germany was
represented. While there is no positive knowledge that these channels
are used for interaction between national delegations, they have at
least potential importance. Another interesting element of the East-
West relationship is the fact that East-West co-memberships in international NGOs are higher than those for intra-East connections. From
this, one could deduce that East European countries generally have
more NGO contacts with Western states than with each other.

There has also been some speculation as to whether joint representation in NGOs by countries of the Western and Communist blocs
may have a beneficial effect on the prospects for international peace.
Louis Kriesberg has undertaken a study of international NGOs in
which both the United States and the Soviet Union were represented.[36]
Analyzing the membership of the more than 1,500 international NGOs
as listed in the 1962-63 edition of the Yearbook of International Organizations, Kriesberg finds that 192 NGOs show joint participation by
the two superpowers. In looking at this figure one should realize
that many of the international NGOs have only a regional focus and
therefore neither the United States nor the Soviet Union would have
an interest in being represented in these organizations. Kriesberg
finds that NGOs concerned with substantive issues about which members of the two countries are apt to have a high consensus are most
likely to have joint representation. When consensus is low, complementarity of interests may be of great significance in joint representation. The NGOs concerned with science, technology, medicine,
and sports were considered to deal with matters about which the
United States and the Soviet Union have relatively high consensus.
Kriesberg points out that significantly these NGOs tend to have a lower
level of activity and less centralized decision-making than do NGOs
dealing with social, economic, moral, or political matters. These
findings indicate some of the limits which national and political differences impose on the role that NGOs can play in the development
of a world community and suggest that at least so far, joint representation by opposing bloc countries in NGOs have made a minimal
contribution toward attaining world peace.[37]

From the foregoing discussion the impression emerges that
NGOs succeed in bringing about some changes in the global interaction
pattern of the international system. However, their impact is

undramatic, diffuse, slow, and does not suggest any single direction.
The input into the international political system emanates from all
functional and geographic segments of the environment as well as
from national and international subsystems. Although one might be
tempted to speculate that the spreading web of NGO activity might
produce the basis for greater integration of mankind and thereby
contribute to higher prospects for international peace, little concrete
evidence is available to sustain genuine hopes for the latter. Nevertheless, as was observed earlier, the number of NGOs and their
activity continues to grow and therefore they will become an increasingly important factor in the future patterns of world politics.

NOTES

1. Cf. Yearbook of International Organizations (13 ed., 1970-
71), p. 1005-6.

2. According to Lyman C. White, International Non-Governmental Organizations (New York: Greenwood Press, 1968), p. 279,
fn. 5, the first international NGO was founded in 1855 and was the
World Alliance of the YMCAs. White contends that the Evangelical
Alliance was not a truly international NGO because "its so-called
members . . . [were] mere subscribers to its publications, without
any voting rights." Others believed that the Rosicrucian Order
founded in 1674 is the first international NGO. Cf. Kjell Skjelsbaek,
"The Growth of International Nongovernmental Organization in the
Twentieth Century," International Organization, XXV, 3 (Summer
1971), 424.

3. Ibid., p. 425.

4. We should note that J. David Singer and Michael Wallace in
"Intergovernmental Organization and the Preservation of Peace:
1816-1864: Some Bivariate Relationships," International Organization XXIV, 3 (Summer 1970), 520-47, use slightly different data for
IGOs founded from those used in Figure 6.1. These disparities,
perhaps due to definitional differences, do not, however, affect
the general growth trend.

5. The curve in Figure 6.2 conforms to the equation:

$$Y = 1.26861 \cdot 10^6 - 1.34083 \cdot 10^3 X + 3.54257 \cdot 10^{-1} X^2$$
$$Y = \text{number of organizations}; X = \text{year}$$

6. See p. 23, and Table 2.1, p. 25.

7. Cf. Ernst B. Haas, The Uniting of Europe (Stanford, Calif.: Stanford University Press, 1968), p. xxxiii.

8. Skjelsbaek, "The Growth of International Nongovernmental Organizations," pp. 425, 426, using different data sources, states that the mean of the number of countries which have individual citizen, national organizations and/or governmental agencies affiliated with international NGOs has risen from 21.0 in 1951 to 25.7 in 1966 (p. 6 and Table 2). Of the NGOs surveyed on this subject 61 percent expect the number of their national branches to rise in the future.

9. For additional analysis see Skjelsbaek, "The Growth of International Nongovernmental Organizations," pp. 430-32.

10. Austria, Finland, Ireland, Sweden, Switzerland, Vatican, Yugoslavia. The authors have felt it important to vary our regional categories from those of Skjelsbaek in order to focus on the significant role netural countries play in the NGO world. All Communist countries have been put into one category. Since their comprehensive data are only available for 1964, no comparisons over time could be made with respect to neutral countries.

11. Yearbook of International Organizations (13th edition, 1970-71), pp. 311, 312, 452, 453.

12. Cf. Article 71 of the United Nations Charter.

13. See Persia Campbell, "Do NGOs Have a Role?," International Development Review, XI, 3, (1969) 34-39; and Walter R. Sharp, The United Nations Economic and Social Council (New York: Columbia University Press, 1969), pp. 39-40.

14. It has been alleged that funds have been provided by the CIA to certain international NGOs. Cf. Campbell, "Do NGOs Have a Role?," pg. 36.

15. Cf. James E. Knott, Freedom of Association (Brussels: Union of International Associations, 1962) p. 67-83.

16. See Sharp, The United Nations Economic and Social Council, pp. 37, 38 and 42; Campbell, "Do NGOs Have a Role?," passim; and Kiichiro Nakahara, "International Pressure Groups and the UN Enlarged ECOSOC" Behavioral Science Research (Tokyo) No. 7 (1970),

pp. 39-49. For a particular roll call vote on admission of three NGOs see page 47. For distribution of voting power in the NGO Committee of ECOSOC see Table 5, page 40. It shows overrepresentation of Western and Eastern Europe. See also Table 4, p. 39.

17. Sixty-one NGOs have 1 special representative; 27 NGOs, 2 representatives, and only 2 have as many as 6 representatives.

18. Campbell, "Do NGOs Have a Role?," p. 39.

19. For examples see J. J. Lador-Lederer, International Non-Governmental Organizations: And Economic Entities (Leyden: A. W. Sythoff, 1963), p. 75.

20. For additional details see White, International Non-Governmental Organizations, pp. 19-32, and Jean Meynaud, Les groupes de pression internationaux (Lausanne: Etudes de Science politique, 1961), pp. 360-71.

21. Ibid., pp. 371-2.

22. Cf. Campbell, "Do NGOs Have a Role?," p. 38.

23. This number will be increased when the United Kingdom, Ireland, Denmark and Norway become EEC members.

24. Journal Officiel des Communautés Européenes, No. L 324/23. December 26, 1969.

25. Campbell, "Do NGOs Have a Role?," p. 39; and Sharp, The United Nations Economic and Social Council, pp. 41-2. See also "The Use of 'Multi-Meetings,'" International Associations, No. 6, 1971, pp. 354-9.

26. Campbell, "Do NGOs Have a Role?," p.37.

27. Skjelsbaek, "The Growth of International Nongovernmental Organization," p. 435.

28. See calculations made by Skjelsbaek, ibid., p. 434 and footnote 31.

29. Quoted by Campbell, "Do NGOs Have a Role?," pp. 34 and 37.

30. Sharp, The United Nations Economic and Social Council, pp. 39 and 40 and footnote 15. Sharp also points out that sometimes delegates simply come "just for the ride" with expenses paid.

31. U.N. Conference on Human Environment, Information Letter, No 1 (June 30, 1971), p. 7.

32. Cf. Merry Bromberger and Serge Bromberger, Jean Monnet and the United States of Europe (New York: Coward-McCann, 1969).

33. Cf. David Mitrany, A Working Peace System (4th ed., London: National Peace Council, 1946.)

34. Skjelsbaek, "The Growth of International Nongovernmental Organization," p. 439.

35. Ibid., p. 440.

36. Louis Kriesberg, "U.S. and U.S.S.R. Participation in International Non-Governmental Organizations," in Louis Kriesberg, ed., Social Processes in International Relations (New York: John Wiley & Sons, 1968), pp. 466-85.

37. See also Skjelsbaek, "The Growth of International Nongovernmental Organization," pp. 441-42.

7

MISCELLANEOUS
TRANSNATIONAL
POLITICAL
GROUPS

In the pursuit of their interests and transnational objectives, MNEs and other NGOs often seek to enlist the aid of various political groups for the transmission of their demands to national governments and IGOs. The most prominent among these groups are political parties, which can be particularly valuable if they have transnational ties and engage in transnational activities. In such cases the parties which may aggregate the interests of several NGOs and might promote some or all of their objectives, are in a position to influence decision-makers in several governments and IGOs in a coordinated fashion thereby enhancing the prospects for success. Of course, instead of employing the "peaceful change" method, NGOs may also attempt to solicit the support of political groups more oriented toward violent change such as liberation fronts or cross-nationally acting radical student organizations. Finally, occasionally foundations operating transnationally may become the carriers of particular NGO demands and interests. While it goes without saying that the transnational activities of the political groups mentioned above can go far beyond the function of being the vehicle of NGO interests and demands, the relationships sketched provide an appropriate line of departure for the sequence which will be employed in this chapter in examining the different groups. The author will therefore proceed first to a discussion and analysis of political parties operating in one way or another across national boundaries.

TRANSNATIONAL PARTIES

Framework for Initiatives

In an examination of border-crossing ties and activities of
political parties a distinction must be made between the parties which
are essentially nationally oriented, operate under national direction
in individual countries, and engage in transnational initiatives only as
a secondary function and those which follow to differing degrees some
kind of central direction or ideology, yet operate also as national
parties in a number of countries.

In the first category fall the Socialists, Christian Democrats,
and Liberals; in the second category the Communists, the Europa
Partei (also known as the European Federalist Party), and perhaps
the Ba'th Party.[1] Originating in Syria, the Ba'th Party has spread
into Iraq and Jordan and, oriented toward socialism, is involved in
the frustrating problem of Arab unification. As for the Communists,
formalized central direction does not exist any more since the dissolution of the Comintern in 1943 and of Cominform in the 1950s, but
the Communist parties in the world nevertheless often look to Moscow
for guidance and approval and remain united, at least basically, with
respect to a central ideology. On the other hand, the doctrinal foundation of many socialist parties has eroded to such an extent that quite
a few, such as the British Labour Party and the Social Democrats in
the Federal Republic of Germany, are slowly becoming parties of
interest aggregation rather than strongly ideologically oriented
organizations.[2]

Since the forcefulness and extent of transnational initiatives
mounted by political parties depends to some degree on the total
number of members and affiliated parties which the different groupings have, Table 7.1 furnishes pertinent figures. Not surprisingly,
the Communist grouping is the largest, with the Socialists and
Christian Democrats following far behind.

Distribution Patterns, Organization,
and Objectives

The Socialists

The transnational grouping of the Socialists is called the
Socialist International which considers itself the direct heir of the

TABLE 7.1

Characteristics of Transnational Party Groupings, 1968

Party Grouping	International Meetings Held Since	Number of National Affiliations	Total Membership
	Parties under essentially national direction		
Socialists	1864/1951[a]	51	15,000,000
Christian Democrats	1965	38	8,000,000
Liberals	1947	14	500,000 (est.)
	Parties under generally centralized direction or ideology		
Communists	1864	88	45,200,000[b]
Ba'th	1965	10 (est.)	no data
Europa Partei	1959	4	no data

a. 1864 refers to meetings under the First International
b. This figure includes the parties in Communist countries where the term "nongovernmental" is not applicable.

Sources: Adopted from David F. Roth, [a]International Political Parties in an Emerging World Order: Towards a Strategy for Realization (mimeo, 1971); and Vereintes Europa, No. 2/3, 1968.

First International founded by Karl Marx in 1864. Even if this claim
is accepted, it needs to be stressed that the split with the Communists
and two World Wars have resulted in several lapses of activity. In
terms of contemporary history, a convenient starting point is the
First Post-War Congress held in Frankfurt in 1951. During this
meeting, the Socialist International declared itself opposed to both
capitalism and communism and dedicated to democracy.[3]

Affiliate parties of the Socialist International are found now in
49 countries located on all continents, but with a major concentration
still in Europe. Table 7.2 shows the world-wide distribution of the
Socialist parties and it should be noted that in Israel and Japan two
of these parties exist and are members of the International. One can
also see from this table that three kinds of memberships are available:
Member Party, Consultative Member, and Observer Member, and
that the number of members has been growing steadily.

Of the 15 million individual members of the International, the
British Labour Party contributes 40 percent, and the Socialist parties
in Australia, Venezuela, Sweden, Madagascar, Austria, and Germany
together make up about 40 percent. In terms of votes (about 70 million)
gained at the most recent elections, Britain, Germany, Japan (the
Socialist Party) and India account for about 60 percent of the total.
Overall, 34 parties play a significant role in each of their country's
political affairs which is a significant factor in assessing the transnational potential of the socialist parties.[4]

The structure of the Socialist International comprises four
organs. The Congress, meeting once every three years, is the largest
body in which all constituent parties are represented and which is
competent to admit and expel members as well as to change the
party statutes. The same kind of representation is allotted to the
Council which meets annually and has extensive powers. The Bureau,
a smaller body with only 18 members, is responsible for day-to-day
operations and controls a Secretariat, located in London.

The main task of the International is liaison between member
parties in order to strengthen relations among them and to achieve
consensus for the coordination of their political attitudes. It also
maintains contacts with the ICFTU. Other bodies performing similar
functions are the occasional meetings of Socialist International Leaders
and the International Union of Socialist Youth. The latter unit claims
116 organizations in 74 countries and thereby has attained a degree of
transnational penetration exceeding that of the parent body.[5]

TABLE 7.2

Membership of the Socialist International,

This Table Shows the Member Parties of the Socialist International and Their Status, as Reported to the Successive Congresses Between 1951 and 1969.

Parties	1951	1952	1953	1955	1957	1959	1961	1963	1966	1969
Aden People's Socialist Party									OM	OM
Argentine Socialist Party	MP	MP	MP	MP	MP	MP	MP	MP	MP	MP
Australian Labor Party									MP	MP
Austrian Socialist Party	MP	MP	MP	MP	MP	MP	MP	MP	MP	MP
Belgian Socialist Party	MP	MP	MP	MP	MP	MP	MP	MP	MP	MP
Progressive Labour Party of Bermuda										OM
British Labour Party	MP	MP	MP	MP	MP	MP	MP	MP	MP	MP
Bulgarian Socialist Party in Exile	MP	MP	MP	CM	CM	CM	CM	CM	CM*	CM
Cameroons Socialist Party								MP*	MP*	CM
Radical Party of Chile									OM	OM
National Liberation Party of Costa Rica									MP	OM
New Democratic Party of Canada[1]	MP	MP	CM	CM	CM	CM	CM	CM	CM	CM
Czech Social Democratic Party in Exile	MP	MP	MP	MP	MP	MP	MP	CM	CM	CM
Danish Social Democratic Party	MP	MP	MP	MP	MP	MP	MP	MP	MP	MP
Dutch Party of Labour	MP	MP	MP	MP	MP	MP	MP	MP	MP	MP
Esthonian Social Democratic Party in Exile	MP	MP	MP	CM	CM	CM	CM	CM	CM	MP
Finnish Social Democratic Party	MP	MP	MP	MP	MP	MP	MP	MP	MP	MP
French Socialist Party	MP	MP	MP	MP	MP	MP	MP	MP	MP	MP
German Social Democratic Party	MP	MP	MP	MP	MP	MP	MP	MP	MP	MP
Greek Socialist League[2]	MP	MP	MP	CM	CM	CM	CM	CM	CM	
Hungarian Socialist Party in Exile	MP	MP	MP	CM	CM	CM	CM	CM	CM	CM
Icelandic Social Democratic Party	MP	MP	MP	MP	MP	MP	MP	MP	MP	MP
All-India Praja Socialist Party	MP	MP	MP	CM	CM	CM	CM	CM	CM	CM
Irish Labour Party	MP	MP	MP	MP	MP	MP	MP	MP	MP	MP
Israel Labour Party[3]	MP	MP	MP	MP	MP	MP	MP	MP	MP	MP
International Jewish Labor Bund[4]	MP	MP	MP	MP	MP	MP	MP	MP	MP	MP
World Union of Socialist Zionists[5]	MP	MP	MP	MP	MP	MP	MP	MP	MP	MP
Italian Socialist Party[6]	MP	MP	MP	MP	MP	MP	MP	MP	MP	MP
People's National Party of Jamaica										MP
Japan Social Democratic Party	MP	MP	MP	MP	MP	MP	MP	MP	MP	MP
Japan Socialist Party										MP
United Socialist Party of Korea									OM	OM

(Continued)

Table 7.2 (Continued)

	1951	1952	1953	1955	1957	1959	1961	1963	1966	1969
Latvian Social Democratic Party in Exile				CM	CM	CM	CM	CM	CM	CM
Lithuanian Social Democratic Party in Exile				CM	CM	CM	CM	CM	CM	CM
Luxembourg Socialist Labour Party	MP	MP	MP	MP	MP	MP	MP	MP	MP	MP
Social Democratic Party of Madagascar									CM	MP
Democratic Action Party of Malaysia									CM	MP
Malayan Labour Party			CM	CM	CM	CM	CM	CM	CM	
Malta Labour Party				MP	MP	MP	MP	MP	CM	MP
Mauritius Social Democratic Party									CM	
New Zealand Labour Party		MP	MP	MP	MP	MP	MP	MP	MP	MP
Norwegian Labour Party	MP	MP	MP	MP	MP	MP	MP	MP	OM	OM
Revolutionary Febrerista Party of Paraguay									OM	OM
Latin American Revolutionary Popular Alliance APRA of Peru									OM	OM
Polish Socialist Party in Exile	MP	MP	MP	CM	CM	CM	CM	CM	CM	CM
Romanian Social Democratic Party in Exile	MP	MP	MP	CM	CM	CM	CM	CM	CM	CM
Saar Social Democratic Party[7]		MP	MP	CM						
San Marino Independent Social Democratic Party							CM	CM	CM	OM
People's Action Party of Singapore				MP	MP	MP	MP	MP	MP	MP
Spanish Socialist Labour Party in Exile	MP	MP	MP	MP	MP	MP	MP	MP	MP	MP
Social Democratic Party of Suedtirol	MP	MP	MP	MP	MP	MP	MP	MP	MP	MP
Swedish Social Democratic Labour Party	MP	MP	MP	MP	MP	MP	MP	MP	MP	MP
Swiss Social Democratic Party	MP	MP	MP	MP	MP	MP	MP	MP	MP	MP
Trieste Socialist Party	MP	MP	MP	CM	CM					
United States Socialist Party	MP	MP	MP	CM	CM	MP	MP	MP	MP	MP
United States Social Democratic Federation	MP	MP	MP	MP	MP	MP				
Uruguay Socialist Party	MP	MP	MP							
Democratic Action Party of Venezuela				CM	CM	CM	CM	CM	OM	OM[8]
Vietnam Socialist Party						MP				
Yugoslav Socialist Party in Exile	MP	MP	MP	CM	CM	CM	CM	CM	CM	CM

KEY:

MP: Member Party
CM: Consultative Member
OM: Observer Member
*: Party banned

NOTES:
[1] Until 1961 member was Co-operative Commonwealth Federation which then merged into the New Democratic Party of Canada
[2] Member was Greek Socialist Party until 1953
[3] Member was Mapai until January 1968, when Mapai, Ahdut Haavoda and Rafi merged to form the Israel Labour Party
[4] International Jewish Bund until 1953
[5] Formerly Zionist Socialist Parties
[6] Member was Social Democratic Party until 1967, when unification with Socialist Party took place
[7] Saar became part of the Federal Republic of Germany on January 1, 1957, and Party merged with German Social Democratic Party
[8] Membership in Venezuela currently suspended

Source: David F. Roth, "International Parties in an Emerging World Order: Toward a Strategy for Realization" (Mimeo., 1971).

The main objectives of the Socialist International include elimination of the veto power of the U.N. Security Council, expansion of United Nations authority, disarmament, creation of an international peace corps, and support for European unification efforts. Being sensitive to the needs of its member parties in the Third World, the International has supported aid to developing countries, expressed its strong approval for the objectives of the United Nations Conference on Trade and Development (UNCTAD), and has opposed the Apartheid policies of South Africa and the African goals of Portugal.

The Christian Democrats

The transnational structures of the Christian Democratic parties are of much more recent origin than those of the Socialist International. Although some liaison between the Christian Democratic parties existed prior to World War II, transnational collaboration came into full bloom in the late 1940s, when strong Christian Democratic parties emerged in Italy, Germany, and France. The first conference of these parties was held in Belgium in 1947. In June 1961 the Christian Democratic World Union was founded which is comprised of the European Christian Democratic Union, the Christian Democratic Organization of America, the Christian Democratic Union of Central Europe, and the International Union of Young Christian Democrats. As can be seen from this membership distribution, Christian Democratic parties are found mainly in Europe and Latin America. The parties in Central Europe are essentially exile organizations. The headquarters of the Christian Democratic Union of Central Europe is, in fact, in New York and its European branch in Rome. Efforts have been made to establish links with parties in other areas of the world, but they have met with little success. One problem is that it is difficult to find the kind of common world-wide ideology from which the Socialist parties benefit. The only party in Asia which joined the Christian Democratic World Union is the Indonesian Catholic Party which affiliated itself in 1967. The Pakindo (Indonesian Protestant Party) has been considering following the same course.[6] It should be pointed out that in Europe the Christian Democrats have played down the emphasis on ideology during the last 10 to 15 years and have successfully become a party of wide interest aggregation.

The structure of the Christian Democratic World Union consists of a World Conference and a World Committee meeting at least twice a year on which all constituent organizations are represented. One associated organization has assumed a measure of importance and should be mentioned. This is the permanent Conference of Presidents and General Secretaries of European Christian Democratic parties which meets at irregular intervals to discuss urgent common problems and which has close links to the Commission of the European Communities.

The Christian Democratic World Union pursues certain common objectives such as the attainment of social justice (defined as just distribution of wealth), and opposition to communism. In addition, the European Christian Democrats have declared themselves as the main champions of European unification and are strong supporters of the Atlantic alliance. The Latin American parties are concerned with reducing Latin America's dependence on the United States and support the elimination of social class differences and a measure of governmental planning. Because of the divergence of some of the goals of the European and Latin American branches of the Christian Democratic World Union, one can hardly expect the emergence of strong common policies. Rather, the World Union has developed primarily into an organization for the exchange of information.

The Liberal Parties

The Liberal parties founded a transnational structure in April 1947 which is called the World Liberal Union, or Liberal International. Despite the intention of this umbrella group, the Liberal parties have never been able to build up a world-wide membership. Outside of Europe the World Liberal Union has member parties only in Canada, Australia, New Zealand, and Israel. There are various exile organizations from Eastern Europe, but their influence today is insignificant. There is no member party in either Iceland or Ireland; and the French Radical Party, formerly oriented toward the objectives of the World Liberal Union, has drifted away. In addition to actual parties the World Liberal Union has also accepted special liberal groups. One example of such a group is found in India.

There are several associated organizations of which the most important is the World Federation of Liberal and Radical Youth. This federation is dominated by Britain and Scandinavia and also has a very left-wing membership from Germany and the Netherlands. The major policy-making organ of the World Liberal Union is the annual Congress. In addition, an Executive Committee meets three times a year, a Secretariat is found in London, and specialized conferences are held at different times. Each year at least one session of the School of Freedom is held in which young liberals from different countries participate in the study of liberal philosophies.

The main aim of the World Liberal Union is to promote liberal ideals and ideas, and to strengthen throughout the nations of the world the belief that liberalism is the only political philosophy capable of defeating the tyranny of totalitarianism in whatever guise it may appear. Specifically, the Union supports greater European unification and United Nations authority. There is also a right-wing, anti-clerical brand of liberalism and some liberal parties, such as the Free Democratic Party in Germany, are split between a more middle of the road faction and one which is oriented basically toward a right-wing philosophy. It should also be noted that the World Federation of Liberal and Radical Youth is opposed to the American position in Viet Nam and strongly supports all anti-colonial initiatives. While the Liberal International has little appeal outside Europe, the Liberal Youth Organization has been able to expand its membership into Latin America, though only to a small degree.[7]

The Communist Parties

Although the various national Communist parties ideally should operate under a central direction, an increasing lack of cohesion has become apparent. Nevertheless, the transnational ties between the Communist parties remains perhaps closer than those of the other party groupings.

Although the Communist Party movements date back to 1864, the relationship amongst Marxist parties assumed greater importance and required redefinition when the Communist Party in the Soviet Union was elevated to power and actually emerged as a governmental organization. The Comintern, founded by Lenin in 1919, became the basic tool to coordinate the strategy and direction of the world revolutionary movement in which the foreign Communist parties in Europe were to play a definite role. Under Bolshevik sponsorship, radical or left-wing factions of the Socialist Democratic parties splintered off to form separate Communist parties which affiliated with the new Third International. At the Second Congress of the Comintern in 1920 statutes were drawn up defining the Communist International as a Universal Communist Party of which the parties operating in each country would form individual sections.[8]

Disagreements between Bolshevik leaders and foreign Communist parties, particularly the German, were frequent. Revolutionary doctrine and strategy, and the role of Soviet diplomacy, were discussed in the World Congress and in the meetings of its executive committee. The participation of foreign Communist parties was by no means a mere formality, and the Soviet state, which was conceived primarily as an instrument of the world revolution, frequently had to adjust its foreign policy to the views of these other parties, over which it did not exercise full control.[9] However, this situation changed in 1928 and until 1953 foreign Communist parties, even after they had assumed power in their own countries, played little part in the formulation of Soviet foreign policy. On the contrary, they became completely subservient to it as pliable and expendable instruments, and as Moscow changed its policy, the foreign Communist parties followed suit even if the new policies were diametrically opposed to the current line.

The dissolution of the Comintern in 1943 did not immediately alter the relationship between Moscow and foreign parties materially. However, in due time the leaders of the satellite countries began to betray signs of uneasiness and independence since they had to consider the interests of their own countries and peoples. To regain some measure of centralized control, Stalin organized the Cominform, ostensibly as an organ of consultation based on the equality and independence of its members, but in reality to root out all tendencies toward independence. It should be noted that Cominform did not operate world-wide, but only covered Eastern Europe and the two largest Communist parties in the West, the Italian and the French.

Significant changes in the relationship between the Communist parties world-wide and the Soviet party appeared in November 1957 during the World Conference of Communist Parties. The Soviet Union, split and divided at home, with its prestige tarnished and its power reduced, had difficulty in preserving its authority over the International Communist movement. The Soviet Union was challenged by China which attempted to introduce China's interests as a prime factor in the International Communist movement. During the early 1960s, the international Communist parties were slowly transformed into a movement grouped around two opposite poles, Moscow and Peking. Leaders in the movement to attain greater independence from Moscow were the Yugoslavian, Albanian, and Romanian Communists. Among the parties outside Eastern Europe the Italian Communists showed increasing manifestations of attempting to go their own way. The invasion of Czechoslovakia in 1968 produced serious repercussions among the Communist parties of the world. Even the French Communist Party, traditionally a docile follower of the zigs and zags of Soviet foreign policy, had to manifest at least its temporary displeasure with the Soviet actions. Even though the Soviet leaders convened repeated world conferences, which served as the major links between the parties and which the Soviet government hoped to use for exerting continuing control over the world-wide Communist Party system, they did not succeed in achieving the cohesion they desired. [10]

Despite the fact that full central direction remains elusive, the global Communist Party apparatus continues to be impressive. Communist parties rule in 14 countries and constitute an emerging and often significant opposition in 35 others. Their membership of some 45 million people is distributed in Europe, Asia, and Latin America. The largest Communist Party is in China, obviously a "governmental" organization, to which some 17 million people belong. The second largest membership is in the Soviet Union whose Communist Party has 13 million people.

The major objectives of the Communist Party movement are to obtain governmental control or participation in the countries in which they function, to reduce what they call the "imperialistic" influence of the United States on a world-wide basis, and to promote within the limits imposed upon them by domestic constraints the foreign policy objectives of the Soviet Union and/or Communist China. In Europe, the objectives of the Communist parties are the dismantlement of NATO, reduction of American influence, and strong opposition to the unification of Europe.

The Europa Partei

The most recent and least important transnational party grouping is the Europa Partei which needs to be examined briefly because of its possible potential for the future. The central direction of the Party is vested in the European Federalist International located in Vienna and founded by Otto Molden in 1959. Several other attempts have been made prior to 1959 and since 1959 to create a truly European party organization. They include the Socialist European Party of Civil Servants of the EEC, the Europa Partei of G. Somer (a lawyer and civil servant in the EEC), two Italian initiatives for a European Federalist Party, and the National European Party proposed by J. Thierart, a Belgain. However, none of these attempts has gone beyond the stage of discussion; only the European Federalist International has established a concrete structure and its national party organizations have fielded candidates for elections.

The first national party organization under the European Federalist International was created in Austria in 1960. Since then, party organizations have been established in Germany, the Netherlands, and Switzerland. In addition, action committees were established in Sweden and France and groups promoting a federal Europe under the Federal International have been formed in Norway and Iceland.

The objectives of the Federalist Union and its parties are a supranational federal state in Europe, principles of fair play in European politics, equal partnership with the United States but no American soldiers in Europe, self-rule for European municipalities, the ethnical independence of European regions, and opposition to Communist policies. These principles have been expanded in a so-called "European Basic Program," the Magna Carta of the Federal International. The individual parties have published their own programs following the principles outlined by the International, which appears to apply central direction in a very relaxed manner.

It should be noted that several national party organizations have participated in elections. The Austrian Party took part in the election for the National Council and gained 21,000 votes in 1962. The next year the Party presented a candidate for the presidential elections and won nearly 4 percent of all Austrian votes (176,000). In Germany the Party participated in 1967 in the elections for a state parliament but could only obtain 0.1 percent of the votes. It did somewhat better in the elections for community councils in Lower Saxony (0.8 percent). A major effort was made during the 1969 elections for the West German Federal Parliament but the German Europa Partei was only able to obtain slightly less than 0.5 percent of the votes cast.[11] Nevertheless, it continues to operate and seeks to participate in the 1973 federal elections in the Federal Republic of Germany.

Initiatives Within the European Community System

The best example of transnational activities by political parties can be seen in Europe. In three major parliamentary bodies, members of various national parties deliberate together, giving them opportunities to engage in various transnational activities. The oldest body is the Consultative Assembly of the Council of Europe which since 1949 has brought together 147 representatives from 18 Member States. In 1954 the Assembly of the Western European Union was formed with 89 representatives from the United Kingdom, France, Germany, Italy, and the Benelux countries. Finally, the European Parliament, successor of the former Common Assembly of the European Coal and Steel Community, meets regularly in Strasbourg and consists of 142 representatives from the six Common Market countries. The number of delegates will be increased to about 200 after the United Kingdom, Ireland, Denmark, and Norway have joined the Common Market. The members of the European Parliament are not seated in accordance with their nationalities, but according to their party affiliations. In keeping with this arrangement the Christian

Democrats of all EEC member countries have their own party organization and caucus, and similar organizational links are in effect
among the Social Democrats and Liberals. Only the French Gaullists
(the UDR, formerly UNR) do not belong to any transnational group
and there are a few Independents not affiliated with a major party
grouping. The recently elected Italian Communists are too few to
form a grouping of their own and have not joined a transnational
group. Table 7.3 provides information on the strength of the various
party groupings in the European Parliament from 1958 to 1970. This
table shows a moderate loss on the part of the Christian Democrats
and a slight increase of the French UDR. The remainder of the
groupings has remained stable while the Independents have suddenly
gained in number during the 1969-70 period.

David Roth has elaborated a party cohesion index average in
the European Parliament for the periods 1958-63 and 1963-66. These
figures can be found in Table 7.4. The cohesion index is calculated
from the percentage deviation of party groups from unanimity in
roll call votes. The higher the percentage of deviation, the weaker
the cohesion. From these figures one may observe that the relative
cohesion is increasing although that of the Christian Democrats and
especially the Liberals has been weakening. Clearly the Socialists
are the most cohesive party grouping and the Liberals the least
cohesive.[12]

In addition to transnational interaction in the European Parliament, the three major European parties meet frequently on a Common
Market-wide basis to exchange views and agree on basic programs
with respect to European problems. These programs generally
express support for political integration and sometimes for the
direct election of the European Parliament. Recent examples of
these transnational party meetings are the meeting in September
1971, of the Christian Democratic group in Catania, Italy, which
expressed itself in favor of strengthening of the powers of the
European institutions; and the meeting during the same month of the
Socialist group of the European Parliament, also in Italy, calling for
a joint attitude among the six Common Market countries with respect
to the monetary crisis.[13] The Gaullist Group in the European Parliament also met in the fall of 1971 but in keeping with the basic opposition of the Gaullist philosophy toward a federal Europe opposed
strengthening the powers of the European Parliament.[14]

Finally, it should be pointed out that sometimes national party
meetings also express themselves with respect to European Community affairs. For example, the Parliamentary Party of the CDU/CSU

TABLE 7.3

Strength of Party Groupings and in the European Parliament, 1958-70

	March 1958	June 1962	1964-65	1965-66	1966-67	1967-68	1968-69	1969-70
Christian Democrats	67	64	62	62	62	63	59	53
Socialists	38	33	36	35	35	34	30	36
Liberals	35[a]	43[a]	25	26	26	26	24	25
UDR (France)	-	-	15	15	15	15	18	18
Independents	2	-	-	-	-	-	1	10
Communists								7

[a]Includes France UNR

Sources: Adopted from Guy van Oudenhove, The Political Parties in the European Parliament (Leyden: A. W. Sijthoff, 1965), p. 259 and data from the European Community Information Service in Washington.

TABLE 7.4

Party Cohesion in the European Parliament, 1958-66

	Percent Seats in European Parliament	Cohesion Index Average (Deviation from unanimity in roll call votes)	
		1958-63	1963-66
Christian Democrats	43.7	15.2	14.9
Socialists	24.7	1.7	2.0
Liberals	18.3	13.7	17.6
UNR-UDT (UDE)	10.6	—	4.5
Average of the Supranational Groups	—	10.2	9.7

Source: Adopted from David F. Roth, "International Political Parties in an Emerging World Order: Towards a Strategy for Realization (Mimeo., 1971).

has specifically demanded the coordination of economic and fiscal policies and the harmonization of the appropriate laws in order to promote transnational business collaboration.[15] Despite these repeated expressions for European unification, the effective responses of the national governments have been less than favorable. This question will be considered next, in the discussion of the effects of transnational initiatives by political parties on national governments and IGOs.

The Effects on National Governments and IGOs

From a theoretical point of view one could be led easily to the assumption that transnational activities of political parties are likely to have a significant impact on the decisions of national governments. Aggregating the interests of economic and social groupings, reflecting selected elite and public opinions, and transmitting specific demands to government decision-makers, political parties could be judged as being highly capable of initiating and implementing social and political transition. On the level of international organization, parties could become an instrument for strengthening IGOs by urging the transfer of jurisdictions and roles to them. Parties could also serve as educational transmission belts to inform national populations of the reforms necessary to strengthen party inputs into IGOs.

However, when one seeks concrete evidence of such actions by political parties and sympathetic responses by national governments, appropriate data on a world-wide basis are very scarce. Most information available regarding the effects or noneffects of party actions on governmental decision-makers can be found in the West European region. For example, a major objective of the party groupings of the Christian Democrats, the Social Democrats, and the Liberals has been the election of the European Parliament by direct universal suffrage.[16] It was hoped that this would lead to strengthening the powers of Parliament, bring about a higher degree of "democratization" of the EEC, and thereby contribute to progress in the process of political integration. However, while over the last ten years the members of the three groupings have been able to induce their colleagues in the national parties and parliaments to adopt various declarations and resolutions favorable to the above objective, no positive actions have been taken by the governments of the Six nor by their parliaments to realize this objective.[17] While in this instance the effectiveness of transnational party groupings to advance the transformation of the European Community system has been very low, changing political conditions in the Common Market may permit a more favorable result in the future.

In assessing the chances for transformation, one must always keep in mind that rhetoric alone is insufficient to produce results even if the political conditions were to improve. Much depends on the prestige of the parliamentarians occupying a seat in the European Parliament and on the responses they can elicit from political elites in various parts of the national institutions. Moreover, studies made on the role that European questions have actually played in elections (the Netherlands elections in 1967 and the West German elections in 1965) suggest that these questions aroused little interest and that their impact on voter motivation was minimal.[18] Therefore, there is not much incentive for elected politicians to bring about changes in the status quo of the Community system, changes whose full consequences for their constituency and for their own position of power cannot be clearly foreseen except that they are likely to be far-reaching.

An example illustrating the interlacement of transnational and national party activities and their effect on an IGO has been the attempt by the Italian and French Communist parties to obtain representation in the European Parliament. Although for many years both parties had spurned any participation in the European Community institutions because they looked upon the Common Market as a manifestation of monopolistic capitalism, the Italian Communist Party considered the time to be ripe in the Spring of 1966 to press its demand for representation in the European Parliament. Some Italian Christian Democrats and Liberals had long ago ceased to be members of their national parliament—some had died in the meantime—yet the Italian Parliament had time and again failed to renew its delegation to the European Parliament. As a consequence the Socialist groups, counting only two Italian members, were underrepresented while the Christian Democrats and Liberals were overrepresented in the European Parliament, a situation which had obvious political disadvantages for the Socialists. Nevertheless, although the Italian Parliament tried to renew its delegation in May of 1966, it failed again and a decision was put off sine die.[19] The Italian Communists were extremely angry and disappointed with this new failure to obtain representation, particularly since Giuseppe Sarragat, at that time President of the Republic, had expressed himself during a news conference in November 1964—he was then Foreign Minister—in favor of Communist representation. Finally, after the elections of 1968 when the Italian Parliament elected new delegates to the European Parliament, the hopes of the Italian Communists were fulfilled and seven members of the Communist Party entered the European Parliament.[20]

The French Communist Party did not fare as well. After the parliamentary election in France in the spring of 1967, the French

Communists put forward four candidates for election to the European Parliament. However, the Communists' candidates were not successful in obtaining the majority of votes necessary for election, which in fact would have required not only the support of the Communist and Socialist members of the Assembly, but also votes from the Christian Democrats and even from some Gaullists.[21]

It should be pointed out that the quest for representation was not motivated by the desire to strengthen the institutions of the Common Market. On the contrary, the long-range purpose of having representatives in the European Parliament was to stop any progress on European unification. So far the seven Communist delegates have presented a low profile during parliamentary deliberations. While they call for the "democratization" of the Community institutions and thereby appeal to those Europeans who see in the reinforcement of the European Parliament a step toward political integration, the Communists mean something else by this term. For them it denotes strengthening the autonomy of the Member States and their legislatures and diminishing the powers of the EEC organs.[22]

While the transnational activities of the Italian and French Communist parties with respect to the Common Market have been crowned by partial success, whose consequences however may not be very significant because of the European Parliament's limited powers, in Latin America such activities by the Communist Party of Cuba seems to have had a more profound effect in Chile and Bolivia. But since, in contrast to the nongovernmental Italian and French Communist parties, their counterparts in Communist dictatorships such as Cuba are part of the governmental apparatus, their activities fall outside the scope of our discussion.

Consequences for the International System

In terms of our criteria of collaboration and conflict in the international system, one could conjecture that the increasing transnational interaction of political parties, especially in Europe, could produce growing trust, cooperation, and new rules for nonviolent conflict management. However, while transnational party interaction has undoubtedly increased, it relates mainly to the harmonization of programs and much less to the coordination of actions on the national level. Therefore, it is doubtful that this interaction has produced a significantly higher level of governmental collaboration within the European Community. At the same time, the transnational activities of the Italian and French Communists demonstrate that collaboration

with other parties on the European level may be more apparent than
real. In fact, one could argue that the purposes of the Communist
parties are rather to bring about a higher degree of conflict inasmuch
as their aims as well as those of other Communist parties in the EEC
are the prevention of unification of Western Europe rather than its
strengthening.

This somewhat pessimistic view, however, should not lead one
to disregard the potential that may flow from the increasing transnational network which the Christian Democrats, the Socialists, and
Liberal parties are creating through their transnational interaction.
It is quite conceivable that these interactions might produce positions
on important issues which would go beyond articulation of demands
and rhetoric. As a consequence, these parties may emerge as forces
which might not only suggest solutions for serious international problems, including those besetting the Third World, but also may play
an active role in implementing these solutions.

NATIONAL LIBERATION MOVEMENTS

The main objective of national liberation movements is the
seizure of governmental power in a particular country. Liberation
movements may be either essentially intranational or they may be
essentially transnational when these movements originate outside
the target countries. The distinction between these two types of
liberation movements is often blurred inasmuch as intranational
liberation movements at times depend on transnational initiatives
toward third countries whose governments are sympathetic to the
movement. On the other hand, transnational liberation movements
may often depend on a substantial core of intranational support.
Major examples of intranational liberation movements are the Viet
Cong in South Viet Nam, the successful seizure of power by the
Communists in China—some observers may argue to the contrary
in this respect—and the anti-colonial liberation movement at the
Gold Coast under Kwame Nkrumah which resulted in an independent
Ghana.[23] Major examples of transnational liberation movements
are the efforts of the Popular Front for the Liberation of Palestine
(PFLP), and Che Guevarra's efforts in Bolivia.

The nongovernmental nature of the transnational movements
which are of main interest to this study is not always clear. In some
cases, established governments are the stimulators of these movements such as is the case of the Cuban government for the activities
of Guevarra supporters in Bolivia. In addition, it seems that some

of the liberation movements consider themselves as either governments
in exile or pregovernmental organizations. However, the fact that
a movement may establish a government in exile does not really obviate the nongovernmental nature of its operations since these governments rarely obtain diplomatic recognition by more than one or two
sympathetic states. J. Bowyer Bell characterizes some of these
liberation movements as covert governments or counterstates.[24]
Nevertheless, this cannot be taken to mean that their essential nongovernmental nature has been eliminated.

Major liberation movements may be found in all parts of the
world, including Europe, inasmuch as the IRA activities in the United
Kingdom appear to be a perfect example of transnational liberation
efforts. The largest number of liberation movements can be detected
in Africa which, in view of the colonial background of this continent,
is not surprising. The most important targets in Africa remain
Rhodesia, Southwest Africa, and the Portuguese colonies. The major
movements are the South African National Congress (ANC); the Zimbabwe African People's Union (ZAPU); the Zimbabwe African National
Union (ZANU); the Pan-African Congress (PAC); the Comité Revolucionário de Mocambique (Coremo); and Govérno Revolucionário de
Angola no Exilio (GRAE). Some of the liberation movements operating
against the Portuguese have founded an alliance by creating the Congress of National Organizations in the Portuguese Colonies (CONCP)
and have set up a secretariat, publicity offices, and a program of
meetings and conferences. In turn, CONCP has negotiated military
cooperation pacts with ANC and ZAPU. On the other hand, ZANU,
PAC, Coremo, and GRAE have formed a coalition of their own.[25]

In Latin America, the Havana based Latin American Solidarity
Organization (OLAS) attempts to tie together the various liberation
movements which are based on Guevarran, Maoist, Trotskyite, and
Castroite dogmas. However, the creation of OLAS does not mean
that the liberation movements in Latin America are operating in a
coordinated fashion. J. Bowyer Bell points out that Latin America
is less coherently organized than Africa where the various liberation
movements sign formal alliances and the special liberation committee
of the OAU provides a coordinating framework.[26] Nevertheless, the
concept of one Latin America is important to Latin Americans because of their common heritage while the concept of one Africa still
suffers from the strong national orientations of the new African
nations.

In the Arab World, the PFLP has several competitors in terms
of seeking to sweep out the Israelis and bring Palestine back under

an Arab government. An Arab national movement has been created which leans toward Marxist-Leninist doctrine and which seeks to bring together the various Palestine liberation movements. Like the Ba'th parties, the Arab national movement urges freedom, unity, and socialism. But success has come to it so far only in Southern Yemen.

The major transnational initiatives applied by all liberation movements are to alienate the population from the present governments, emphasize their commitment to world revolution, and attempt to manipulate whatever indigenous unrest and revolutionary spirit exists in the target countries. Partisans are organized into guerilla fighters who use sabotage and terror to undermine the control of the government. At the same time, propaganda efforts are made to destroy the legitimacy of the present government and to establish whenever possible a rival regime through the creation of "parallel hierarchies." Loyalties to the government and at times to the state are often challenged through transnational appeals. Any other conceivable method of informal penetration of the governmental and societal fabric is attempted while at the same time the liberation movement will seek recognition, and perhaps respectability through external support and backing.[27]

The effects on target governments depend to a large degree on the military power they possess and their political and economic stability. Israel's superior counter insurgency organization has been an effective barrier to the efforts of the Arab liberation movements. Nevertheless, the PLFP and perhaps other organizations with similar goals succeeded in hijacking and damaging Israeli planes and those of other Western countries and Israel has not been able to prevent various acts of sabotage. This has put Israel and other Western nations affected by Arab sabotage in the unenviable position of having to negotiate with the Arab liberation leadership. On the other hand, weak and politically unstable Bolivia while having great difficulties in coping with the liberation efforts of Che Guevarra eventually succeeded in suppressing them. The Portuguese colonies in Africa have been able so far to resist African liberation movements through the extensive use of military power, but the last word may not have been written about success and failure of the Portuguese.

The effects on host countries also depend on their economic and political stability. For example, King Hussein of Jordan, troubled by economic and political problems, has been forced to tolerate the provocative and often turbulent presence of the PFLP supporters. Lebanon had to risk civil war when it attempted to control the Fedayen. Syria responded to the demands of the liberation movement supporters

by creating their own variety of revolutionaries. Tanzania and
Zambia have attempted to regulate carefully the activities and contacts of liberation movements operating from their country against
targets in South and Portuguese Africa.

Of course, in some cases, host governments do not suffer at
all from national liberation movements operating on their soil. On
the contrary, governments of countries such as Cuba are the main
supporters and manipulators of liberation movements and thereby
provide them with a degree of legitimacy in the eyes of people in
the target countries.

The consequences of national liberation movements for the
international system so far have been disruptive and have increased
the level of conflict existing in several regions of the world. While
attempts have been made to consider the national liberation movements as aspects of a world-wide revolution, the ties between the
national liberation efforts have been mainly emotional rather than
organizational.[28] Thus even from the point of view of fundamental
change of the international system through a global revolution, which
might have an integrative effect on the world as a whole, no real
impact can be detected at present.

RADICAL STUDENT MOVEMENTS

Although some of the radical students leading student movements
in Western Europe, North America, and Japan have all shown a commitment to revolution and anarchism, it is not clear that these movements engage purposely in transnational initiatives and seek to promote transnational objectives in a coordinated fashion. We have witnessed Daniel Cohn-Bendit mounting the ramparts in Berlin, Frankfurt,
and Paris. We have seen former Berkeley students like Marshall
Bloom among the hard-core radical leadership in the London School
of Economics at Oxford. But beyond these manifestations of common
leadership and apparent high degree of parallelism in objectives and
methods in various countries where students have challenged the traditional order, there is little evidence that these movements are controlled or instigated by a central headquarters. While the East
German Communists may have from time to time provided some
monetary support to the radicals in West Berlin and while occasional
assertions have been made that the Chinese Communists were putting
funds into radical student movements, no proof for the existence of
a global conspiratorial scheme has been offered[29] despite voices in
the United States to the contrary.[30]

The initial chief objective of student movements in Western Europe and Japan has been a change in the archaic structure of the universities, while in the United States the main demand was a higher degree of participation in the decision-making process of the university. Beyond that, one finds in all countries a revulsion against what is called the "materialistic consumer society," considerable alienation from established authority, and a frequently voiced desire to remake society by either revolution or otherwise in order to improve the "quality of life." It should be noted that the Soviet system of government and its economy has been as much a target of attack as the Western capitalistic systems. Some student governments feel that the cultural revolution in China may show the way to a better life for the peoples of the world.

While the Western industrially advanced countries have been the main arenas of the radical student movements, there have been occasional outbreaks of student unrest also beyond the Iron Curtain, although this was confined mainly to countries such as in Czechoslovakia where some political and social ferment already had occurred. Some very occasional reports from the Soviet Union about student unrest have also been received. On the other hand, the developing countries have witnessed very little student unrest. As Joseph A. Califano reports, one Israeli student told him he did not have time for such nonsense and had to build a nation and fight a war. According to Califano, young Kenyans and Tanzanians also reject the student revolution as such and are primarily concerned with obtaining an education and building their own countries.[31] Clearly nationalism is very much alive in Israel and the Third World countries of Africa and Asia while among the youth in Western Europe and Japan nationalism is often a dying proposition.

There is no doubt that the radical student movements had definite effects on the governments of the countries in which they were operating. The university structures in Western Europe have undergone a remarkable change through the enactment of new laws in France, Germany, and other Western European states. In fact, one could argue that the legislators in these countries often overreacted to the demands of the students and that the reforms instituted have created a new kind of instability in the operation of universities. In the United States and Canada the universities have also responded favorably to the requests of the students for greater participation in the decision-making process. However, the state legislators in the United States and Congress often looked upon these favorable responses of university administrations with displeasure and a certain amount of backlash to the radical student activities has emerged.

As far as the more political claims of the student movements
are concerned, Western governments in general have attempted to
accommodate the desire expressed by the student movements for
greater participation in the political process. The demands for a
higher quality of life including reduction of pollution and a greater
social consciousness on the part of the governments have been recognized almost everywhere in the industrialized world but how much
positive action toward these goals will be taken remains to be seen.

The consequences for the international system as a whole are
initially perhaps more disruptive than constructive, although the
strong expressions for peace to which all radical student movements
are committed could have favorable longrange implications for the
international system. With respect to regional subsystems, it is
interesting to note that in Western Europe the original fervor for
unification manifested for example by pulling out frontier stakes and
other symbols of the national separation has largely subsided. While
some measure of rhetoric continues to flow from the student movements
for European unity, political unification seems to be considered acceptable only if it were carried out through a high degree of democratization of central institutions and were accompanied by a move away
from the present capitalist system and civil service technocracy toward
a much higher level of social consciousness.[32]

TRANSNATIONAL ACTIVITIES OF CHURCHES

When one thinks of transnational activities undertaken by religious
denominations, it is the Roman Catholic Church which comes foremost
to one's mind. However, other churches also pursue transnational
initiatives mostly through more than 60 church-related NGOs such as
the Baptist World Alliance or the World Methodist Council. The
Roman Catholics have also formed a number of NGOs used for the
pursuit of transnational objectives.

The Roman Catholic Church has at its disposal both governmental
and nongovernmental means to influence governments and people of
the countries of the world. Possessing a small geographical territory
in Rome, called the State of the Vatican City, the Holy See is accorded
under international law a legal status similar to that of a state. As
a consequence, the Vatican operates a full-fledged diplomatic apparatus
and has diplomatic representatives accredited in many capitals of the
world. These representatives, called nuncios or internuncios, perform duties as officials of a sovereign state and are authorized to
conclude treaties such as concordats and other diplomatic duties.[33]

The nongovernmental structure of the Catholic Church consists of the hierarchy of bishops and missionaries which serves the more than 500 million Catholics residing within the borders of other nation-states all over the world. To reach these Catholics, the Holy See initiates various kinds of border-crossing transactions. These transactions may take the form of pastoral policies, educational activities, or missionary work. This provides access for the Catholic Church to politically sovereign territories, securing credence for the pursuit of Catholic religious work and preserving and strengthening the ties between local churches and the center in Rome. Overarching these nongovernmental transnational activities are the formal concordats concluded by many states with the Holy See. These concordats are designed to provide the best conditions possible for the protection of the church, for the extension of its influence, and for the provision of special privileges of the clergy.

The transnational social and political initiatives undertaken by the Catholic Church support a variety of objectives including social reform in Latin America, opposition to "secular faiths" including communism, the organization of Catholic action groups in France and Italy, and the foundation of youth organizations (for example the Jeunesse ouvrière chrétienne movement founded by Joseph Cardinal Cardjin in Belgium).[34] In support of these initiatives in particular countries the Holy See may mobilize resources from other parts of the Catholic system and deploy or at least offer them to local Catholic hierarchies. In other words, the power of the Catholic Church is such that it can provide full orchestration for its initiatives in various parts of the world by bringing to bear on it human and material resources at the disposal of its world-wide system.

The extensive capabilities available to the Catholic Church are lacking when it comes to the transnational activities of other religious denominations. In the first place, the number of people in the world espousing religions other than the Catholic Church is much smaller with the possible exception of the Buddhists. Secondly, these religious denominations do not have the governmental structure and resources which the Catholic Church possesses. Most of the transnational activities of other churches are carried out through NGOs, but these NGOs cannot muster even a small percentage of the resources of the Catholic Church. For example, the Baptist World Alliance has an annual income of only $156,000 (1968). While it has members on all contentents, totaling 26 million people, its power to mount effective transnational initiatives is quite weak. The World Methodist Council has only a staff of two paid individuals and therefore is in a similar weak condition as is its Baptist counterpart. These conditions prevail

in almost all other religious NGOs. An umbrella group of the various
NGOs is the World Council of Churches founded in 1948. Its purpose
is to facilitate common action between churches in the international
arena, promote the growth of ecumenical and missionary consciousness in members of all churches, and establish and maintain relations
with national and regional church councils. The membership of this
Council is made up of churches in 79 countries. The Holy See sends
official observers to the World Council of Churches, although it does
not officially belong to this organization. The Catholics recognize
the need for religious coalitions and alliances with other Christian
denominations, but progress toward such coalitions is slow.

An interesting international and transnational initiative pursuit
by the churches to influence the international system has been the
effort to pull the United States armed forces out of Viet Nam. Various
national church organizations in the United States, the National Council
of Churches, and the World Council of Churches brought increasing
pressure to bear on the United States government to attain this goal.
A number of resolutions were adopted in the United States and by the
World Council of Churches for this purpose. This project included
a corollary effort to strengthen the United Nations and bolster the
activities of the disarmament conference in Geneva.[35]

The effects on governments of the transnational initiatives
mounted by churches can be seen with greater clarity when they
involve Roman Catholic activities than those engaged in by the other
churches. Although "governmental" and "nongovernmental" initiatives
of the Catholics cannot be clearly separated, one can observe full
acceptance by some states such as Colombia, to complete rejection
as practiced by many of the Communist bloc countries.[36] Between
these extremes are several additional types of situations confronting
the totality of initiatives of the Roman Catholic Church. One important group of states, most of which are Catholic countries, limit the
Holy See's influence over internal church affairs by denying rights
of patronage. At the same time, these states agree to the general
protection of the Church and carry on full-fledged diplomatic relations
with the Vatican. Examples of this type of relationships are Argentina,
Peru, Spain, and Venezuela. The other group of nation-states in the
middle range between full acceptance and complete rejection of Catholic
initiatives are those which have established and institutionalized the
principle of separation of church and state, e.g. Brazil, Chile, France,
Mexico, Portugal, and the United States. Although the governments
of these countries accept no responsibility for protecting, preserving,
or promoting the Catholic faith, they do not deny the Church opportunities to conduct nongovernmental transactions across their boundaries.[37]

With respect to the efforts of various church groups to halt
the war in Viet Nam, the initial effects were less than satisfactory.
Only after other groups in the American society began to support this
objective, did the American government begin to respond favorably
to the demand for winding down the Viet Nam War.

In terms of collaboration and conflict affecting the international
system, most transnational church initiatives should be judged as
supportive of world-wide understanding and collaboration. The
efforts of the Catholic Church to reduce the wide gap existing between
the rich and the poor of Latin America through social reforms cannot
but have favorable consequences for the Latin American regional
subsystem. The attempts to bring about peace in Viet Nam staged by
American and international church groups also tend to promote greater
harmony in the international system, although the long-range consequence may be different if a significant shift in the power relationship in Southeast and South Asia should ensue. The efforts of the
Catholic Church in the Communist countries, while initially creating
conflicts within individual countries and perhaps among the Communist
subsystem, could culminate eventually in producing a more integrated
society. Of course, no final judgment can be made at the present
time.

FOUNDATIONS WITH INTERNATIONAL ACTIVITIES

The last category of organizations engaging in transnational
initiatives is the group of foundations that undertake activities outside
the countries in which they are headquartered. [38] According to the
Foundation Directory of 1967, about 21 percent (or 160 million) of
the grants from the 237 largest American foundations were for international activities, compared to 2 percent (or 9 million) of the grants
from 6,566 intermediate and small foundations. Moreover, the number of foundations which made international grants increased from 33
in 1963 to 152 in 1966. Some European foundations, especially the
Volkswagen Foundation, which approaches the organization and size
of the large American foundations also have begun to offer grants for
international activities. [39]

The two most important American foundations supporting international activities are the Ford Foundation and the Rockefeller Foundation. The Ford Foundation had assets of approximately $3.6 billion
in 1968 and the Rockefeller Foundation somewhat less than $1 billion.
One-fifth to one-quarter of the Ford Foundation budget has been spent
on international activities. This number is nearly half of that contributed by all other foundations combined, but only a very small

portion of governmental resources for such purposes as foreign aid
or cultural exchange.[40] Nevertheless, these two foundations have
sufficient resources to make a significant impact in the areas where
grants have been given. Most foundations making grants abroad
operate from their home headquarters although short-term study
missions are sent to areas of activities from time to time. Only
the Ford and Rockefeller Foundations have resident staffs abroad
to develop and supervise foreign programs.

The objectives of the foundations vary from time period to
time period. After World War I the Rockefeller Foundation was
interested in eradicating disease and working toward a world in
which political differences were irrelevant in the face of human
suffering. The Ford Foundation between 1951 and 1959 devoted
$500 million to development assistance. A high priority of the Ford
Foundation since World War II was the assurance of a lasting peace.
As a consequence, transnational initiatives were aimed at the miti-
gation of tensions which threaten world peace, the development among
peoples of the world of the understanding and conditions essential to
permanent peace, the improvement and strengthening of the United
Nations and its specialized agencies, and the improvement of the
structure and procedures by which the United States government and
private American groups could participate in world affairs.[41]

An area of special concern for the Ford Foundation was the
Third World.[42] Support was given to help newly independent countries
such as Ghana to improve their economic and political foundations.
Favoring liberalism, pluralism, and rational scientific and techno-
cratic reform the Ford Foundation made contributions to the Congress
Party in India and the Christian Democratic Party in Chile. It also
supported economic planning and agricultural policies even in countries
with military governments such as Pakistan and Brazil.[43]

In some cases the Ford Foundation allied itself with other
foundations and governmental agencies in order to support various
activities in developing countries. Some of these alliances have led
to a division of labor between the foundation and assistance agencies.
Finally, the foundation has encouraged with advice and money the
growth of various institutions in the Third World, including planning
ministries, science councils, development banks, and foundations in
foreign countries.[44]

The effects of foundation activities on foreign governments
depends to a large degree on the attitude of the governmental leaders.
While they may appreciate the funds and expertise offered by the

foundations, they may also be concerned with unwanted interference in the affairs of their countries. As a consequence, some of the governments want to control all grants made by private institutions and would like to supervise the activities that flow from these grants. Nevertheless, Ford Foundation advisors have played major roles in Asia and Africa in shaping governmental policies regarding population measures, agricultural problems, and education.

Although foundations will attempt to work with current governments, they may take the side of the victims of government repression in certain cases. For example, in São Paulo, where several distinguished social scientists were forcibly retired, the Ford Foundation helped to establish an independent center for continuing their research. Two other "retirees" were made consultants to the Foundation. In 1966, when the military regime in Argentina violently intervened at the University of Buenos Aires, physically assaulting professors and students, the Ford Foundation helped scores of Argentine scientists to resettle in other Latin American countries more respectful of academic freedom.[45]

In Western Europe the Ford Foundation has attempted to support political unification by providing grants to centers especially interested in the process of political integration. Despite these efforts, however, the organizations selected for this purpose have not been fully successful in achieving the objectives pursued by the Ford Foundation.

It is very difficult, if not impossible, to judge the consequences of foundation grants for the international system. In general one can say that the transnational initiatives of foundations are too sporadic and too insufficiently financed to make a lasting impact. The lagging transformation of the European Community system into a more unified political structure is a pertinent example. Clearly, other actors have more powerful resources at their disposal to checkmate foundation initiatives, particularly in controversial fields. One could speculate that only in cases where foundations have strong allies will they be able to produce significant consequences in the international system.

NOTES

1. Transnational parties of minor importance are the World Anti-Communist League, the Inter-American Association for Democracy and Freedom, and the International Peasant Union.

2. See Roy C. Macridis and Robert E. Ward, Modern Political

Systems: Europe (2nd ed., Englewood Cliffs, N.J.: Prentice-Hall, 1968, 2.), pp. 18-21; Gabriel A. Almond and James S. Coleman, The Politics of Developing Areas (Princeton, N.J.: Princeton University Press, 1960), pp. 38-45; and Otto Kirchheimer, "The Transformation of the West European Party Systems," in Joseph L. Palombara and Myron Weiner, Political Parties and Political Development (Princeton, N.J.: Princeton University Press, 1966), pp. 177-200.

3. Cf. Stanley Henig, ed., European Political Parties (New York: Praeger Publishers, 1970), p. 529.

4. Ibid., p. 530.

5. Ibid., p. 531.

6. Yearbook of International Organizations (13th edition, 1970-71), p. 66. See also Hennig, European Political Parties, pp. 522-33 and David F. Roth, "International Political Parties in an Emerging World Order: Toward a Strategy of Realization," (mimeo 1971,).

7. Yearbook of International Organizations (13th edition, 1970-71), p. 738.

8. Vernon V. Aspaturian, "The Soviet Union and International Communism," in Roy C. Macridis, ed., Foreign Policy in World Politics (3rd ed., Englewood Cliffs, N.J.: Prentice-Hall, Inc., 1967), pp. 216-245, especially p. 217.

9. Ibid., p. 217.

10. Cf. William E. Griffith, Communism in Europe (Cambridge, Mass.: M.I.T. Press 1964), passim.

11. For additional details see Gunter Mudrich, "A New Path: To a United Europe by Means of One Supra-National Party," Paper presented at the College of Europe, Bruges, Belgium (mimeo., May 6, 1969).

12. Roth, "International Political Parties," p. 22.

13. Agence Europe, September 9, 1971, and September 10, 1971.

14. Agence Europe, October 1, 1971.

15. Sueddeutsche Zeitung, June 20, 1969.

16. For documentation on this subject see Parliament Europeen, Pour l'election du Parlement europeen au suffrage universel direct, Septembre 1969.

17. In Germany the inter-party working group of the Bundestag created to promote direct election to the European Parliament was dissolved after eight months of activity, seemingly because the prospects for such election were not good. (Cf. Die Welt, November 6, 1971.)

18. J.K. DeVree, "Le thème européen dans les élections générales de 1967 au Pays-Bas" (Europa Institute of the University of Amsterdam) (Mimeo); and Alfred Jaeger, "Das Thema 'Europa' im Bundestagswahlkampf 1965" (Forschungsinstitut fuer Politische Wissenschaft and Europaeische Fragen and der Universitaet zu Koeln) (Mimeo).

19. Cf. "Communists in the Communities?," Common Market, xi, 6 (June 1966), pp. 111-13.

20. Werner Feld, "The French and Italian Communists and the Common Market: The Requests for Representation in the Community Institutions," Journal of Common Market Studies, VI, 3, 1968, 250-266, and European Community, February 1969, pp. 6-8.

21. Ibid.

22. Cf. editorial, Agence Europe Bulletin, November 24, 1971.

23. Cf. Eric R. Wolf, "Peasant Rebellion and Revolution," p. 48; John R. McLane, "Archaic Movements and Revolution in Southern Vietnam," p. 68; and C. L. R. James, "Colonialism and National Liberation in Africa: The Gold Coast Revolution," p. 102, all in Norman Miller and Roderick Aya, ed., National Liberation: Revolution in the Third World (New York: The Free Press, 1971).

24. J. Bowyer Bell, "Contemporary Revolutionary Organizations," International Organization, XXV, 3 (Summer 1971), 503.

25. Ibid., p. 507.

26. Ibid., p. 509.

27. For greater details see Andrew M. Scott, The Functioning of the International Political System (New York: The Macmillan Company, 1967), pp. 191-202.

28. Bell, "Contemporary Revolutionary Organizations," p. 515.

29. Joseph A. Califano, Jr., The Student Revolution: A Global Confrontation (New York: W. W. Norton & Company, 1970), p. 53.

30. Most Europeans and Japanese have rejected such claims (Ibid., p. 63).

31. Ibid., pp. 54-55.

32. Cf. the interesting book by Norbert Gansel, ed., Uberwindet den Kapitalismus oder Was wollen die Jungsozialisten? (Hamburg: Rowohlt, 1971), especially pp. 126-37. See also James Robert Huntley, "Student Unrest in Europe and America: Some Implications for Western Society," Res Publica, XII, 2, 1970, pp. 171-84.

33. For full details see Robert A. Graham, Vatican Diplomacy: A Study of Church and State on the International Plane (Princeton, N.J.: Princeton University Press, 1959), pp. 127-54.

34. For details see Ivan Vallier, "The Roman Catholic Church: A Transnational Actor," International Organization, XXV, 3 (Summer 1971), 479-502.

35. For details see James L. Adams, The Growing Church Lobby in Washington (Grand Rapids, Michigan: William B. Eerdmans Publishing Company, 1970), pp. 204-244.

36. Despite the rejection of Catholic initiatives, Catholics are permitted to carry on regular sacremental activities in many of the Communist countries and in countries with large pre-World War II Catholic populations such as Poland some accommodations are made toward the Catholic hierarchy. Cuba not only has accepted a Papal Nuncio, but has authorized an ambassador accredited to the Vatican.

37. See Vallier, "The Roman Catholic Church: A Transnational Actor," pp. 485-89.

38. The term "foundation" designates organizations that have broadly defined charitable purposes, substantial capital assets, and income derived from gifts, bequests, and capital investments. They are granted tax-exempt status by the Internal Revenue Code. For details see Irving Louis Horowitz and Ruth Leonora Horowitz, "Tax-Exempt Foundations: Their Effects on National Policy," Science, Vol. CLXVIII, April 10, 1970, pp. 220-28.

39. Of the 32 foundations with assets exceeding $1 million, 29 are American. For other details see Foundation Directory (New York: Russell Sage Foundation, 1967); Directory of European Foundations (Turin: Agnelli Foundation); and Philanthropic Foundations in the United States: A Brief Description (New York: Foundation Center, 1969).

40. Peter D. Bell, "The Ford Foundation as a Transnational Actor," International Organization, XXV, 3 (Summer 1971), 465-78.

41. Ibid., p. 468.

42. Cf. Horowitz and Horowitz, "Tax-Exempt Foundations," pp. 224-5.

43. Bell, "The Ford Foundations," p. 471.

44. Ibid., p. 474.

45. Ibid., p. 477.

8

In the introduction to this book (Chapter 1) a number of questions were raised concerning which some tentative answers must be furnished. How extensive are the capabilities of nongovernmental entities to influence world politics and how effectively are these capabilities employed? Does the emergence of these new forces necessitate a modification in the concept of the international system? What possible impact does the totality of nongovernmental forces have on the regional and global integration of polities and ultimately on the maintenance of international peace? And finally there is the question of whether or not the transnational pursuit of various interests by nongovernmental entities would give rise to world-wide pluralism which might strengthen the forces of functionalism and perhaps gradually undermine the sovereign powers of the nation-state.

INVOLVEMENT IN WORLD POLITICS
AND THE INTERNATIONAL SYSTEM

The data presented in this book are incontrovertible evidence of the tremendous growth in the number of nongovernmental entities with transnational designs, although not all categories of these entities have shared uniformly in this growth. The upward trend in the number of these entities, which began around the turn of the century, accelerated sharply during the last two decades and in conformance with this trend, the number of transnational initiatives mounted by nongovernmental organizations has also increased enormously. Although the economic, human, and organizational resources available to these entities for transnational initiatives vary widely, the data suggest a considerable increase of total resources when all

categories of nongovernmental units are taken together. Clearly,
MNE and other border-crossing business enterprises rank highest
on this score, but international labor, certain traditional NGOs, church
groups, and liberation movements have also enhanced their transnational capabilities since World War II. The successful exploitation
of these capabilities in terms of inducing the favorable allocation
of values by governmental and IGO actors which in turn would bring
about changes in the world-wide pattern of transnational interactions
depends also on the motives impelling border-crossing initiatives.
Given the nature of man it is only realistic to assume that the profit
motive underlying the initiatives of MNEs and other border-crossing
business ventures instills greater vigor into the transnational efforts
of these entities than does the satisfaction of economic and social
needs of members and perhaps mankind in general which motivate
many traditional NGOs. Strong emotional factors and doctrinaire
considerations which are characteristic of liberation movements,
certain political groups, and church organizations may also provide
special impetus to the transnational initiatives of these entities.

The effectiveness of nongovernmental forces to bring about
changes in the political international system including altered relationships among governmental actors and IGOs has been suggested by a
number of cases related in the preceding chapters. An interesting
example of MNE initiatives reaching the highest levels of government
has been the meeting of Prime Minister Trudeau of Canada and
President Nixon in December 1971. The pervasive fear of U.S.
domination by American MNE investments in Canada prompted
Trudeau to bring up this matter when the economic and monetary
relations between the two countries were discussed at that time. In
response to the Prime Minister's concern, President Nixon felt
compelled to declare that the United States "would do nothing that
would make Canada feel it was a colony of America." In turn, with
an eye to his audience, Trudeau stated that Nixon" had recognized
the entire freedom of Canada."[1]

American investments in France, as has been shown, also have
caused the apprehension of the French government which either
denied authorization for investments or insisted on specific changes
in the proposed investment project. Beyond that, the French government attempted to inject restrictions on American investments
into the proposed industrial policy for the European Community
which was elaborated by the Commission in 1970.

While in many instances MNEs pursue the strategy of presenting
a low profile and projecting the image of the good cooperative citizen

in host countries, the Peruvian examples of aggressive initiatives by American MNEs illustrate how both host and parent governments are compelled to respond to these initiatives by taking positions and actions that bear on or bring about changes in the international system. Of course, even the strategy of the low profile adopted by an MNE does not mean that it does not seek value-allocating behavior of one or more governments in the international field. The corporate management may simply consider such a strategy more productive in terms of end results and, as has been shown, a great variety of multi-level strategies including different coalitions are available to nongovernmental entities to pursue their transnational initiatives.

In the field of labor instances have also been presented depicting the direct involvement of governments in response to transnational initiatives with likely consequences for the international system. One example was the unsuccessful attempt by the Jamaican government, cooperating with Alcoa, to deny entry to USW organizers seeking to help Jamaican labor unions in a strike against that company.

While the transnational initiatives of many traditional NGOs may be less effective than those of international business and liberation movements in compelling publicized reaction and action of national governments bearing on their external relations, changes of a primarily technical nature on the part of these governments have been brought about by these NGO initiatives. These changes, as has been observed, are usually undramatic and often escape the public-at-large, yet in a minor way they affect the political international system none the less.

All in all, it is becoming obvious that in quantitative and qualitative terms the border-crossing initiatives of nongovernmental forces are increasingly significant factors for the global pattern of transnational interactions. In the formulation and implementation of their foreign policies all national governments and IGOs must take into account these initiatives which become important inputs into their respective decision-making processes. By either taking advantage of the opportunities presented by the nongovernmental entities and their initiatives or by seeking to curb or bypass these activities, governmental and IGO decision-makers initiate or contribute to shifts in the power relationships among the governmental actors of the international system. By being able to induce value-allocating action and reaction of governments and IGOs in the international system, nongovernmental entities clearly deserve actor status, but this status is qualitatively different for those of national governments since they cannot "authoritatively" allocate values but depend on

governments for this. Even if one were to argue that certain nongovernmental entities (large MNEs) could practically control the allocation of values by some small state governments, the allocation remains "authoritative" in the sense of being formally in the hands of
official decision-makers. Moreover, new alliances with other governments or other nongovernmental entities may reduce or eliminate the
existing "outside" control and reinstate the full power position and
authority of the government. Finally, the governmental decision-
makers can always attempt to fall back on sources of power other
than those springing from the economy which in particular countries
may be weak indeed. Such sources are the armed forces, the bureaucracy, and the people of the country themselves.

This leads to a brief discussion of the often proclaimed demise
of the nation-state. It is tempting to argue that the spreading web
of multinational nongovernmental organizations is gradually tying
down the nation-state in the manner of the Lilliputians placing in-
numerable ropes over the sleeping Gulliver with the result that the
government's latitude of decision-making becomes increasingly restricted. However, although the national governments must and do
take into account the growing number of transnational initiatives when
formulating and implementing foreign policy, the autonomy of the
nation-state displays remarkable persistence despite the fact that
many governments are unable fully to perform anymore their traditional functions of ensuring the economic well-being and security
of their citizens.[2] Two main reasons account for this persistence.
First, national political and administrative elites want to assure the
continued enjoyment of their vested interests by all means at their
command, and second, large segments of the public look upon the
state as a countervailing force against powerful transnational entities
such as MNEs, international labor organizations, or liberation movements which are perceived as a threat to the status quo or whose
aims or potential benefits are not fully understood. As a consequence,
diplomats and soldiers as representatives of the national governments
are apt to remain the main agents for shaping the international system,
although executives of MNEs, leaders of international labor organizations, and directors of NGOs are likely to become increasingly
influential, though indirect participants in the process of change which
the international political system is continually undergoing.

From the foregoing discussion one may draw the following conclusions. Many of the nongovernmental entities have indeed become
powerful forces in influencing and molding world politics and their
dramatic increase in numbers makes it imperative for national governments and IGOs to pay close attention to their demands and

activities.   The notion of the international system as developed in
Chapter 1 is not obsolete at present but requires some refinements.
A fundamental distinction must be made between governmental and
nongovernmental actor status in the political international system.
Since by definition nongovernmental actors cannot make "authoritative" allocations of value, they depend on governmental actors for
such actions and therefore occupy a lower status rank in the system.
However, nongovernmental actors are often powerful and influential
initiators of changes in the global pattern of the system and since by
now they are much more numerous than the governmental actors,
they have become a major source for the dynamics of the system.

REGIONAL AND GLOBAL INTEGRATION

Having reached some general conclusions regarding the power
and influence of nongovernmental forces in the world political arena
and their standing as an actor in the international system, consideration must now be given to an assessment of their impact on integration.
The preceding chapters have already made appraisals of this topic
with respect to the different categories of nongovernmental forces
examined and have expressed the author's view that these forces can
make a greater contribution to regional integration than to global
integration.   Looking now at this question from the perspective of the
impact which the totality of transnational initiatives undertaken by
nongovernmental entities have on integration, the author can find no
reason to change his opinion.   It seems to him that the links forged
and the ropes tied by the nongovernmental Lilliputians across the
bodies of a number of nation-states within an international region can
have more profound consequences for the transformation of the regional subsystem involved than such links and ties have on a world-
wide level.   Several reasons support this argument.   Within a geographically defined international region, transnational economic in-
terrelationships and interpenetration can be established with relative
ease if basically common economic philosophies prevail and the countries involved have had a high level of trade with each other.   Moreover, within such a region common historical and cultural traditions
are likely to exist which, reinforced by today's border-crossing mass
communications in the form of television, radio, and perhaps tourism, [3]
tend to lead to a wider sharing of common values.   In the event that
in such regions formal economic integration schemes are pursued by
intergovernmental agreement, a high level of economic interdependence can be created through the transnational initiatives of various
nongovernmental actors.   In turn the intensity of interdependence may
spawn political consequences that will be the more profound, the more

the nongovernmental actors coordinate their initiatives and the wider the circle of societal groups which perceive to obtain increasing benefits from the growing regional interdependence. In view of the common cultural and historical traditions and the possibility that common values are likely to be shared more extensively, loyalties may be slowly detached from the nation-state and shifted to regional symbols and institutions which are looked upon as providing greater material benefits in the future than those available from the national authorities. The emergence of new regionally oriented groups of elites benefiting from the growing interdependence, and the formation of alliances among these groups for purposes of furthering the process of regional integration will also have favorable implications for the political unification of the region and for reducing the importance and influence of the nation-state apparatus in the area.

However, the scenario and sequence of events as depicted above is likely to proceed very slowly as regional developments in Europe and elsewhere have demonstrated. Growing interdependence, as was pointed out, is likely to conjure up in the minds of national decision-makers fears of increased dependence and loss of autonomy in decision-making. Moreover, national political, administrative, and business elites, apprehensive of losing their vested interests and their positions of power and influence, oppose the process of integration as it progresses into the political sphere and use nationalistic sentiments as a potent tool to bolster this opposition. In Europe, some national officials seek to evade decisions made by the European Community institutions or attempt to recapture competences which had been transferred to the Community as in the case of the Common Agricultural Policy.[4] The CAP offers also a good example of the fragility of regional interdependence. Although monetary union is now an intermediate term goal of the European Community member states (1980), Germany's insistence on floating the mark in the spring of 1971 followed by similar action of the Netherlands upset the precarious alignment of Common Market currencies necessary to insure common prices for farm commodities throughout the EEC, a basic institutionalized principle of the CAP. It also necessitated the introduction of an intra-Community system of border controls, levies, and refunds entirely incompatible with the intended system of agricultural interdependence in the Common Market. Despite the new alignments of currencies following the official devaluation of the dollar in December of 1971, it is doubtful that common prices for farm commodities can be reintroduced at an early date. The major reason for this doubt is the political sensitivity of the issue since as the result of the upward valuations of the German mark and the Dutch guilder farmers in the two countries have less revenue for their products if, as is likely, the currencies of the remaining four member states would be taken as a guide for their prices. While it is theoretically possible for the German and Dutch governments to pay subsidies to their farmers in compensation for the losses the latter would incur, the new burdens on the national budgets seem to be unacceptable at least for the federal government of Germany which has to consider the forthcoming elections in 1973.[5] The example of the CAP also makes clear that the imposition of constraints caused by interdependence is acceptable only if the distribution of benefits and costs flowing from it approach some kind of equitableness. Groups perceiving to suffer harm from growing interdependence such as organized labor's apprehension that it will sustain injury from transnational capital movements and multinational production facilities of MNEs are likely to use their political clout to fight integration and enlist the aid of their national political allies in government and other sectors of the society to safeguard the eminence of the national decision-making process.

While the foregoing discussion has highlighted some of the problem areas which any contribution toward regional integration by the various nongovernmental forces must face, the regional scenario described earlier is apt to provide the needed societal conditions and climate to enable these primarily functionalist forces to move economic and political integration forward, even if only by small increments. These favorable conditions do not exist on the global level. From a purely rational point of view it is perfectly proper to argue that a global industrial state with absolute freedom of movement for persons, goods, and capital, would benefit the people of the world and that MNEs, labor, and national governments have converging interests in the promotion of economic and social welfare goals whose attainment is also pursued by many other nongovernmental entities. However, there is some doubt whether MNEs, while idealizing a world without frontiers, may really want it since their strength often flows from taking advantage of differing national labor and other costs as well as from different tax structures. Moreover, in the absence of the favorable conditions that exist in a regional level and considering the complexities, objectives, and expectations prevailing in the practice of national politics, the web of the totality of nongovernmental forces and their transnational initiatives is likely to have little, if any, impact on global integration, the culmination of which might be one worldwide government. Several additional factors reinforce this view. The interests and objectives of major groups of nongovernmental entities may not be acceptable to large unorganized segments of society, whose members may see themselves as being deprived of determining their own fate. The desire for political participation so forcefully articulated all over the world by the frequently very idealistic young might make them extremely suspicious of a political organization of the globe based on the convergence and reconciliation of material interests.

Finally, the improvement of the quality of life, which large numbers of the people of this world are now seeking so urgently, may turn out to be nothing but a mirage if the world were ruled by technocracies acting merely in accordance with the satisfaction of group interests among which the economically most powerful may obtain the lion's share of advantages. Even if an international institution within or outside the United Nations could be established to control the giant MNEs with the help of organized labor and the national governments, no assurance could be given that some kind of collusion among the three "partners" might not endanger or harm the aspirations of large segments of mankind. For all these reasons many people of the world will continue to look upon the nation-state as the guarantor of their interests and wishes, particularly since despite many failings its government is regarded as close to them, its political system whatever it may be is familiar, and channels are well known through which demands and petitions can be sent to legislators and administrators even if the responses often may be negative.

While in the author's judgment the contribution which nongovernmental forces are capable of making toward global integration is minimal, they may be able to help in preventing a possible disintegration of the international system. Karl Deutsch warns of the self-closure of political systems which can occur when the channels of a system such as a nation-state toward the outside world gradually shrink and the intake of information from the international system is reduced. [6] If one considers that the ratio of international trade to national income has steadily grown smaller not only for the United States but many other industrialized countries,[7] one is obviously witnessing the narrowing of a significant channel of nation-states to the outside world. The same holds true of a decrease in the proportion of mail crossing national boundaries or when a smaller proportion of the population of a state can read or speak a foreign language. These tendencies toward self-closure are counteracted by the manifold transnational initiatives of nongovernmental entities which strengthen the channels of nation-states linking each other and thereby serve to maintain and broaden the intercourse in the international system.

THE ASSURANCE OF PEACE

In his analyses of the consequences which the transnational initiatives of the various categories of nongovernmental entities appear

to have for the international system in terms of collaboration and
conflict the author has discovered that the intrusion of these initiatives into the national political system was apt to generate tension
among the countries involved. Despite the many beneficial effects
of these initiatives for the community of nations, differing perceptions
of what constitute benefits or drawbacks gave rise to tendencies for
conflict and of course liberation movements by their very nature produce conflict. However, with the exception of liberation movements,
the tensions and conflicts engendered by transnationally operating
nongovernmental forces are unlikely to result in the outbreak of wars.
They may cause ruffled feelings between governments, unfriendly
diplomatic acts, and perhaps mild forms of economic retaliation, but
are unlikely to go beyond this level of hostility.

On the other hand, the totality of transnational relations resulting
from the initiatives of nongovernmental entities which is growing from
year to year, is likely to have a moderately positive effect on the
maintenance of international peace. Border-crossing collaboration
of various kinds will draw an increasing number of people of different
nationalities and ethnic and cultural backgrounds into activities which
provide better mutual understanding of their different traits and are
likely to reduce their long-held and deeply-ingrained prejudices. The
important aspect of this collaboration is working together for specific
shared goals which furnishes the cutting edge for the reduction of conceptual and cultural differences and thereby is a much more effective
means for this purpose than for example international tourism which
in fact might sharpen national prejudices. The positive contribution
which nongovernmental forces can make toward regional integration
is significant in this context inasmuch as it may well set into motion
a learning process of transnational collaboration which transcends the
regional framework and has global impact. In this connection, transideological enterprises and contacts between labor organizations assume an increasingly significant role since they contribute to long-
range changes of previously hostile attitudes among peoples of countries on both sides of the ideological fence. Though membership in
NGOs straddles the Iron Curtain, investigation has produced little
concrete evidence that this produces positive behavioral changes in
governmental decision-making of countries in opposing camps.

Despite the favorable implications for the maintenance of international peace which one can detect as springing from the expanding
net of nongovernmental initiatives and activities, one must realize
that international society remains essentially a dog-eat-dog reality.
When it comes to important strategic interests of countries perceived
as vital by the nation's decision-makers, war will be resorted to as
the Israeli-Arab and the India-Pakistan conflicts have demonstrated
so clearly. Threats to a country's security, imagined or real, assume

paramount importance. In the emotion-charged atmosphere of "high politics" the forces of functionalism represented by the activities of nongovernmental entities rapidly lose out.

One might speculate what would happen if powerful MNEs would threaten to withhold or shift their resources from countries which insist on military solutions for conflicts and disputes with third countries. While theoretically such a threat could make an impact on the decision-making of medium-sized and small countries, it may also be counterproductive since it would heighten the feeling of dependence of national political and administrative elites and reduce the prospects for sound national decision-making in a difficult and precarious situation. Imposed interdependence to keep the governments peaceful may create intolerable situations for the governmental decision-makers. Moreover, it is very doubtful that MNE managements could be induced to use their economic power for the purpose of safeguarding peace in such a direct manner although they may stand to benefit financially from such action. At least so far, MNEs have preferred to present a low profile in most international situations involving conflict-laden high politics and to conceal their power as much as possible under the guise of the good corporate citizen. What stance they might take in the future when as predicted by some observers only a relatively few MNEs will dominate the international business scene, is impossible to predict. It is not inconceivable that the role of a potent peace maker in the world might add to the global legitimacy that MNEs must have if they want to win over public opinion which is likely to become increasingly critical of the MNEs' accumulation of economic and political power.

INTERNATIONAL PLURALISM

The pluralistic nature of society in terms of a multiplicity of competing groups and social institutions is an essential ingredient of the political system in Western democracies. While the subject of the group has been central to the study of politics for many years, it has been the relationship of groups and social institutions to the government within the context of the state which has been the major focus of investigation. [8] Some students of politics have asserted that within the political system the role of government is predominant, with groups placed in a position of petitioning the government for action favorable to the group or attempting to induce the government to decide on such action. Others see government only as an umpire between contending parties or perhaps as a primus inter pares with no more power than any one of the institutional groupings in society.

On the international plane many nongovernmental entities examined in this book, especially the traditional NGOs, perform functions very similar to those of national interest groups but no central
government exists to play the roles described above. Moreover,
MNEs and transnational business ventures articulate interests and in
view of their powerful resources are in a strong position to present
coordinated demands. In turn, some of these interests and demands
may be aggregated by international NGOs and as the extent and power
of transnational parties grow, the latter may also serve as transmission belts for the demands of the various transnational nongovernmental actors. In the absence of world or regional governments, the
only agencies in the international arena to arbitrate contending group
interests, at present, are U. N. agencies and regional IGOs. Since
in general the scope of these agencies is severely circumscribed and
their authority very limited, the targets for the demands of international nongovernmental entities must be the national governments
which are the chief authoritative allocators of values nationally and
internationally. That this is, in fact, the case has been shown in the
discussion of international business, labor, and the traditional NGOs—
all of which are well aware that favorable action by national governments is essential for the success of their transnational initiatives.

What is seen emerging then is indeed a growing international
pluralism which, however, for the arbitration and reconciliation of
conflicting interests and demands depends mainly on the decisions of
the national authorities. As the number of transnational nongovernmental actors expands and the quantity and urgency of their demands
rise, the attention of national decision-makers will have to be focused
more and more on the disposal of these demands by either approving,
denying, or modifying them. In these decisions the public interest,
national as well as international, must not be neglected, which is
often a difficult task. [9] If these demands are met at an increasing
rate, the transnational nongovernmental forces are likely to be gradually strengthened and to acquire a higher level of legitimacy since
they will be regarded by the public in many countries as being more
and more capable of satisfying needs and expectations. This, in turn,
will enhance their position of influence vis-à-vis the national political
and administrative elites while at the same time the positions of power
of the territorial nation-states are being slowly eroded. Whether
this scenario will actually be played out cannot be determined at this
time, but it suggests that international pluralism can constitute a
powerful force and new political reality in world politics that may
lead to further changes in the international system and require new
conceptualizations. However, much empirical research needs to be
done before this new world of international pluralism can be understood

and analyzed. Moreover, there is much divergence of opinion as to what the world of the future should be and what it can be. The search for a new order based on humanistic values rather than the pursuit of national interests suggests that new paths in normative theory must also be examined and tested. The common good of all mankind needs to be defined before the forces inherent in international pluralism can be given free rein.

NOTES

1. Time, December 20, 1971, p. 7.

2. Cf. John H. Herz, "The Territorial State Revisited: Reflections on the Future of the Nation-State, " in James N. Rosenau, International Politics and Foreign Policy (rev. ed. ; New York: The Free Press, 1969) pp. 76-89.

3. It is not quite clear whether international tourism reduces or in fact strengthens national prejudices toward the people of the countries visited. While many American political scientists such as Karl W. Deutsch, "Transaction Flows as Indicators of Political Cohension," in Philip E. Jacob and James V. Toscano, The Integration of Political Communities (Philadelphia: Lippincott, 1964), pp. 75-97, assumed that tourism was one of the elements promoting greater integration, recent studies undertaken in Europe cast doubt on this proposition.

4. This became clear in interviews of German Federal and State officials conducted by the author (October-November 1971) and is corroborated by Professor Donald J. Puchala in his Report to the Carnegie Endowment for International Peace on his Research conducted in September 1971.

5. See also Journal of Commerce, December 15, 1971.

6. For details see Karl W. Deutsch, The Nerves of Government (New York: The Free Press, 1966), pp. 214-44.

7. See Karl W. Deutsch and Alexander Eckstein, "National Industrialization and the Declining Share of the International Economic Sector, 1890-1959, " World Politics, XIII, 2 (January 1961), 267-99.

8. Cf. David Truman, The Governmental Process (New York: Knopf, 1951).

9. For a full discussion of this problem see Edward N. Megay, "Anti-Pluralist Liberalism: The German Neo-Liberals, " Political Science Quarterly, LXXXV, 3 (September 1970), 422-42.

BIBLIOGRAPHY

BOOKS AND PERIODICALS

Adams, James L. The Growing Church Lobby in Washington. Grand Rapids, Michigan: William B. Eerdmans Publishing Company, 1970.

Agence Europe Bulletin, July 4, 9, 25, 1966 and August 27, September 9, 10, October 1, November 22, 24, 1971.

Agence Europe Document, April 29, May 30, 1969.

Almond, Gabriel A. and James S. Coleman. The Politics of Developing Areas. Princeton, N.J.: Princeton University Press, 1960.

Almond, Gabriel A. and Sidney Verba. Civic Culture. Boston: Little, Brown and Company, 1965.

Balekjian, W. H. Legal Aspects of Foreign Investment in the European Community. Manchester, England: Manchester University Press, 1967.

Barber, Richard J. The American Corporation. New York: E. P. Dutton & Co., 1970.

Beard, Charles A. An Economic Interpretation of the Constitution of the United States. New York: Macmillan, 1960.

Behrman, Jack N. National Interests and the Multinational Enterprise: Tensions Among the North Atlantic Countries. Englewood Cliffs, N.J.: Prentice-Hall, 1970.

Bromberger, Merry and Serge Bromberger. Jean Monnet and the United States of Europe. New York: Coward-McCann, 1969.

Buckley, Walter, ed. Modern Systems Research for the Behavioral Scientists. Chicago: Aldine Publishing Company, 1968.

Califano, Joseph A., Jr. The Student Revolution: A Global Confrontation. New York: W. W. Norton & Company, Inc., 1970.

CEE. Reportoire des organismes communs crees dans le cadre des Communautes europeenes, 1960.

CEE. Reportoire des organismes communs crees dans le cadre des Communautes europeenes, 1970.

Cooper, Richard N. The Economics of Interdependence: Economic Policy in the Atlantic Community. New York: McGraw-Hill, 1968.

Coplin, William D. Introduction to International Politics. Chicago: Markham Publishing Company, 1971.

Dawson, Richard E. and Kenneth Prewitt. Political Socialization. Boston: Little, Brown and Company, 1969.

Dell, Sidney. A Latin American Common Market. London: Oxford University Press, 1966.

Deutsch, Karl W. The Nerves of Government. New York: The Free Press, 1966.

DGB Report, March 1971.

DGB Report, No. 9/10, October, 1971.

Die Welt, November 1, 1971.

Directory of European Foundations. Turin: Agnelli Foundation.

Donner, Frederick G. The World-Wide Industrial Enterprise: Its Challenge and Promise. New York: McGraw-Hill, 1967.

Dougherty, James E. and Robert L. Pfaltzgraff, Jr. Contending Theories of International Relations. Philadelphia: J.B. Lippincott Co., 1971.

Drucker, Peter F. The Age of Discontinuity. New York: Harper & Row, 1969.

Dunning, John H. American Investment in British Manufacturing Industry. London: George Allen and Unwin, Ltd., 1958.

_____. The Role of American Investment in the British Economy. London: PEP, 1969.

Easton, David. A Framework for Political Analysis. Englewood Cliffs, N.J.: Prentice-Hall, Inc., 1965.

Engler, Robert. The Politics of Oil. Chicago: University of Chicago Press, 1961.

European Community, February 1969.

European Community, June 1969.

Feld, Werner J. Transnational Business Collaboration Among Common Market Countries. New York: Praeger Publishers, Inc., 1970.

Fortune, LX, No. 3 (August 15, 1971).

Foundation Directory. New York: Russell Sage Foundation, 1967.

Friedman, Wolfgang C. and George Kalmanoff. Joint International Business Ventures. New York: Columbia University Press, 1961.

Gansel, Norbert, ed. Uberwindet den Kapitalismus oder Was wollen die Jungsozialisten? Hamburg: Rowohlt, 1971.

Gottfurcht, Hans. Die Internationale Gewerkschaftsbewegung im Weltgeschehen. Cologne: Bund-Verlag, 1962.

Graham, Robert A. Vatican Diplomacy: A Study of Church and State on the International Plane. Princeton, N.J.: Princeton University Press, 1959.

Griffith, William E. Communism in Europe. Cambridge, Mass.: M.I.T. Press, 1964.

Haas, Ernst B. The Uniting of Europe. Stanford, Calif.: Stanford University Press, 1968.

Hamburg, Handelskammer. Deutsche Direktinvestitionen Im Ausland, May 1969.

Hellmann, Rainer. The Challenge to U.S. Dominance of the International Corporation. Translated by Peter Rouf. New York: University of Cambridge, Mass., Dunellen, 1970.

Henig, Stanley, ed. European Political Parties. New York: Praeger Publishers, 1970.

Jacob, Philip E. and James V. Toscano. The Integration of Political Communities. Philadelphia: Lippincott, 1964.

Jessup, Philip C. Transnational Law. New Haven: Yale University Press, 1956.

Johnstone, Allan W., United States Direct Investment in France: An Investigation of the French Charges. Cambridge, Mass: M.I.T. Press, 1965.

Journal Officiel des Communautés Européenes, No. L 324/23, December 26, 1969.

Kindleberger, Charles P. American Business Abroad. New Haven: Yale University Press, 1969.

_____, ed. The International Corporation: A Symposium. Cambridge, Mass.: M.I.T. Press, 1970.

Knott, James E. Freedom of Association. Brussels: Union of International Associations, 1962.

Kolde, E. J. International Business Enterprise. Englewood Cliffs, N.J.: Prentice-Hall, 1968.

Kriesberg, Louis, ed. Social Processes in International Relations. New York: John Wiley & Sons, Inc., 1968.

Lador-Lederer, J.J. International Non-Governmental Organizations: And Economic Entities. Leyden: A.W. Sythoff, 1963.

Litvak, Isaiah A. and Christopher J. Maule. Foreign Investment and the Experience of Host Countries. New York: Praeger Publishers, Inc., 1970.

Lodge, George C. Spearheads of Democracy. New York: Harper & Row Publishers, 1962.

Macridis, Roy C., ed. Foreign Policy in World Politics. Engelwood Cliffs, N.J.: Prentice-Hall, 1967.

_____ and Robert E. Ward. Modern Political Systems: Europe. Englewood Cliffs, N.J.: Prentice-Hall, 1968, 2nd ed.

Maerker, Rudolf and Christian Uhlig. Tasks, Organizations, and Aims of Trade Unions. Stuttgart: BZ-Druck, 1967.

Magdoff, Harry. The Age of Imperialism: The Economics of U.S. Foreign Policy. New York: Monthly Review Press, 1969.

Mauritius. 4-Year Plan for Social & Economic Development, 1971.

McClelland, Charles A. Theory and International System. New York: Macmillan Company, 1966.

Miller, Norman and Roderick Aya, ed. National Liberation: Revolution in the Third World. New York: The Free Press, 1971.

Mitrany, David. A Working Peace System. 4th ed.; London: National Peace Council, 1946.

The Multinational Company and National Development: A Lamp Anthology. New York: Standard Oil Company of New Jersey, 1970.

Norman, John. Labor and Politics in Libya and Arab Africa. New York: Bookman Associates, 1965.

Palombara, Joseph L. and Myron Weiner. Political Parties and Political Development. Princeton, N.J.: Princeton University Press, 1966.

Parliament Europeen. Pour l'élection du Parlement européen au suffrage universel direct, Septembre, 1969.

Parsons, Talcott and Edward A. Shils, eds. Toward a General Theory of Action. New York: Harper and Row, Torchbooks, 1962.

Penrose, Edith T. The Large International Firm in Developing Countries: The International Petroleum Industry. London: George Allen & Unwin, Ltd., 1968.

Philanthropic Foundations in the United States: A Brief Description. New York: Foundation Center, 1969.

Reuter, Paul. Economic Origins of Jeffersonian Democracy. New York: Macmillan, 1915.

Rolfe, Sidney, and Walter Damm, eds. The Multinational Corporation in the World Economy. New York: Praeger Publishers, 1970.

Rosenau, James N. International Politics and Foreign Policy. Rev. ed; New York: The Free Press, 1969.

_____. Linkage Politics. New York: The Free Press, 1969.

Safarian, A. E. Foreign Ownership of Canadian Industry. Toronto: McGraw-Hill Co. of Canada, 1966.

Scott, Andrew M. The Functioning of the International Political System. New York: Macmillan Company, 1967.

Sharp, Walter R. The United Nations Economic and Social Council. New York: Columbia University Press, 1969.

Stein, Eric. Harmonization of European Company Laws National Reform and Transnational Coordination. Indianapolis: Bobbs Merrill Co., Inc., 1971.

Sueddeutsche Zeitung, June 20, 1969.

Svarlien, Oscar. Introduction to the Law of Nations. New York: McGraw-Hill, 1955.

Tanzer, Michael, The Political Economy of International Oil and the Underdeveloped Countries. Boston: Beacon Press, 1969.

Truman, David. The Governmental Process. New York: Knopf, 1951.

UAW-Solidarity Report, July 1968 and October 1969.

UN Conference on Human Environment, Information Letter, No. 1, June 30, 1971.

Vaupel, James W. and John P. Curran. The Making of Multinational Enterprise. Boston: Division of Research, Graduate School of Business Administration, Harvard University, 1969.

Vernon, Raymond. Sovereignty at Bay: The Multinational Spread of U.S. Enterprises. Harvard Multinational Enterprise Series. New York: Basic Books Publishers, 1971.

Yearbook of International Organization. 10th edition, 1964-65; 12th edition, 1968-69; 13th edition, 1970-71.

Yearbook of National Account Statistics, United Nations.

PERIODICAL ARTICLES AND BOOK SELECTIONS

Allison, Graham T. "Conceptual Models and the Cuban Missile Crisis," American Political Science Review, LXIII, 3 (September 1969).

Aspaturian, Vernon V. "The Soviet Union and International Communism," in Roy C. Macridis, ed., Foreign Policy in World Politics. 3rd edition, Englewood Cliffs, N. J.: Prentice-Hall, 1967, pp. 216-45.

Bell, J. Bowyer. "Contemporary Revolutionary Organizations," International Organization, XXV, 3 (Summer 1971), p. 503.

Bell, Peter D. "The Ford Foundation as a Transnational Actor," International Organization, XXV, 3 (Summer 1971), pp. 465-78.

Bertin, Gilles Y. "Foreign Investment in France," in Isaiah A. Litvak and Christopher J. Maule, Foreign Investment and the Experience of Host Countries. New York: Praeger Publishers, Inc., 1970, pp. 105-22.

Blanplain, Roger. "American Involvement in Belgium," in Alfred Kamin, ed., Western European Labor and the American Corporation. Washington, D. C.: The Bureau of National Affairs, 1970, pp. 455-65.

Bradshaw, Marie T. "U. S. Exports to Foreign Affiliates of U. S. Firms," Survey of Current Business, XLIX 49, 5, (May 1969), pp. 34-51.

Bywater, William, "Why Free Trade is Unfair to U. S. Workers," New York Times, January 3, 1971.

Campbell, Persia. "Do NGOs Have a Role?," International Development Review, XI, 3 (1969), pp. 34-39.

Cox, R. W. "Labor and Transnational Relations," International Organization, XXV, 3 (Summer 1971), pp. 554-84.

Damm, Walter, "The Economic Aspects of European Direct Investment in the United States" in Sidney E. Rolfe and Walter Damm, ed.,

The Multinational Corporation in the World Economy. New York: Praeger Publishers, 1970, pp. 35-51.

de Jong, H. W. "De Concentratiebeweging in de Westeuropese Economie," Economisch-Statistische Berichten, January 22 and 29 and February 5 and 12, 1969.

Deutsch, Karl W. "Transaction Flows as Indicators of Political Cohesion," in Philip E. Jacob and James V. Toscano, The Integration of Political Communities. Philadelphia: Lippincott, 1964, pp. 75-97.

_____ and Alexander Eckstein, "National Industrialization and The Declining Share of the International Economic Sector, 1890-1959," World Politics, XIII, 2 (January 1961), pp. 267-99.

Dunning, John H. "Foreign Investment in the United Kingdom," in Isaiah A. Litvak and Christopher J. Maule, Foreign Investment and the Experience of Host Countries. New York: Praeger Publishers, 1970, pp. 205-55.

_____. "Technology, United States Investment, and European Economic Growth," in Charles P. Kindleberger, ed., The International Corporation: A Symposium. Cambridge, Mass.: M. I. T. Press, 1970, pp. 141-76.

Feld, Werner, "The French and Italian Communists and the Common Market: The Request for Representation in the Community Institutions," Journal of Common Market Studies VI, 3 (March 1968), pp. 250-66.

_____. "National Bureaucracies of the EEC Member States and Political Integration: A Preliminary Inquiry," 139 in Robert Jordan, ed., International Administration: Its Evolution and Contemporary Applications. London: Oxford University Press, 1971.

_____. "The Utility of the EEC Experience for the People's Democracies in Eastern Europe," in J. Lukaskewski, ed., The People's Democracies After Prague. De Tempel (Bruges, Belgium), 1970.

Gannon, James P. "More U. S. Mining Help Foreign Workers to Pressure American Company Overseas," The Wall Street Journal, December 7, 1970, p. 30.

Goldberg, Paul M. and C. P. Kindleberger. "Toward a GATT for Investment: A Proposal for Supervision of the International Corporation," Law and Policy in International Business, 2, 2 (Summer 1970), pp. 295-325.

Herz, John H. "The Territorial State Revisited: Reflections on the Future of the Nation-State," in James N. Rosenau, International Politics and Foreign Policy. Rev. ed., New York: The Free Press, 1969, pp. 76-89.

Heymann, Philippe. "Une question de vie ou de mort: une politique industrielle européene, Communauté Europeene, No. 140, Mars 1970.

Horowitz, Irving Louis and Ruth Leonora Horowitz. "Tax-Exempt Foundations: Their Effects on National Policy," Science, Vol. 168 (April 10, 1970), pp. 220-228.

Huntley, James Robert. "Student Unrest in Europe and America: Some Implications for Western Society," Res Publica, XII, 2 (1970), pp. 171-84.

Hymer, Stephen and Robert Rawthorn. "Multinational Corporations and International Oligopoly: The Non-American Challenge," in Charles P. Kindleberger, ed., The International Corporation: A Symposium. Cambridge, Mass.: M.I.T. Press, 1970.

Jacoby, Neil H. "The Multinational Corporation," The Center Magazine, III, 3 (May 1970), pp. 37-55.

Jager, Elizabeth R., "The Conglomerate Goes Global," AFL-CIO American Federationist, January 1970.

James, C. L. R. "Colonialism and National Liberation in Africa: The Gold Coast Revolution," in Norman Miller and Roderick Aya, ed., National Liberation: Revolution in the Third World. New York: The Free Press, 1971.

Johnson, Harry G. "The Efficiency and Welfare Implications of the International Corporation," in Charles P. Kindleberger, ed., The International Corporation: A Symposium. Cambridge, Mass.: M.I.T. Press, 1970, pp. 35-56.

_____ "The Multinational Corporation as Development Agent," Columbia Journal of World Business, V, 3 (May-June 1970), pp. 25-30.

Judge, A. J. N. "Multinational Business Enterprises," in Yearbook of International Organizations, 1968.

Kaiser, Karl, "Transnationale Politik," Politische Vierteljahresschrift, Vol. 10, Special Issue, 1969.

Khatkhate, Deena R. "Management in Development Countries," Finance and Development, No. 3, 1971, pp. 8-14.

Kriesberg, Louis. "U.S. and U.S.S.R. Participation in International Non-Governmental Organizations," in Louis Kriesberg, ed., Social Processes in International Relations. New York: John Wiley & Sons, 1968, pp. 466-485.

Leontiades, James, "The European Challenge: A Response," Columbia Journal of World Business, 4, 4 (July-August, 1970).

Litvak, Isaiah A. and Christopher J. Maule. "Foreign Investment in Canada," in Isaiah A. Litvak and Christopher J. Maule, ed., Foreign Investment: The Experience of Host Countries. New York: Praeger Publishers, 1970, pp. 76-104.

Magdoff, Harry. "The Logic of Imperialism," Social Policy, September-October 1970, pp. 20-29.

Mayer, Lawrence A. "Into a Time of Stagflation," Fortune, August 1971, pp. 144-49.

McLane, John R. "Archaic Movements and Revolution in Southern Vietnam," in Norman Miller and Roderick Aya, ed., National Liberation: Revolution in the Third World. New York: The Free Press, 1971.

Megay, Edward N. "Anti-Pluralist Liberalism: The German Neo-Liberals," Political Science Quarterly, LXXXV, 3 (September 1970), pp. 422-442.

Meynen, Johannes, Wolfgang Friedmann, Kenneth Weg. "Joint Ventures Revisited," Columbia Journal of World Business, I, 2 (Spring 1966), pp. 19-29.

Miles, Edward. "Transnational Processes and International Organization: Outer Space and the Oceans," International Organization, XXV, 3 (Summer 1971).

Muret, Charlotte. "The Swiss Pattern for a Federated Europe," in International Political Communities, An Anthology. Garden City, N.Y.: Doubleday, 1966, pp. 149-73.

Nakahara, Kiichiro. "International Pressure Groups and the UN Enlarged ECOSOC," Behavioral Science Research (Tokyo), No. 7, 1970, pp. 39-49.

Neunreither, Karlheinz. "Wirtschaftsverbaende im Prozess der europaeischen Integration," in C. J. Friedrich, Politische Dimensionen der europaeischen Gemeinschaftsbildung. Koeln and Opladen: Westdeutscher Verlag, 1968, pp. 358-442.

Nye, J. S. and Robert D. Keohane. "Transnational Relations and World Politics: An Introduction", International Organization, XXV, 3 (Summer 1971).

Perlmutter, Howard V. "Attitudinal Patterns in Joint Decision Making in Multinational Firms—Nation State Relationships," in M. F. Tuite, M. Radnor, and R. Chischolm, eds., International Decision Making. Chicago, Aldine Publishing Company, 1972).

_____. "Emerging East-West Ventures: The Transideological Enterprise," Columbia Journal of World Politics, September-October 1969, pp. 39-50.

_____. "The Toruous Evolution of the Multinational Corporation," Columbia Journal of World Business, No. 4, 1969.

Polk, Judd. "The Rise of World Corporations," Saturday Review, November 22, 1969, pp. 32 ff.

Powrie, Thomas L., "Foreign Investments in Canada," in Sidney E. Rolfe and Walter Damm (eds.), The Multinational Corporation in the World Economy. New York: Praeger Publishers, 1970, pp. 86-106.

Puchala, Donald J. "Patterns in West European Integration," Journal of Common Market Studies, IX, 2, (December 1970), pp. 117-42.

Rolfe, Sidney E. "The International Corporation in Perspective," in Sidney E. Rolfe and Walter Damm (eds.), The Multinational Corporation in the World Economy. New York: Praeger Publishers, 1970.

Rose, Sanford. "The Rewarding Strategies of Multinationalism,"
Fortune, September 15, 1968, pp. 100 ff.

Shaw, Robert d'A., "Foreign Investment and Global Labor", Columbia
Journal of World Business, VI, 4, (July-August 1971), pp. 52-62.

Singer, J. David. "The Global System and its Sub-Systems: A
Developmental View," in James N. Rosenau, Linkage Politics,
New York: The Free Press, 1969, pp. 21-43.

Platig, E. Raymond. "International Relations as a Field of Inquiry,"
in James N. Rosenau, ed. International Politics and Foreign
Policy. New York: The Free Press, 1969, pp. 6-19.

_____ and Michael Wallace. "Intergovernmental Organization and
the Preservation of Peace: 1816-1864: Some Bivariate Relationships," International Organization XXIV, 3 (Summer 1970), pp.
520-47.

Skjelsbaek, Kjell. "The Growth of International Nongovernmental
Organization in the Twentieth Century," International Organization, XXV, 3 (Summer 1971), pp. 420-442.

Speeckaert, G. P. "Multinational Business Enterprises," Yearbook
of International Organizations, 13th ed., 1970-71, pp. 1028-89.

Streeten, Paul. "Obstacles to Private Foreign Investment in the
LDCs," Columbia Journal of World Business, V, 3, (May-June
1970, pp. 31-39.

Sukijasovic, Miodrag. "Foreign Investment in Yugoslavia," in Isaiah
A. Litvak and Christopher J. Maule, Foreign Investment and
the Experience of Host Countries. New York, Praeger Publishers, 1970.

Vallier, Ivan. "The Roman Catholic Church: A Transnational Actor,"
International Organization, XXV, 3 (Summer 1971), pp. 479-502.

Vernon, Raymond. "Economic Sovereignty at Bay," Foreign Affairs,
XLVII, 1 (October 1968) pp. 1110-22.

_____. "Future of the Multinational Enterprise," in Charles P.
Kindleberger, ed., The International Corporation. Cambridge,
Mass. M.I.T. Press, 1970.

_____. "Multinational Enterprises and National Sovereignty," Harvard Business Review, XLV 2 (March-April, 1967), pp. 156-72.

Vetter, Heinz O. "The Lessons of the ICFTU Congress," DGB Report, III, 4 (1969), p. 38.

_____. "The Trade Unions as a Link Between the Nations", DGB Report (1970), Vol. IV, No. 7/8, p. 65.

Waltz, Kenneth N. "The Myth of Interdependence, " in Charles P. Kindleberger, The International Corporation: A Symposium. Cambridge, Mass.: M.I.T. Press 1970, pp. 205-223.

Wolf, Eric R., "Peasant Rebellion and Revolution, " in Norman Miller and Roderick Aya, ed., National Liberation: Revolution in the Third World. New York, The Free Press, 1971.

REPORTS

Behrman, Jack N., "The Multinational Enterprise and Nation States: the Shifting Balance of Power, " (Conference on the Multinational Corporation, held at the Department of State, February 14, 1969, pp. 19-21.

_____. "The Multinational Enterprise: Its Initiatives and Governmental Reactions, " March 1971, (mimeo.)

Blake, David H., "Multinational Corporations, International Unionism, and Global Integration, " Paper presented at the Research Conference on the Multinational Corporation in the Global Political System at the University of Pennsylvania, April 22-23, 1971 (mimeo., 1971).

DeVree, J. K., "Le thème européen dans les elections générales de 1967 au Pays-Bas, " Europa Institute of the University of Amsterdam (mimeo).

Evan, William M., "Multinational Corporations and International Professional Associations as Mechanisms for Integration of the International System, " paper presented at ISA Convention, Puerto Rico, March 1971.

Galloway, Jonathan F., "Multinational Enterprises As Worldwide

Interest Groups, " Paper delivered at the Annual Meeting of the
American Political Science Association, September 1970.

_____. "The Role of Multinational Enterprises in the Integration
of Western Europe and the North Atlantic Countries, " Paper
presented for the Research Conference in the Multinational
Corporation in the Global Political System, at the University of
Pennsylvania, April 22-23, 1971.

Goldberg, Paul M. , "The Evolution of Transnational Companies in
Europe," unpublished Ph. D. dissertation, Sloan School of
Management, M. I. T. June 1971.

Goodsell, Charles T. , "The Multinational Corporation As Transnational
Actor: Observations Based On Peru," Remarks at the Annual
Meeting of American Political Science Association, September
9, 1971.

Heginbotham, Erland, "The Multinational Corporation and International
Production: Some Common Misconceptions, " conference on
multinational corporations held at the University of Pennsylvania,
spring 1971.

Hymer, Stephen H. , "The Efficiency (Contradictions) of Multinational
Corporations. " Economic Growth Center, Yale University
(mimeo. , 1970).

Jaeger, Alfred, "Das Thema 'Europa' im Bundestagswahlkampf 1965, "
Forschungsinsitut fuer Politische Wissenschaft und Europaeische
Fragen and der Universitaet zu Koeln (mimeo).

Kapoor, Ashok, "The Multinational Enterprise and the Nation State
in Asia, " Paper presented at the Research Conference on the
Multinational Corporation in the Global Political System, University of Pennsylvania, April 1971 (mimeo. , 1971).

Mennis, Bernard and Karl P. Sauvant, "Multinational Corporations
and the Prospects for Regional Integration, " Paper presented
for the Research Conference on the Multinational Corporation
in the Global Political System, at the University of Pennsylvania
April 22-23, 1971, (mimeo. , 1971).

Mudrich, Gunter, "A New Path: To a United Europe by Means of
One Supra-National Party," Paper presented at the College of
Europe, Bruges, Belgium May 6, 1969 (mimeo.)

Nye, J. S., "Multinational Enterprise and Prospects for Regional
and Global Integration, 1971," Paper presented for the Research
Conference in the Multinational Corporation in the Global Political
System, at the University of Pennsylvania, April 22-23, 1971
(mimeo., 1971).

Perlmutter, Howard V., "Towards Research on and Development of
Nations," Address before the symposium on "International
Collective Bargaining" sponsored by the International Institute
of Labour Studies of the ILO, 29, April 1969, Geneva, Switzerland.

Phlips, Louis, "Effects economiques de la concentration industrielle:
Essai d'analyse empirique," (mimeo., 1969).

Roth, David F., "International Political Parties in an Emerging
World Order: Towards a Strategy for Realization" (mimeo,
1971).

Vernon, Raymond, "Foreign Enterprises and Developing Nations in
the Raw Materials Industries" (mimeo., 1969).

Congress of National Organizations in the Portuguese Colonies (CONCP), 231
Congress of Parents and Teachers, 60
Congress Party in India, 239
Consultative Assembly of the Council of Europe, 224
Consultative Assembly of the Council of European Coal and Steel Community, 224
COPA (Comité des Organisations Professionelles Agricoles de la C.E.E.), 200
Cox, R.W., 153, 166
Crete, 186
Cuba, 186, 229, 230, 233
Cyprus, 30, 182
Czechoslovakia, 162, 186, 222, 234

de Gaulle, Charles, 127
Denmark, 29, 30, 32, 186, 224
Deutsch, Karl, 252
Dominican Republic, 160
Drucker, Peter, 47
Dulles, John Foster, 61
Dunning, John H., 74

East Africa, 81
Eastern Europe, 96, 123, 142, 162, 182, 183, 186, 208, 220, 221, 222
East Germany, 208
Economic and Social Committee (of the EEC), 205
ECOSOC, 181, 194, 195, 200, 203, 205
Ecuador, 101
Egypt, 186
Eisenhower, Dwight D., 61
Engler, Robert, 61
Ente Nazionale Idrocarburi (ENI), 32
ethnocentric orientation, 54, 57, 79, 107
Euratom, 6
Eurodollar, 83
Europe, 24, 25, 26, 27, 34, 38, 39, 46, 47, 51, 52, 80, 83, 85, 92, 98, 100, 101, 125, 127, 132, 133, 134, 135, 136, 137, 139, 140, 141, 153, 154, 155, 156, 161, 162, 163, 166, 168, 182, 183, 184, 199, 200, 216, 219, 220, 221, 222, 223, 224, 225, 227, 228, 229, 230, 231, 238, 250
European Christian Democratic Union, 219, 220

European Coal and Steel Community, 6
European Committee of the Christian Metal Workers Union, 155
European Communities Commission, 80, 100, 133, 134, 220, 246
The "European Company" Statute, 133
European Confederation of Agriculture, 198
European Confederation of Free Trade Unions, 5
European Economic Community, 3, 5, 6, 21, 38, 41, 42, 70, 75, 79, 82, 85, 88, 99, 108, 118, 122, 125, 126, 127, 128, 131, 132, 135, 136, 137, 139, 140, 141, 155, 156, 157, 158, 161, 168, 181, 183, 188, 199, 200, 206, 223, 224, 225, 227, 228, 229, 230, 240, 246, 250
EEC Treaty, 200
European Federalist International, 223, 224
European Federation of Free Trade Unions, 168
European Free Trade Association, 25, 38, 41, 42, 181
European Parliament, 6, 224, 225, 226, 227, 228, 229
Europa Partei, 6, 214, 215, 223, 224
European Patent Law, 133, 140
European Secretariat (WCL), 168
Export Control Act of 1949, 90

Farbenfabrieken Bayer AG, 32, 138
Farbewerke Hoechst AG, 32, 124, 125, 134, 135, 138
Federal Trade Commission, 61
Federation of Women's Clubs, 60
Fiat, 5, 15, 95, 96, 106, 135, 138, 155, 156, 158
Finland, 30, 186
First World Automotive Conference, 155
Force Ouvrière de la Metallurgie, 154, 156
Ford Foundation, 6, 21, 238, 239, 240
Ford Motor Company, 32, 34, 70, 87, 153, 157
Forrestal, James, 61
Foundation Directory of 1967, 238
France, 6, 14, 28, 29, 30, 31, 32, 40, 43, 44, 45, 71, 74, 75, 76, 82, 84, 85, 88, 89, 91, 100, 121, 122, 123, 124,

National European Party, 223
National Foreign Trade Council, 60
Nationalism, 127, 137, 164
National Liberation Fronts, 6, 213,
  230, 231, 232, 233, 246, 248, 253
Netherlands, 27, 30, 32, 34, 40, 75, 88,
  125, 127, 128, 157, 186, 220, 223, 228,
  250
New Caladonia, 77, 155
New Zealand, 39, 48, 148, 149, 184,
  220
NGO Conference, 201
North Africa, 186
North America, 149, 175, 182, 186,
  233
North Atlantic Treaty Organization
  (NATO), 223
Nye, J.S., 11, 15

OAS, 198
OAU, 231

Pakindo (Indonesian Protestant
  Party), 219
Pakistan, 39, 80, 81, 186, 239, 253
Pan-African Congress (PAC), 231
Panama, 186
Parliamentary Party of the CDU/CUS,
  225
Parsons, Talcott, 8
Parten, J.R., 61
Parti Socialist Europeen, 6
Pauley, Edwin W., 61
Peace of Westfalia, 3
Pechiney, 28, 32, 121, 138
Perlmutter, Howard V., 22, 54, 95,
  96, 106, 136
Peru, 58, 59, 60, 101, 104, 163, 186,
  237, 247
Peruvian Telephone Company, 58
Pfaltzgraff, Robert, 7
Philips' Gloeilampenfabrieken, 22,
  26, 34, 155
Phillipines, 77, 80, 160, 186
Platig, E. Raymond, 9
pluralism, 7, 204, 239, 245, 254, 255,
  256
Poland, 96, 121, 186
"political front" unions, 153
polycentric organization, 23, 52, 53,
  54, 55, 57, 78, 79, 136
Popular Front for the Liberation of
  Palestine (PFLP), 230, 231, 232

Portugal, 27, 30, 77, 152, 159, 186,
  219, 231, 232, 237
Portuguese Africa, 233

Rapoport, Anatol, 8
Renault, 14, 100, 123, 138
Reuter, Paul, 140
Rhodesia, 26, 231
Rockefeller Foundation, 238, 239
Roman Catholic Church, 235, 236,
  237, 238
Romania, 122, 186, 222
Romanian General Trade Union
  Federation, 162
Rome, 32, 235, 236
Roth, David, 225
Roussel-Uclaf, 124
Royal Dutch Shell, 31, 32, 34, 59
Rusk, Dean, 59
Russo-Japanese War, 176

Salvador, 186
Sarragat, Giuseppe, 228
Saviem, 123
School of Freedom, 220
Second Congress of the Comintern,
  221
Second Development Decade, 206
Servan-Schreiber, J-J, 36
Scandinavia, 220
Shaw, Robert d'A., 166
Shell Oil, 34
The Shell Transport and Trading
  Company, Ltd., 31, 32
Siemens, 138
Singapore, 81, 164
Singer Company, 32, 152
Skjelsbaek, Kjell, 32, 182, 203, 207
Social Democratic Party of
  Germany, 214
Socialist Democratic parties, 221,
  224, 225, 226, 227, 228, 229, 230
Socialist European Party of Civil
  Servants, 223
Socialist International Congress,
  216
Somer, G., 223
South African National Congress
  (ANC), 231
South America, 44, 81, 149
Southeast Asia, 166, 238
South Korea, 77, 81, 163, 164, 207
South Rhodesia, 77

WERNER J. FELD, Professor of Political Science and Chairman of the Department of Political Science at Louisiana State University in New Orleans, has been a close student of European integration and international organizations since 1960. He is the author of <u>Transnational Business Collaboration Among Common Market Countries</u>: <u>Its Implication for Political Integration</u> (Praeger, 1970), <u>The European Common Market and the World</u> (1967) and <u>The Court of the European Communities</u>: <u>New Dimension in International Adjudication</u> (1964). In addition, he has published a number of articles on various aspects of the European Community and international politics.

Professor Feld received a degree in law from the University of Berlin and a Ph.D. in political science from Tulane University. He was Fulbright Professor at the College of Europe during the academic year 1968-69 and was Visiting Professor at Johns Hopkins University in Bologna.